RACE AND ETHNICITY IN THE 21ST CENTURY

Race and Ethnicity in the 21st Century

Edited by

Alice Bloch
City University London, UK

and

John Solomos
City University London, UK

First published 2010 by
PALGRAVE MACMILLAN

Palgrave Macmillan in the UK is an imprint of Macmillan Publishers Limited, registered in England, company number 785998, of Houndmills, Basingstoke, Hampshire RG21 6XS.

Palgrave Macmillan in the US is a division of St Martin's Press LLC, 175 Fifth Avenue, New York, NY 10010.

Palgrave Macmillan is the global academic imprint of the above companies and has companies and representatives throughout the world.

Palgrave® and Macmillan® are registered trademarks in the United States, the United Kingdom, Europe and other countries.

ISBN-13: 978–0–230–00778–9 hardback
ISBN-13: 978–0–230–00779–6 paperback

This book is printed on paper suitable for recycling and made from fully managed and sustained forest sources. Logging, pulping and manufacturing processes are expected to conform to the environmental regulations of the country of origin.

A catalogue record for this book is available from the British Library.

A catalog record for this book is available from the Library of Congress.

10   9   8   7   6   5   4   3   2   1
19   18   17   16   15   14   13   12   11   10

Printed and bound in Great Britain by
CPI Antony Rowe, Chippenham and Eastbourne

For Nikolas, Daniel and Rachel

Contents

Notes on Contributors

Editors

Alice Bloch is Professor of Sociology in the Department of Sociology, City University London. She has published widely in the areas of refugee studies, migration and researching hidden and/or vulnerable groups, including *The Migration and Settlement of Refugees in Britain* (2002). She is currently working on a research project exploring the social and economic lives of young undocumented migrants.

John Solomos is Professor of Sociology in the Department of Sociology, City University London. He is Director of the Centre on Race, Ethnicity and Migration. Before that he was Professor of Sociology in the Faculty of Humanities and Social Science at South Bank University, London, and he has previously worked at the Centre for Research in Ethnic Relations, University of Warwick, and Birkbeck College, University of London, and University of Southampton. He has published on various aspects of race and ethnic studies, including *The Changing Face of Football: Racism, Identity and Multiculture and the English Game* (co-author with Les Back and Tim Crabbe, 2001), *Race and Racism in Britain* (4th Edition, 2010) and *Race, Ethnicity and Social Theory* (2010). He has also edited a number of books including *Racialization: Studies in Theory and Practice* (co-editor with Karim Murji, 2005) and *Theories of Race and Racism: A Reader* (2nd Edition; co-editor with Les Back, 2009). He is co-editor of the international journal *Ethnic and Racial Studies*, published ten times a year.

Contributors

Sundas Ali is a DPhil student in Sociology at Nuffield College, University of Oxford. She initially studied at the University of Bristol where she obtained an MSc in International Relations and a BSc in Economics and Econometrics. Her research interests include identity, immigration, inequalities and social cohesion. She has carried out research for the Aga Khan Development Network on the social inclusion of minorities in Britain, for Prof. Timothy Garton Ash at the European Studies Centre, Oxford on his book *Muslims in Europe*, for the Centre on Migration, Policy and Society, Oxford on migrant health and social care workers, and for the Ageing Institute, Oxford on the effects of economic inequalities on health. She convenes the Social Sciences' Graduate Research in Progress Seminar series at Oxford and is currently organising a conference on the Orientalism at War project at the DPIR, Oxford and Defence Academy, Cambridge. She is also working with a team of Oxford researchers on an ethnic minority election survey to be conducted in parallel with the main BES.

Myria Georgiou teaches media at the Department of Media and Communications, London School of Economics and Political Science (LSE). Her research focuses on media, migration, diaspora and transnationalism. She has researched and published books and articles on transnational audiences across Europe and the US, on culturally diverse cities and urban communication, and on the representation of minorities in the press. Her books include *Diaspora, Identity and the Media* (2006); she has co-edited *Transnational Lives and the Media* (2007) and she is currently working on a book titled *Media and the City* (forthcoming).

David Gillborn is Professor of Education at the Institute of Education, London, and editor of the international journal *Race, Ethnicity and Education*. He has written widely on racism in education, including the books *Racism and Education: Coincidence or Conspiracy?* (2008, Routledge) and *Rationing Education* (with Deborah Youdell, 2000, Open University Press).

Malcolm Harrison is Professor of Housing and Social Policy at the University of Leeds, and has published widely on housing and ethnicity, urban policies, disability and welfare systems. His latest completed project investigated the responses of higher education institutions to disabled students and their needs. His books include *Housing, 'Race' and Community Cohesion* (2005).

Anthony Heath is Professor of Sociology at the University of Oxford, Fellow of Nuffield College and Fellow of the British Academy. His research interests cover social stratification, ethnicity, electoral behaviour and national identity. He has published many books and over 100 scientific papers. His most recent book, *Unequal Chances: Ethnic Minorities in Western Labour Markets* (edited with Sin Yi Cheung), was published in 2007. He is currently carrying out projects evaluating the affirmative action programme in Northern Ireland and on the decline of traditional identities in Britain, and is working with a team of European colleagues on a comparative study of ethnic minority education. He has carried out work for the Department for Communities and Local Government on social cohesion, for Lord Goldsmith's Citizenship Review on national identity and for the Department for Work and Pensions on employer discrimination, and is currently working with UNDP in Bosnia and Herzegovina on social capital and human development.

Patricia Hynes is Senior Research Officer at the NSPCC working in partnership with the University of Bedfordshire on research into trafficked children and young people. Her current research interests are in the areas of forced migration, refugee and asylum policy, trafficking, social exclusion and inclusion, human rights and the ethics of conducting research with migrant populations. Her publications include *The Issue of 'Trust' or 'Mistrust' in Research with Refugees: Choices, Caveats and Considerations for Researchers* (UNHCR Working Paper No. 98, 2003), *Contemporary Compulsory Dispersal: The Absence of Space for the Restoration of Trust* (Journal of Refugee Studies, 2009) and *The Social Exclusion and Dispersal of Asylum Seekers: Between Liminality and Belonging* (Policy Press, forthcoming).

Eugene McLaughlin is Professor of Criminology in the Department of Sociology, City University London. He has written extensively on police governance and reform, police-race relations, criminal justice policy and criminological theory. His current research concentrates on the theory and practice of policing and security in multi-pluralist societies and the news media, crime and public policy. His most recent book is *The New Policing* (2007).

James Nazroo is Professor of Sociology at the University of Manchester. He initially trained at St. George's Hospital Medical School, where he obtained a BSc (medical sociology) and MBBS, then studied at Royal Holloway and Bedford New College for an MSc in Sociology of Health and Illness, and finally studied for his PhD in Sociology at UCL. Before coming to Manchester, he was Professor of Medical Sociology in the Department of Epidemiology and Public Health at UCL. Issues of inequality, social justice and underlying processes of stratification have been the primary focus of his research activities, which have centred on gender, ethnicity, ageing and the intersections between these. His work on ethnic inequalities in health began with describing differences in health across and within broad ethnic groupings and assessing the contribution that social disadvantage might make to these differences. Central to this has been developing an understanding of the links between ethnicity, racism, class and inequality. This work has covered a variety of elements of social disadvantage, including socioeconomic position, racial discrimination and harassment, and ecological effects. It also covers a variety of health outcomes, including general health, mental health, cardiovascular disease and sexual health. He has increasingly focused on comparative analysis (across groups, time and place) to investigate underlying processes, involving collaborations with colleagues in the US, Canada, Europe and New Zealand, as well as the UK.

Deborah Phillips is Reader in Ethnic and Racial Studies in the School of Geography at the University of Leeds. She has published on aspects of 'race' and housing, discourses on ethnic segregation and integration, and community cohesion. Her recent publications include 'Parallel lives? Challenging discourses of British Muslim self-segregation' (2006, *Environment and Planning D: Society and Space* 24), *Housing, 'Race' and Community Cohesion* (2005, with M. Harrison and others) and 'British Asian Narratives of Urban Space' (2007, *Transactions of the Institute of British Geographers*, with C. Davis and P. Ratcliffe).

Nicola Rollock is a Researcher at the Institute of Education, University of London where she is working on an ESRC project "The Educational Strategies of the Black Middle Classes". Her research interests include race equality and broader issues around social justice in education and the criminal justice system. She is author of *The Stephen Lawrence Inquiry 10 Years On* and *Failure by any other name? Educational Policy and the continuing struggle for Black academic success* both published by the Runnymede Trust.

Catherine Rothon is Medical Research Council Special Training Fellow at the Centre for Psychiatry, Barts, and the London School of Medicine and Dentistry, University of London. She studied for her first degree in History at the University of Cambridge. Her doctorate, awarded in 2005 by the University of Oxford, focused on ethnic differentials in educational achievement in Britain. Her research interests include educational inequalities, ethnicity, mental health and racial prejudice.

Rosemary Sales is Emeritus Professor of Social Policy at Middlesex University and a member of the Social Policy Research Centre. Her current research interests are in immigration and refugee policy and in new migration flows. She has been involved in a number of research projects on these themes both at European level and focusing on London. Recent projects have included studies of new Chinese migration to London, of London's Chinatown, the migratory strategies of recent Polish migrants to London and skilled migration and migrant integration in Europe. Her recent publications include *Understanding Immigration and Refugee Policy: Contradictions and Continuities* (2007) and *Growing Up with Risk* (2007; co-edited with B. Thom and J. Pearce).

Satnam Virdee is Professor of Sociology at the University of Glasgow. His current research interests focus on mapping the relationship between racism and capitalist modernity; racism, class and labour markets; and the study of racist and anti-racist collective action. His forthcoming book *Racism, Resistance and Radicalism*.

Preface

The subject matter of this book represents an important field of both scholarly and policy-related debate in contemporary societies. Certainly over the past two decades or so we have seen a rapid growth in both the range of books covering this field and the public policy debates about the role of race and ethnicity as social and political issues. It is in this context that we started talking about producing a collection that provides an overview of current scholarship around key facets of race and ethnicity at the beginning of the 21st century. Beyond providing an overview of specific issues we encouraged our contributors to write chapters that both provide an insight into the main threads of theoretical debate and empirical research and are written in an accessible and informative style. We hope that collectively we have succeeded in these objectives and that the book will become a point of reference for students, researchers and practitioners alike working in this ever-changing field. All chapters have been written in a style that prioritises accessibility and we hope this will enhance the value of the book as a whole. As an aid to using individual chapters we have included at the end of each chapter some suggestions for key texts that explore the concerns of each chapter from a range of perspectives.

The production of an edited book such as this one is inevitably a collective effort by the editors and the contributors of the individual chapters. We have worked closely with all the contributors at a number of stages and we are grateful for the ways in which they have worked with us in producing and then revising their chapters. They have responded to our various requests with grace and we hope they can see that the final versions of all the chapters link up well together.

As editors we would also like to acknowledge the support and encouragement of our colleagues and students in the Department of Sociology at City University. The Department has provided us with a vibrant intellectual environment that has given us the space to think and talk about these issues and to edit this book together. More generally, we have been encouraged in our efforts by our broader network of friends in the Department and in the wider scholarly communities, including Claire Alexander, Suki Ali, Leah Bassel, Martin Bulmer, Kirsten Campbell, Milena Chimienti, Patricia Hill Collins, David Goldberg, Michael Keith, Kate Nash, Marco Martiniello, Eugene McLaughlin, Sarah

Neal, Liza Schuster, Amal Treacher and Frank Webster. We have also bene-fitted from the support of our publishers at Palgrave Macmillan, particularly Catherine Gray, Emily Salz and Beverley Tarquini.

Alice Bloch
John Solomos

CHAPTER 1

Key Questions in the Sociology of Race and Ethnicity

ALICE BLOCH AND JOHN SOLOMOS

We have edited *Race and Ethnicity in the 21st Century* with two core objectives in mind. First, we see it as a resource for students and scholars of race and ethnicity. It is for this reason that we have sought to cover what are seen as the substantive core issues in the making of race and ethnic relations in contemporary societies. Second, we wanted to bring together authors who could write with a sense of depth and authority about the specific issues covered by their chapters. All the authors included in this volume have carried out extensive empirical and conceptual research in their main areas of scholarship and this is reflected in the individual chapters. More generally, however, we see this volume as helping readers to think about key facets of contemporary race and ethnic relations on the basis of current research and utilising a range of theoretical and conceptual perspectives. Another way to make this point would be to say that we wanted to raise questions for our readers and help them to think about them from a range of angles rather than provide them with a uniform perspective.

In the current climate there is both intense public debate and mobilisation around the issues we cover in this book. This is evident in the heavily politicised debates we see about such questions as immigration, asylum, policing, education, public housing and related issues. It is also evident in the social constructions of migrant and minority communities as 'social problems' or 'enemies within' as well as in the seemingly common-sense acceptance of the argument that many Western societies have become 'too diverse' for their own good (Hansen 2007; Hartmann and Gerteis 2005). In this climate of fear and uncertainty it has also been evident that there has been a loss of historical perspective about both the background to current preoccupations and the reasons why multiculturalism as a set of policies and initiatives emerged in the first place. The various chapters in this book seek to address this loss of perspective by situating the present situation within a broader historical context. In doing so they give voice to the need to see debates about racial and ethnic inequality as part of an ongoing struggle to define the boundaries of solidarity and civic belonging in modern societies (Alexander 2003, 2006).

In our role as editors of this book we set ourselves two main tasks. First, in this chapter we want to provide some of the background context for the substantive chapters by providing an analytical overview of the changing research and theoretical agendas in the field of race and ethnic studies. Our main concerns here are to provide a critical account of some of the key facets of the sociological study of race and ethnicity. Second, we shall supplement this introductory overview by focusing in the concluding chapter on providing an overview of some of the common themes and questions that arise from the substantive chapters and the issues that are likely to come to the fore in the coming period of the 21st century. It is to the first of these tasks that we now move on to.

Changing contours of race and ethnicity

The role of racial and ethnic differences in British society has been a source of policy and scholarly debate ever since the post-1945 period, though it has become a significant part of social scientific research in the period since the 1970s (Bleich 2003; Solomos 2003). In terms of public policy, however, questions about racial and ethnic difference have been part of the social policy agenda from the 1960s onwards, with the development of policies aimed at promoting the social and cultural integration of racial and ethnic minorities, and anti-discrimination legislation aimed at tackling forms of exclusion in areas such as employment and housing and in the promotion of multicultural policies in fields such as education. Indeed, from the 1960s onwards there has been both a growing awareness of Britain as an ever-more complex multicultural society and an intense public debate about issues such as immigration, race relations policies and the changing boundaries of national identity and Britishness. According to Robin Cohen, it is precisely this 'fuzzy frontier' between the British and others that has been at the heart of policy debates about race and immigration in the decades since the 1960s (Cohen 1994). We have seen a wide range of legislation on issues such as immigration, race relations, nationality, urban policy, criminal justice and human rights that has helped to shape public discourses about race and ethnicity in the wider society.

As historical accounts have begun to uncover, however, this is not to say that debates about race and ethnicity can be seen simply as the product of the past five decades or so. Britain's role as a major global power and territorial empire goes back a number of centuries, and issues of race and difference have in this sense been part of our history and culture for a number of centuries (Holmes 1988; Rich 1990; Walvin 2000, 2007). For the purposes of this chapter, however, our primary focus will be on the contemporary period, and specifically on how questions about race and ethnic relations have been discussed within academic discourses and in the wider society.

The analysis in this chapter is framed by two overarching themes. First, and here we draw on conceptual debates within sociology about race and ethnicity, it attempts to clarify the meanings that have been attached to race and ethnicity. In doing so we shall focus specifically on some facets of debates that have emerged particularly in sociology over the past three decades (Back and Solomos 2009). Second, we shall attempt to delineate the political context within which the conceptual debates have taken place. This is an important issue to include in any analysis of theories of race and ethnic differences, since it seems evident in Britain and from a comparative perspective that questions about race and ethnicity are inevitably part of political discourses as well as embedded in academic and scholarly research.

Studying race, ethnicity and racism

The study of ethnic and racial relations has seen many transformations in the period since the 1960s. From being a relatively small field of research and scholarship, with the possible exception of sociological analysis in the United States, we have seen a noticeable growth of books and journals specialising in this area and a marked increase in both undergraduate and postgraduate teaching in this field. As a field of research it has also become more noticeably global in its focus. Over the past three decades we have seen the development of a diverse range of research that is going all over the globe on aspects of race and ethnic diversity (Goldberg and Solomos 2002). These changes in research agendas are in many ways not surprising, since the past three decades have witnessed intense social and political debate about race and ethnic issues in various parts of the globe. It is because of this changing geopolitical and social environment that we have seen intense debate about the boundaries of what it is that we study when we research race and ethnicity in the contemporary environment. Researching questions about race, ethnicity and racism inevitably draws scholars into questions about the nature of the social, cultural and economic realities that are being examined. It is also important to note that research in this field has inevitably been politicised, at least in the sense that it has been heavily influenced by wider political pressures and realities.

Early research on race and ethnic relations emerged within the sociological tradition of the United States in the early part of the 20th century. It is interesting to note in this regard that a historical overview of the origins and development of the American sociological tradition highlights the changing role of race and ethnicity as the focus of study and research, going back to the beginnings of sociology as an academic discipline in universities such as Chicago (Calhoun 2007). More specifically, a number of authors have noted both the centrality of race as a field of study in American sociology and the tensions that this gave rise to in a society that was deeply structured by the legacies of slavery, segregation and racism (Collins 2007; Winant 2007).

The study of race, racism and ethnicity became a core theme in the British sociological tradition, and to a more limited extent in other social science disciplines, in the period from the 1980s onwards. The work of earlier scholars such as Michael Banton and John Rex helped to establish the roots of the sociological study of race and ethnicity within British sociology during the 1960s and 1970s (Banton 1967; Rex 1970). Given their foundational role in shaping the study of race and ethnicity in Britain it is perhaps not surprising that both Banton and Rex feature prominently in subsequent discussions of the origins and limitations of research in this field (Malešević 2004). It remained the case, however, that as late as the 1970s race and ethnicity remained relatively marginal subfields of study within the social sciences. Indeed, in the early stages of research on race in Britain there was a noticeable scepticism about the need for a specific sub-field of race and ethnic studies (Cohen 1972).

In the period from the 1980s, however, there has been a noticeable expansion of scholarly research and debate during the past three decades, often influenced by radical forms of sociological theory and shaped in some ways by the changes that we have seen in the past three decades (Alexander and Knowles 2005; Centre for Contemporary Cultural Studies 1982; Knowles 2003). Events such as the urban riots of the 1980s, new patterns of migration and minority formation, and public tensions about religious and cultural diversity have all played a role in influencing new scholarship and public debate. The establishment of journals specialising in this field and of research groupings and centres and the appointment of academics specialising in these areas of research highlighted the institutionalisation of race and ethnicity as fields of research in the social sciences.

This growth of research and scholarship certainly helped establish race and ethnicity as fields of sociology and other disciplines. It also led to intense debate about what it was that social scientists working on these issues should actually be studying. From the 1980s onwards a proliferation of different schools of thought has come to the fore as a feature of this field, meaning that in practice there is little agreement among researchers about what it is that is subsumed under terms such as 'race', 'ethnicity' and 'racism' (for a recent overview of some of these debates see Carter and Virdee 2008). As with other sub-fields of contemporary sociology and the social sciences more generally there has been a process by which often-hostile theoretical debates have helped to influence both researchers and students alike. This is a point made, for example, by Bev Skeggs in her critical overview of feminist debates about sociology over the past few decades (Skeggs 2008).

A key question that has been at the heart of contemporary debates is the following: How has the category of race come to play such an important role in shaping contemporary social relations? This is not to say that there is agreement about how best to answer this question. On the contrary, scholars and researchers show little sign of agreeing about what it is we mean when we use notions such as race, racism, ethnicity and related social categories. Many of the questions raised in these debates take us to the following: Is race a suitable social category? What do we mean when we talk of racism as shaping the structure of particular societies? What role have race and ethnicity played in different historical contexts? Is it possible to speak of racism in the singular or racisms in the plural? These questions are at the heart of many of the theoretical and conceptual debates that dominate current debates, and yet what is interesting about much of the literature about race and racism is the absence of commonly agreed conceptual tools or even agreement about the general parameters of race and racism as fields of study.

Although 'race' and 'ethnicity' are terms often used in conjunction or in parallel to refer to social groups which differ in terms of physical attributes accorded social significance in the case of race or in terms of language, culture, place of origin or common membership of a descent group without distinguishing physical characteristics in the case of ethnicity, there is no equivalent term to 'racism' in relation to ethnicity. Perhaps ethnic conflict is analogous, but this is more of a descriptive term of certain consequences of the existence of different ethnic groups which may or may not occur. Racism as a concept is much more closely tied to the concept of race, and is a reminder that where members of society make distinctions between different racial groups, at least some members of that society are likely to behave in ways which give rise to racism as a behavioural and ideational consequence of making racial distinctions in the first place (Mosse 1985). Unfortunately the opposite does not hold. A society which denied or did not formally acknowledge the existence of different racial groups would not necessarily thus rid itself of racism (Goldberg 2008).

Over the past three decades there has been intense debate about the very language that we use in talking about race and racism (Bulmer and Solomos 2004; Essed and Goldberg 2002). Over the past decade or so the shifting boundaries of race and ethnicity as categories of social analysis have become evermore evident. In particular, there has been a plethora of studies that provide new perspectives on difference, identities, subjectivities and power relations. In this environment ideas about race, racism and ethnicity have become the subject of intense debate and controversy. Yet it is paradoxically the case that there is still much confusion about what it is that we mean by such notions, as evidenced by the range of terminological debates that have tended to dominate much discussion in recent years (Alexander and Knowles 2005; Bulmer and Solomos 2004). In the course of these debates it has become evident that a number of questions remain to be analysed and fully understood: What factors explain the mobilising power of ideas about race and ethnicity in the contemporary environment? What counter-values and counter-ideas can be developed to undermine the appeal of racist ideas and movements? Is it possible for communities that are socially defined by differences of race, ethnicity, religion or other signifiers to live together in societies which are able to ensure equality, justice and civilised tolerance? While it is not possible in a single collection such as this one to address all of these questions in detail, the various substantive chapters that follow do address them in the context of the specific arenas that they analyse.

Changing research strategies and agendas

One of the most important features of research and scholarship on race and ethnicity in the past three decades has been the emergence of a wide range of research strategies, theoretical paradigms and research agendas. It is perhaps not surprising in this context that there is little agreement among scholars working in a range of social science disciplines about the boundaries of what it is that we study when we carry out research on race and ethnicity. A good example of this lack of consensus can be found in the ways in which the issue of racial and ethnic identities has been analysed in contemporary scholarship and research.

The question of identity has been at the heart of both historical and contemporary accounts of race. George Mosse's historical reconstruction of the origins and evolution of modern racism makes the important point that race as a discursive formation relies on the definition of racial identities and their essential characteristics (Mosse 1985). In the contemporary context the question of identity and belonging has become an even more central aspect of racialised discourses and mobilisations. In the past few decades the ebb and flow of migration processes has helped to highlight the role of identity in shaping the experiences of racial and ethnic minorities. The preoccupation with identity can be taken as one outcome of concerns about where minorities in contemporary societies actually belong.

At a basic level, after all identity is about belonging, about what we have in common with some people and what differentiates us from others. Identity gives one a sense of personal location, and provides a stable core of one's individuality; but it is also about one's social relationships, one's complex involvement with others, and in the modern world these have become even more complex and confusing. Each of us lives with a variety of potentially contradictory identities, which battle within us for allegiance: as men or women, black or white, straight or gay, able-bodied or disabled. The list is potentially infinite, and so, therefore, are our possible belongings. Which of them we focus on, bring to the fore and identify with depends on a host of factors. At the centre, however, are the values we share or wish to share with others (Alcoff 1996; Anthias 2002; Appiah 2006).

Part of the problem, however, is that if one looks into the construction of racial and ethnic identities from a historical as well as a contemporary angle it becomes clear that they are not simply imposed from above. They are also chosen, and actively used, albeit within particular social contexts and constraints. Against dominant representations of others there is resistance (Appiah and Gates Jr 1995; Appiah and Gutmann 1996). Analysing resistance and agency re-politicises relations between collectivities and draws attention to the central constituting factor of power in social relations. But it is possible to overemphasise resistance; to validate others through validating the lives of the colonised and exploited. Valorising resistance may also have the unintended effect of belittling the enormous costs exacted in situations of unequal power, exclusion and discrimination. While political legitimacy, gaining access or a hearing, may depend on being able to call up a constituency and authorise representations through appeals to authenticity, it provides the basis for policing the boundaries of authenticity wherein some insiders may find themselves excluded because they are not authentic enough.

For example, stressing race and ethnic differences can obscure the experiences and interests that women may share as women. We therefore need to ask the following: Who is constructing the categories and defining the boundaries? Who is resisting these constructions and definitions? What are the consequences being written into or out of particular categories? What happens when subordinate groups seek to mobilise along boundaries drawn for the purposes of domination? What happens to individuals whose multiple identities may be fragmented and segmented by category politics?

One of the problems with much of the contemporary discussion of identity politics is that the dilemmas and questions outlined above are not adequately addressed. This is largely because much discussion is underpinned by the presumption that one's identity necessarily defines one's politics and that there can be no politics until the subject has excavated or laid claim to his/her identity. Inherent in such positions is the failure to understand the way in which identity grows out of and is transformed by action and struggle (Kumar 2008; Parekh 2008). This is one of the dangers of the preoccupation of exactly who is covered by specific racial and ethnic categories in contemporary British society.

By way of example, the usage of the notion of black to cover a variety of diverse communities has been increasingly rejected by scholars in favour of other categories such as Asian, Muslim or African Caribbean. Yet others have sought to argue for a notion of black grounded in 'race-ial' particularity. But the danger of these approaches is that one is presented with no more than a strategy of simple inversion wherein the old bad black essentialist subject is replaced by a new good ethnic or cultural essentialist subject whose identity is constructed as fixed by cultural, religious or ethnic characteristics.

Migration, mobilities and diversity

Ever since the 1960s successive British governments have accepted, with varying degrees of enthusiasm, the core idea that policies and initiatives on race and immigration should work on the principle of helping migrants to integrate into society and developing the capacity of the society as a whole to live with difference. In general terms, we have seen the emergence of a range of national and local policies that articulated a philosophy of multiculturalism, albeit in a context where there has been little agreement about what the term 'multiculturalism' actually means, both conceptually and in practice (Favell 2001; Lentin 2005). It has come to encompass a startling variety of viewpoints ranging from left to right, from academic to policy-oriented. What one finds, therefore, are a number of overlapping debates, a number of multiculturalisms, which one should be wary of eliding together into some singular phenomenon.

There are clearly quite divergent perspectives in the present political environment about how best to deal with all of these concerns. There is, for example, a wealth of discussion about what measures are necessary to tackle the inequalities and exclusions that confront minority groups. At the same time there is clear evidence that existing initiatives are severely limited in their impact and have failed to bring about a major improvement in the socio-political position of minorities. The application of the models outlined above in Germany, France and Italy has had a limited impact – discrimination is ubiquitous, racist violence is on the increase and segregation is a fact of life for a large proportion of minorities in each country.

Until recently policy debates in Britain, unlike some other European societies, seldom looked seriously at the issue of political and citizenship rights of migrants and their descendants. This was partly because it is widely assumed that such issues are not as relevant in this country given that many of those who came to Britain in the post-war period were British citizens and entitled in theory to participate politically. In Germany, where citizenship and its attendant political rights have traditionally been harder for migrants to acquire, it was seen by those on the Left in particular as an important means of promoting integration. However, ethnic minorities in Britain and elsewhere are questioning whether they are in fact fully included in and represented through political institutions (Back et al. 2004; Solomos and Back 1995). It is not surprising, therefore, that an important concern in recent years has been with the substance of citizenship and of the rights of minorities. In this environment there is a growing awareness of the gap between formal citizenship and the de facto restriction of the economic and social rights of minorities as a result of discrimination, economic restructuring and the decline of the welfare state.

This gap constitutes both evidence of a continuing failure of policy and an ongoing challenge not solely to policy-makers but also to scholars of these issues to rethink and reformulate responses to inequality and discrimination. The British government's 2002 White Paper on *Secure Borders, Safe Havens: Integration with Diversity in Modern Britain* acknowledged some of these failures, referring to divided and fractured communities, lacking a sense of common values or shared civic identity. In this it echoed some of the debates around *l'Affaire du Foulard* in France in which Islam was presented as a threat to the cohesion of the Republic, and a consensus emerged that a higher individualist price had to be exerted from French Muslims for their citizenship and membership in the French polity. In Britain, the emphasis of the White Paper was on the duties of newcomers to conform to develop a sense of shared identity. Racism and discrimination were mentioned only in passing and without any discussion.

The significance of issues of identity, difference and culture for minority and majority populations and the relationship between identity, difference and culture needs to be located within a broader reconceptualisation of substantive democracy that can include a place for the rights of minorities. The value of such a politics is that it makes the complicated issue of difference fundamental to addressing the discourse of substantive citizenship; moreover, it favours looking at the conflict over relations of power, identity and culture as central to a broader struggle to advance the critical imperatives of a democratic society. Of key importance to such a struggle is the need to rethink and rewrite difference in relation to wider questions of membership, community and social responsibility.

Controversies about the rights to citizenship of migrants and refugees have provided us with an insight into some of the real political tensions that remain about how we can define the boundaries of citizenship and belonging in contemporary societies. The growing public interest about the role of fundamentalism among sections of the Muslim communities in various countries has given a new life to debates about the issue of cultural differences and processes of integration. It is interesting to note in this regard that justifiable concerns about the rights of women are being exploited both to attack some minorities and to undermine a commitment to multiculturalism. By highlighting some of the most obvious limitations of multiculturalism and anti-racism in shaping policy change in this field such controversies have done much to bring about a more critical debate about the role and impact of policies which are premised on notions such as multiculturalism. They have also highlighted the ever-changing terms of political and policy agendas about these issues and the fact that there is little agreement about what kind of strategies for change should be pursued.

The preoccupation in much of the literature in this field with issues of identity and the assertion of the relevance and importance of understanding the role of new ethnicities has not resolved the fundamental question of how to balance the quest for evermore specific identities with the need to allow for broader and less fixed cultural identities. Indeed, if anything, this quest for a politics of identity has helped to highlight one of the key dilemmas of liberal political thought. Yet what is quite clear is that the quest for more specific, as opposed to universal, identities is becoming more pronounced in the present political environment. The search for national, ethnic and racial has become a pronounced, if not dominant, feature of political debate within both majority and minority communities in the postmodern societies of the early 21st century.

One of the dilemmas we face in the present environment is that there is a clear possibility that new patterns of segregation could establish themselves and limit everyday interaction between racially defined groups. The growing evidence of a crisis of race and of racialised class inequalities in the United States is a poignant reminder that the Civil Rights Movement and other movements since then have had at best a partial impact on established patterns of racial inequality and have not stopped the development of new patterns of exclusion and segregation. But it is also clear that there is evidence that within contemporary European societies there is the danger of institutionalising new forms of exclusion as a result of increased racial violence and racist mobilisations by the extreme Right.

Given our experiences in quite diverse local and national political environments, who would argue with any real faith that we can ignore them? Can we be sure that the resurgence of racist nationalism does not pose a very real danger for the possibility of civilised coexistence between groups defined as belonging to different racial, ethnic and national identities? One of the great ironies of the present situation is that transnational economic, social and political relations have helped to create a multiplicity of migrant networks and communities that transcend received national boundaries. Categories such as migrants and refugees are no longer an adequate way to describe the realities of movement and settlement in many parts of the globe. In many ways the idea of diaspora as an unending sojourn across different lands better captures the reality of transnational networks and communities than the language of immigration and assimilation. Multiple, circular and return migrations, rather than a single great journey from one sedentary space to another, have helped to transform transnational spaces by creating new forms of cultural and political identity.

This point can be illustrated by reference to some research on the changing debates about race and racism within the context of football culture in England. In research that was carried out in the late 1990s and early 2000s among football supporters, players and administrators the emphasis was on the need to explore the ways in which changing discourses about race and nation were emerging as part of English football culture during this period (Back, Crabbe and Solomos 2001). Drawing on empirical research among football supporters, players and administrators the researchers argued that the everyday experiences of race and racism in sport are not already predetermined. In the rituals of sporting life the relationship between race, nation and inclusion is repeatedly stated and defined through the feelings of identity and belonging that are manifest between teams and their devoted supporters. In everyday social environments such as sport, race and nation function not as given entities but social forms that are staged through big games and repeated sporting dramas. Their form and quality are defined through the performance itself and continuities are established through repetition. From this perspective race is not a given but the process in which racial difference is invoked and connected with issues of identity, entitlement and belonging. Through focusing on the repeated or cyclical nature of these processes in sport, it is possible to identify moments in which ruptures occur that may challenge the tenets of racial exclusion (Burdsey 2006; Hartmann 2003).

Research such as this confronts precisely the question of how racial identities are constructed and refashioned in everyday contexts. It is within the everydayness of sport that we can find the micro-enactment of inclusion/exclusion, group definition and identity. Even in the definition of rivalries within sport there is recognition. The ways in which sporting cultures put the world together implicitly constructs limits on the levels of participation from Britain's diverse minority communities. This involves also facing the vexed question about how to define and conceptualise racism. Research on sport highlights the complex ways in which racial ideologies can be cast through either the racialised body (i.e. that racial difference can be connected with athletic prowess and, by implication, also cerebral function) or the ossified notions of culture that are defined in the relationship between particular cultural groupings and their relationship to sport and sporting cultures (Carrington 2008).

Part of the point of raising this example here is to suggest that we need to see research on race and ethnicity as not merely concerned with the macrolevel social analysis of these phenomena but as grounded in the everydayness of how race and ethnicity is experienced by individuals, groups, communities and within institutions (Essed 1991, 2000). It is perhaps research of this kind that can show us something about the ways in which ideas about race and racial difference work in specific contexts that we can begin to advance our conceptual frameworks in directions that can make them more sensitive to the nuanced and complex varieties of racism in contemporary societies.

Mapping the book

The eight substantive chapters that follow have been organised in such a way that they cover the issues that have played a key role in shaping race and ethnic relations in contemporary Britain as well as other societies. This is not to say that they exhaust the range of issues that could potentially be covered in a book of this kind, but we have sought to cover what are seen as the key arenas in which questions about race and ethnicity have been an important issue in public debate.

The first substantive chapter by Malcolm Harrison and Deborah Phillips is focused on the role of housing and residence in shaping the experiences of minority communities in Britain and other European countries. Housing and residence has been an area of major scholarship and research in the field of race and ethnic studies for some time now, going back to classic studies such as Rex and Moore's account of Birmingham in the 1960s (Rex and Moore 1967). In this chapter we find both an overview of previous scholarship and a critical analysis of contemporary patterns and processes that draws on current empirical research. It also highlights the importance of comparative analysis of these issues if we are to develop an understanding of both the commonalities and the differences between national experiences. The question of how to compare the experiences of diverse societies is an issue that is also touched upon in some of the other chapters and we shall also return to it in the concluding chapter.

The next chapter, by Patricia Hynes and Rosemary Sales, continues the focus on residence and locality by looking at the experiences of asylum seekers and refugees over the past decade. Starting off from the policy of dispersal that has been at the heart of state responses to asylum and refuge in Britain, along with other countries, Hynes and Sales are able to explore both the origins of this policy and the tortuous routes through which it was put into practice. They highlight the importance of notions of social cohesion and managed migration in shaping both official and public discourses about asylum seekers and the limitations of governmental policies in dealing with the complexities of this important social phenomenon.

Following on from the analysis of housing and residence, the chapter by Satnam Virdee focuses on the role of employment and labour market discrimination in structuring the class position of racial minorities in Britain. Virdee's starting point is a radical critique of both earlier studies of this issue and of the underlying assumptions of the public policy agenda in this area. He begins with an overview of research on employment and the class-positioning of minorities from the mid-1960s onwards. In the course of the chapter he moves on to review evidence about the continuing role of disadvantage as well as evidence of mobility by some minority communities in the labour market.

A recurrent theme in studies of race and ethnicity from the 1970s onwards has been the question of policing minority communities, particularly in socially deprived inner city localities. The chapter by Eugene McLaughlin focuses particularly on the changing context of race and policing in the aftermath of the Macpherson Report on the murder of Stephen Lawrence (Macpherson 1999). In a wide-ranging analysis of developments over the past decade McLaughlin provides an insight into the important role of debates about youth and gang culture, new patterns of migration and terrorism in influencing the development of policy in this field. In developing his account of the changing contours of race and policing in the current period he seeks to emphasise the need for an analytic frame that is sensitive to the volatility of policy agendas in this field. A case in point is his account of the ways in which popular fears about street crime and youth gang cultures become part of wider sets of racialised discourses about the role of the police and the breakdown of public order.

The focus of James Nazroo's chapter is on the issue of ethnic differences in health, in terms of both morbidity and mortality. Nazroo's chapter draws empirically on research in the United Kingdom, though he also covers some aspects of research in other countries, and seeks to both describe and explain the ethnic patterning of health. His account emphasises the need for a more nuanced and complex analysis of the evidence about the interplay between race and ethnicity and health outcomes. While arguing forcefully that ethnic health inequalities are a product of racialised social relations, Nazroo reiterates the need to locate such inequalities within a broader economic and social analytical frame.

The centrality of education and schooling in shaping the experiences of minority children has been a subject of much debate and research for a number of decades. The chapter by David Gillborn and Nicola Rollock provides a critical overview of current qualitative and quantitative research in this field. Their analysis shows that race inequities continue to scar the English educational system. Worse still, education policy appears to be actively implicated in the processes that sustain, and in some cases extend, race inequity. Some of the processes can appear subtle; for example, concerning teachers' differential expectations and the cumulative effects of internal selection within schools.

The last two substantive chapters have a somewhat broader focus than the previous six chapters. Myria Georgiou's chapter is concerned with the role of media representations of ethnic and racial diversity. Drawing on a wide range of research evidence, she provides a critical account of the variety of ways in which the mediated construction of minority communities plays a vital role in shaping race and ethnic relations in societies such as the United Kingdom. In addition, however, she provides an analysis of what actions have been taken to tackle such issues as the negative stereotyping of minorities in the press and other popular media.

Finally, the concluding substantive chapter by Anthony Heath, Catherine Rothon and Sundas Ali focuses on the variety of ways in which ethnic minorities identify themselves and also on the way they see themselves in relation to British society. In the aftermath of events in the current decade this is a question that is at the heart of debates about religious diversity, social cohesion and citizenship. It is also an issue that has given rise to much speculative discussion that has not drawn on available research findings. The focus of the chapter on using detailed empirical research, from data sources such as the British Social Attitudes Survey, is a challenge to the limitations of such speculation. A good example of this approach can be found in the dissection of the evidence about the commitment of minority communities to a sense of belonging to British society.

Conclusion

The analysis outlined in this chapter has sought to set the scene for the substantive chapters that follow by outlining key facets of current academic and policy debates about race and ethnicity. We began by looking at some of the key theoretical perspectives that have emerged in academic discourses and attempted to link these debates to trends and developments in the contemporary social and political environment. Perhaps the main point that we want to emphasise in conclusion is that this is a field that is constantly being refashioned by the emergence of new patterns of racialisation, migration and minority formation. Part of the dilemma we face at the present time is that there is a relative dearth of research on the everyday experiences of race, ethnic and cultural diversity in specific social and cultural environments. This is partly because the preoccupation with developing sophisticated theoretical narratives has led to a neglect of empirically focused research, whether at the local, national or transnational level.

This is even more evident in the ways in which the question of racism, and the mechanisms through which it is produced and reproduced within contemporary societies, has been handled in contemporary sociological theories. We have seen very little empirically focused research in recent years on the ways in which race is actually experienced in particular communities and localities and how racist mobilisations actually take shape in specific situations. It is only through such an analysis that we can begin to imagine a politics that challenges racism and the processes of exclusion on which it is based.

It is evident from the context and the reference points of this introduction and the following substantive chapters that the arguments developed here engage closely with current debates and controversies within the British academic and policy environment. It may well be that some of the points raised here need to be thought of somewhat differently within a broader set of theoretical debates about the changing nature of contemporary forms of racism. It is certainly the case that much can be learned from all of us reflecting on the concerns and preoccupations, as well as the terms of discourse, of our different national scholarly traditions in this field (Winant 2006). It seems to us, however, that part of our concern throughout this dialogue should be a critical interrogation about what it is that we are doing when we are researching issues such as racism, immigration and multiculturalism in our current social and political environment. Such a critical self-awareness is important if we are to understand the shifting patterns of race and ethnic relations in the coming period.

References

Alcoff, L. M. (1996). 'Philosophy and Racial Identity'. *Radical Philosophy* 75: 5–14.

Alexander, C. E. and Knowles, C. (2005). *Making Race Matter: Bodies, Space, and Identity*. Basingstoke: Palgrave Macmillan.

Alexander, J. C. (2003). *The Meanings of Social Life: A Cultural Sociology*. New York: Oxford University Press.

Alexander, J. C. (2006). *The Civil Sphere*. New York: Oxford University Press.

Anthias, F. (2002). 'Where Do I Belong? Narrating Collective Identity and Translocational Positionality'. *Ethnicities* 2 (4): 491–514.

Appiah, K. A. (2006). 'The Politics of Identity'. *Daedalus* Fall: 15–22.

Appiah, K. A. and Gates Jr, H. L. (eds) (1995). *Identities*. Chicago: University of Chicago Press.

Appiah, K. A. and Gutmann, A. (1996). *Color Conscious: The Political Morality of Race*. Princeton: Princeton University Press.

Back, L., Crabbe, T. and Solomos, J. (2001). *The Changing Face of Football: Racism, Identity and Multiculture in the English Game*. Oxford: Berg.

Back, L., Keith, M., Khan, A., Shukra, K. and Solomos, J. (2004). 'Black Politics and the Web of Joined-up Governance: Compromise, Ethnic Minority Mobilisation and the Transitional Public Sphere'. *Social Movement Studies* 2 (1): 31–50.

Back, L. and Solomos, J. (eds) (2009). *Theories of Race and Racism: A Reader*, 2nd Ed. London: Routledge.

Banton, M. (1967). *Race Relations*. New York: Basic Books.

Bleich, E. (2003). *Race Relations in Britain and France: Ideas and Policymaking since the 1960s*. Cambridge: Cambridge University Press.

Bulmer, M. and Solomos, J. (eds) (2004). *Researching Race and Racism*. London: Routledge.

Burdsey, D. (2006). '"If I Ever Play Football, Dad, Can I Play for England or India?" British Asians, Sport and Diasporic National Identities'. *Sociology* 40 (1): 11–28.

Calhoun, C. J. (2007). *Sociology in America: A History*. Chicago: University of Chicago Press.

Carrington, B. (2008). '"What's the Footballer Doing Here?" Racialized Performativity, Reflexivity, and Identity'. *Cultural Studies <=> Critical Methodologies* 8 (4): 423–52.

Carter, B. and Virdee, S. (2008). 'Racism and the Sociological Imagination'. *British Journal of Sociology* 59 (4): 661–79.

Centre for Contemporary Cultural Studies (1982). *The Empire Strikes Back: Race and Racism in 70s Britain*. London: Hutchinson.

Cohen, P. S. (1972). 'Need There Be a Sociology of Race Relations'. *Sociology* 6 (1): 101–8.

Cohen, R. (1994). *Fuzzy Frontiers of Identity: The British Case and the Others*. London: Longman.

Collins, P. H. (2007). 'Pushing the Boundaries or Business as Usual? Race, Class, and Gender Studies and Sociological Inquiry' in Calhoun, C. (ed.) *Sociology in America: A History*. Chicago: University of Chicago Press.

Essed, P. (1991). *Understanding Everyday Racism: An Interdisciplinary Theory*. Newbury Park: Sage.

Essed, P. (2000). *Diversity: Gender, Color, and Culture*. Amherst: University of Massachusetts.

Essed, P. and Goldberg, D. T. (eds) (2002). *Race Critical Theories: Text and Context*. Oxford: Blackwell.

Favell, A. (2001). 'Multiethnic Britain: An Exception in Europe'. *Patterns of Prejudice* 35 (1): 35–58.

Goldberg, D. T. (2008). *The Threat of Race: Reflections on Racial Neoliberalism*. Malden, MA: Wiley-Blackwell.

Goldberg, D. T. and Solomos, J. (eds) (2002). *A Companion to Racial and Ethnic Studies*. Oxford: Blackwell.

Hansen, R. (2007). 'Diversity, Integration and the Turn from Multiculturalism in the United Kingdom' in Banting, K., Courchene, T. J. and Seidle, F. L. (eds) *Belonging? Diversity, Recognition and Shared Citizenship in Canada*. Montreal: Institute for Research on Public Policy.

Hartmann, D. (2003). 'What Can We Learn From Sport if We Take Sport Seriously as a Racial Force? Lessons from C. L. R. James Beyond a Boundary'. *Ethnic and Racial Studies* 26 (3): 451–83.

Hartmann, D. and Gerteis, J. (2005). 'Dealing with Diversity: Mapping Multiculturalism in Sociological Terms'. *Sociological Theory* 23 (2): 218–40.

Holmes, C. (1988). *John Bull's Island*. Basingstoke: Macmillan.

Knowles, C. (2003). *Race and Social Analysis*. London: Sage.

Kumar, K. (2008). 'The Question of European Identity: Europe in the American Mirror'. *European Journal of Social Theory* 11 (1): 87–105.

Lentin, A. (2005). 'Replacing "Race", Historicizing "Culture" in Multiculturalism'. *Patterns of Prejudice* 39 (4): 379–96.

Macpherson, W. (1999). *The Stephen Lawrence Inquiry*. London: Stationery Office.

Malešević, S. (2004). *The Sociology of Ethnicity*. London: Sage.

Mosse, G. L. (1985). *Toward the Final Solution: A History of European Racism*. Madison: University of Wisconsin Press.

Parekh, B. (2008). *A New Politics of Identity: Political Principles for an Interdependent World*. Basingstoke: Palgrave Macmillan.

Rex, J. (1970). *Race Relations in Sociological Theory*. London: Weidenfeld & Nicolson.

Rex, J. and Moore, R. (1967). *Race, Community and Conflict: A Study of Sparkbrook*. Oxford: Oxford University Press.

Rich, P. B. (1990). *Race and Empire in British Politics*. Cambridge: Cambridge University Press.

Skeggs, B. (2008). 'The Dirty History of Feminism and Sociology: Or the War of Conceptual Attrition'. *Sociological Review* 56 (4): 670–90.

Solomos, J. (2003). *Race and Racism in Britain*, 3rd Ed. Basingstoke: Palgrave Macmillan.

Solomos, J. and Back, L. (1995). *Race, Politics, and Social Change*. London: Routledge.

Walvin, J. (2000). *Making the Black Atlantic: Britain and the African Diaspora*. London: Cassell.

Walvin, J. (2007). *The Trader, the Owner, the Slave: Parallel Lives in the Age of Slavery*. London: Jonathan Cape.

Winant, H. (2006). 'Race and Racism: Towards a Global Future'. *Ethnic and Racial Studies* 29 (5): 986–1003.

Winant, H. (2007). 'The Dark Side of the Force: One Hundred Years of the Sociology of Race' in Calhoun, C. (ed.) *Sociology in America: A History*. Chicago: University of Chicago Press.

CHAPTER 2

Housing and Neighbourhoods: A UK and European Perspective

MALCOLM HARRISON AND DEBORAH PHILLIPS

Introduction

A great deal has been written in recent decades about ethnicity and urban housing, and the first aim of this chapter is to pull together what is already known about the overall picture of conditions and trends in the UK. To enhance the story, however, we also go beyond previous commentaries, by placing this experience alongside and within a broader European context. Drawing on recent research (Harrison et al., 2006), we will evaluate UK trends and achievements within a wider comparative frame.

This chapter starts by examining the patterns and processes of change in minority ethnic housing and settlement in the UK. The record on ethnicity and racism reveals a mixture of failures and successes. On the one hand, minority ethnic groups have faced persistent problems of poor quality accommodation, disadvantaged neighbourhoods, and limited choice. People from minority ethnic backgrounds have appeared in disproportionately high numbers amongst the homeless in recent years, while there is still evidence of severe racist threats and abuse for those seeking accommodation in some white-dominated social rented housing areas. On the other hand, progress has been made by particular households and communities, with a degree of suburbanisation into more prosperous places, and many successful efforts by activists to put ethnic relations nearer to the heart of public policy debates.

Having reviewed the UK position, the chapter turns to the broader European scene. This wider perspective helps in three ways. First, it reinforces the point that processes and patterns of discrimination and exclusion are not random, but have a systematic and persistent character. Similar racist practices occur in the housing field within countries that are very different. Cross-national comparison indicates striking similarities in the housing experiences of minority ethnic groups across Europe, despite diversity of social, cultural and political contexts. Similar mechanisms of housing discrimination and disadvantage are found in different countries, and people seen as 'different' are often subjected to exclusion and ill-treatment, ranging from being refused a property to physical attacks aimed at keeping households out of a particular locality. It is clear that the UK often conforms to a much more general pattern of experiences.

Second, we can see that there is now considerable diversity in the housing experiences of the more established minority ethnic groups in most European countries, reflecting differences in social class, ethnicity, generation, family type and gender. Distinct ethnic clusters persist in some of the poorest urban neighbourhoods, but the passing decades have seen successive generations moving into a wider range of housing circumstances, property types and areas. Again, we can see that a UK picture is paralleled at least to a degree in other places. The rate of progress of particular minority ethnic groups varies, however, and may well be different in differing settings. Some scholars in Europe refer to an 'ethnic hierarchy' (as in Sweden), or 'differential incorporation' (as in the UK: see Harrison with Davis, 2001). This may occur within (and perhaps sometimes between) countries or cities, giving rise to different patterns of disadvantage for specific groups in differing contexts.

Third, we want to remind readers that the UK has in many ways been one of Europe's pioneers in its strategies and methodologies for equality and diversity. Britain is relatively strong on law, data, monitoring, and research. When compared with several European Union counterparts, the UK has developed a set of policies and regulatory methodologies that appear relatively advanced and comprehensive (although this does not necessarily apply to the management of asylum and refugee issues). This is not to suggest that good intentions are always carried through to successful implementation, for they are not. There are also still numerous problems needing more attention, gaps in the information base, and inadequate depth in UK research enterprises. Nonetheless, it is important to look at other European situations in order to be fully aware of what has been achieved in Britain.

UK housing experiences: general trends and patterns

The earliest accounts of the experiences of minority ethnic groups in the housing market reveal how newly arriving immigrants had little choice but to occupy the bottom end of the market, ending up in poor private rental properties or, in the case of South Asians, purchasing cheap, deteriorating inner-city terraced housing abandoned by white households moving to the suburbs. Distinct ethnic clusters developed in the inner cities, the product of a number of often inter-related factors, namely the newcomers' poverty and lack of knowledge of the housing market, the pattern of job opportunities open to them, the desire for clustering for social and cultural reasons, and the often blatant discrimination faced by black minority ethnic groups (and some white immigrants) in the early post-war years.

The details of housing experiences in the very unwelcoming environments facing minorities were analysed in a group of 'classic' housing and 'race' studies, running roughly from the 1960s to the end of the 1980s. The Commission for Racial Equality (CRE) played an important investigative role, along with aca-demic researchers (see CRE, 1984, 1984a, 1985, 1985a, 1987, 1988, 1988a, 1990, 1990a). Research in several cities indicated that minority ethnic households were disadvantaged through direct and indirect discrimination when encoun-tering public sector housing allocation processes (Henderson and Karn, 1987; Phillips, 1986; Sarre et al., 1989; Simpson, 1981). Minority ethnic households often ended up in inferior dwellings or areas. There was also discrimination in private sector markets, with 'gatekeepers' such as estate agents contributing to segregation by 'steering' minority households away from areas favoured by white people. Individual private landlords could simply tell a potential renter from a minority community that a flat had already been let to someone else (saying 'sorry, it's gone'), even though this might be untrue. Across all hous-ing sectors it was relatively easy for direct or indirect discrimination to occur, since monitoring and equality codes were by today's standards primitive or non-existent. Given the potency of white racism, 'no-go' areas developed that minority households were reluctant to live within, or even pass through. Mean-while, some areas with substantial minority ethnic settlement came to be treated as representing relatively high risks for mortgage lending, so that purchasers and sellers within them faced problems of delays, extra costs, or even a rel-ative 'mortgage famine'. The term 'red-lining' was borrowed from the USA to describe the negative delineation of such areas by building societies (for mortgages see CRE, 1985a; Harrison and Stevens, 1981).

By contrast, today's UK housing policy and practice environments are markedly different from those of earlier periods. Practices and policies in social rented housing provision in particular have undergone a considerable shift in response to criticisms and developments in law and guidelines. Many overt dis-criminatory practices of earlier decades could not occur in UK social renting now, as the decision-making environment is far more regulated (although this is not so much the case for the private sectors). Furthermore, as well as improv-ing existing services, the UK has paralleled US Affirmative Action with more modest (but less contested) strategies for Positive Action. The latter have helped 'bring through' able minority ethnic personnel in the labour market, with Positive Action Training in Housing schemes being important contributors (see Julienne, 2001), along with innovations such as mentoring schemes for housing workers. Another policy (begun in the mid-1980s) was to support the development of black and minority ethnic (BME) housing associations. Some observers have suggested that overall progress in the UK housing sector has been greater than in several other spheres. For instance, while equal opportunities have not yet been secured in housing employment, a Cabinet Office report at the start of this decade claimed housing to be 'one of the best service sectors in terms of minority ethnic employment' (2000, p. 62). Nonetheless, very few people from minority ethnic groups have as yet found their way into top housing jobs in local government or housing associations (*Housing Today*, 22nd April, 2005).

Of course, implementation of equality policies is not always effective, and there are many topics on which monitoring data are scarce, or where staffing and services remain inadequate. Furthermore, new forms of discrimination can develop as organisations and tasks shift; for example, discriminatory practices might arise in the control of anti-social behaviour or the treatment of young people in housing. In the private sectors, a slowly emerging issue over the last 15 years has been the performance of mortgage lenders, banks and insurers in relation to religious or cultural minorities, where particular living arrangements and religious requirements may not have been well catered for. Some efforts have been made to respond to Islamic financing preferences. Meanwhile, however, there may be an absence of facilities or cover for specific low-income housing districts, so that the term 'red-lining' has reappeared in press reporting, this time being applied to insurance companies (see *The Guardian*, 14 November 1998; 30 January 1999).

Although UK public policy has responded positively to the multicultural environment that has developed in urban areas, this response has been overlaid recently by fears about geographical segregation and separatism in lifestyles and social organisation, and by the potential for new manifestations of conflict. Interest in integration and community relations is an old concern that was evident especially in some earlier phases of 'race relations' work in Britain, but has now been given something of a 'makeover'. In particular, a high-profile debate has taken place about an apparent lack of community cohesion, following disturbances on the streets of northern England at the start of the 21st century (see Harrison et al., 2005). As argued elsewhere (Phillips, 2006), popular and political discourses have tended to attribute ethnic segregation to cultural/religious differences (between British Asians and whites), and to downplay institutional or wider structural constraints on ethnic mixing. Significantly (especially given public anxieties about the national identity and citizenship of 'alien others'), the persistence of visible minority ethnic clustering within inner-city areas is frequently portrayed as a 'problem' to be tackled by policy solutions. This has resonances with political themes in some other EU countries.

Change and continuity in neighbourhood clustering and disadvantage

When considering arguments about community cohesion it is important to recognise that there have been numerous ongoing changes in the housing and settlement patterns that can be observed over the post-war years. Certainly, it is a mistake to rely on a static image of minority ethnic settlement segregation, or to assert that the dominant driver of residence patterns is deliberate 'self-segregation' by minority ethnic households. Over time, a combination of factors has been operating to facilitate significant shifts in residence, and specific positive trends have improved market positions and widened housing and neighbourhood options. Amongst key factors enabling movement beyond established areas of settlement have been the following:

- The impact of both structural and individual/household change.
- 'Race' relations legislation and 'race equality' initiatives (mainly within the social housing sector), with a more responsive social housing sector.
- Changing housing demands from a socially, culturally, demographically, and economically maturing population, with growing minority ethnic empowerment through socio-economic advancement and greater skills in negotiating the housing market.
- Generational differences in housing aspirations and strategies.
- The role of minority ethnic creativity in bringing advancement.

Thus – and despite the continuities of clustering in established areas of settlement – socio-economic developments have brought greater social and spatial mobility to minority ethnic populations, and have resulted in loosening ties (voluntary and imposed) to particular (usually inner city) locations. One of the most obvious signs of this has been the growing number of minority ethnic households moving to the suburbs and other areas not traditionally associated with minority ethnic settlement in the UK. As Rees and Butt's analysis of geographical change over the 1981–2001 period concludes, the modest deconcentration of minority ethnic groups evident between 1981 and 1991 'swelled in the 1991–2001 decade to more significant shifts' (Rees and Butt, 2004, p. 185). For those households searching within private housing markets, access to finance and information has greatly improved in overall terms since the early days of widespread institutional exclusion, landlord hostility, and vendor discrimination. The lowering of barriers by these 'gatekeepers', coupled with greater disposable income, has resulted in increasing numbers of black and minority ethnic households moving well up the property ladder as social class differences have widened.

Of course, this positive pattern of change is only half the story. We can also see some worrying continuities between the early post-war years and now. The 2001 Census indicates that there are still major inequalities between white British and black minority ethnic groups when considered in terms of access to good quality housing in all tenures, levels of overcrowding, and representation within disadvantaged residential neighbourhoods. There remains real concern about material disadvantages and barriers being encountered by minority ethnic residents living in deprived urban areas. Central government acknowledges the situation, endorsing the view that 67 per cent of people from black minority ethnic communities live in the 88 most deprived districts in England, compared to 37 per cent of the white population (see Home Office, 2004). The English House Condition Survey (2001) found that black and minority ethnic households are nearly three times (27 per cent) as likely to live in 'poor' neighbourhoods as whites (10 per cent). Qualitative research on the housing circumstances of people of South Asian origin living in inner Bradford in 2002 depicts the everyday experiences behind these statistics. As one young Pakistani man said, 'I'm sure a white person walking into my house would think "do people live here"? .... I'm sure they'd do that on every other house on my street' (see Phillips and Harrison, 2005, p. 182). If we add to this the finding already noted at the start of this chapter that black minority ethnic groups are disproportionately represented amongst the homeless (representing 26 per cent of those accepted as homeless by local authorities between January and March 2004, but only 8 per cent of the general population, according to Department of Communities and Local Government (DCLG) statistics), and take into account the power of racist harassment to shape housing choices, it is clear that a pattern of minority ethnic disadvantage in housing persists.

Demographic projections suggest that, by 2011, the number of households headed by someone of minority ethnic origin in the UK will increase by 39 per cent compared with 18 per cent for white heads of households. This reflects the age structure of the minority ethnic population, family size, and overcrowding levels. Overcrowding is likely to increase as younger family members marry. Research into the views of five minority ethnic groups in Leeds (Law et al., 1996) and, more recently, British Asian families in Leeds and Bradford (Phillips et al., 2007) has pointed to the complexity of processes influencing household formation and re-formation. Decisions on whether or not to move out of the parental home reflect financial pressures, changing views of family life and perceived housing options. The desire for extended family living under one roof, and thus large accommodation, persists amongst many British Asian families, perhaps especially Muslims. This restricts housing choices across the social classes. The search by middle-class families for suburban housing, for example, is often governed by the desire for property with sufficient room to build an extension. Nevertheless, the potential for the formation of smaller households is also evident for all minority ethnic groups. The greatest pressure for new household formation lies with British Pakistani and Bangladeshi families, because of their youthful age structure and the high incidence of overcrowding within the traditional inner areas of terraced housing. However, these groups also currently occupy the weakest position in the housing and employment markets, and may thus encounter difficulties in securing decent, affordable, and large enough accommodation in their preferred locations.

Although concentration in difficult localities and environments is a salient policy concern, the reasons for persistent ethnic clustering in the more deprived areas of our inner cities remain open to debate. Over the decades, the salience of minority ethnic choice versus constraint and the power of individual agency versus institutional discrimination in shaping geographies of ethnic settlement within cities have been hotly contested (for a review of the debates see Phillips, 1998; Ratcliffe, 1996; Sarre et al., 1989). Those favouring 'choice based' explanations have emphasised the role of social and cultural heritage and attachments when making housing and neighbourhood decisions. In contrast, others have stressed the constraints imposed on minority ethnic people's choices by racism, poverty, institutional discrimination, the fear of racist harassment in certain areas, and cultural/familial obligations. Acknowledging both the main lines of argument here, we suggest that spatially segregated living (in low quality environments and housing) very often arises through an accumulation of *bounded choices*. These reflect both cultural values or affiliations, and practicalities in terms of support (especially for those with limited English), as well as real and perceived constraints on where minority ethnic people can live.

There is an additional point to make about locality choices. Despite the low housing and environmental quality of many established areas of minority ethnic settlement, a degree of long-term voluntary geographical segregation amongst households need not necessarily be problematic in itself. Simpson, Phillips and Ahmed (2007) have drawn a distinction between 'benign' and 'dysfunctional' segregation. 'Benign segregation' occurs when new generations stay close to their parental home and opt to live in neighbourhoods where they can easily draw on, and contribute to, their social and cultural networks. 'Dysfunctional segregation' occurs when people of different heritage remain apart due to inequality in the housing market or due to perceived and real racialised territories that influence people's housing choices.

As far as racism's effects are concerned, we need to emphasise that harassment continues to be extremely problematic. This is in spite of the fact that the need to tackle it has been acknowledged time after time, and over many years. Although tensions can arise between people from different minority groups as well as with the white mainstream, it is racism within white social housing neighbourhoods that is often seen as the crucial practical issue (Phillips and Harrison, 2005). Chahal (2005) has indicated the ingredients required to create effective response and prevention strategies, but we also need to bear in mind broader events and trends that help sustain racism. Some media and political commentaries, both on asylum seekers and on Islam, may have contributed to a climate of hostility. Going further, competition for scarce social rented dwellings may be contributing to the maintenance of 'race hate'. At the very least, current situations of severe rationing and delays in access – in a process where tenancy allocation is quite properly needs-led – may have been exacerbating feelings of grievance amongst white households that could be built on by racist activists to claim legitimacy. In a context of long-standing constraints placed on new building for social housing tenancies, observers suggest that the UK now has an 'affordability crisis' (for instance, see David Orr, Chief Executive of the National Housing Federation, in *The Guardian*, 18 May 2007). At the same time, newer migrant groups and young households within some established BME communities are likely to be seeking affordable rented dwellings in substantial numbers, and to be able to demonstrate their need for it. The advent of 'choice-based lettings' (in which property vacancies are widely advertised) may have made allocations and shortages more visible, at the same time as potentially helping to open up access to social renting for more minority ethnic households. It could remain especially difficult to deal with hate crime in environments marked by low incomes, inadequate educational pathways, poor job opportunities, and difficulties in securing good housing. In any event, the persistence of spatial separations between groups cannot be understood without taking account of the patterns of white housing choices and racist practices.

Differences amongst minority groups: a complex and shifting pattern

Whilst acknowledging the housing improvements and ongoing problems shared across different minority groups, we also need to highlight the importance of diversity. Housing histories have varied between differing groups or communities, with distinctions in terms of tenure, housing types and quality, household sizes, and overall settlement patterns. In effect, each group has had its own settlement geography, which has shifted over time. Regional or localised housing and labour market effects may also shape opportunities, and the generational differences mentioned above may bring challenges, conditions, and options different from those faced by previous generations of households.

As time has passed, the social rented sector has come to play important roles in the housing of particular ethnic groups. The 2001 Census indicates that 'Black Caribbeans' and Bangladeshis (especially those living in London) are now well represented in social housing (see Table 2.1), a sector in which minority ethnic groups were once acutely disadvantaged by formal and informal rules and direct discrimination. Social renting is today also a significant potential resource for female-headed households in general, reflecting its vital role for groups with limited options in private markets. Housing associations (including those that are BME-led) have performed significant functions in offering important routes for minorities into affordable housing. Tenure patterns are further complicated by regional market conditions. In London these conditions have long made movement into ownership difficult, a factor giving impetus to the social renting options. In addition, there are variations nationally and locally within groups as well as between them.

One way of looking at the situation is to think in terms of 'difference within difference' (Harrison with Davis, 2001). On the one hand, there are persistent shared problems across and within ethnic groups. On the other hand, we can see much variety in households' opportunities and options, as well as in current conditions and experiences. At the detailed level, lines of differentiation affecting housing may change over time. Perhaps a plausible argument about

Table 2.1 Housing Tenure by Ethnic Group in England and Wales, 2001 (Percentages)

	Owned outright	Owned with a mortgage or loan	Rented from council	Other social rented	Rented privately	Other[1]	All tenures (=100%) (millions)
White							
British	25	46	12	5	8	4	45.5
Irish	26	37	14	7	11	5	0.6
Other White	19	32	8	5	28	8	1.3
Mixed							
White and Black Caribbean	7	34	28	16	10	5	0.2
White and Black African	7	32	22	14	18	7	0.1
White and Asian	15	47	12	7	14	6	0.2
Other mixed	12	40	15	9	16	6	0.2

Asian or Asian British							
Indian	27	52	5	3	10	3	1.0
Pakistani	27	43	9	6	12	4	0.7
Bangladeshi	9	29	33	15	10	4	0.3
Other Asian	16	43	9	7	19	7	0.2
Black or Black British							
Black Caribbean	12	36	25	15	7	5	0.6
Black African	5	20	33	17	18	7	0.5
Other Black	7	28	30	20	9	5	0.1
Chinese or other							
Chinese	21	37	8	4	18	12	0.2
Other	11	28	12	8	30	11	0.2
All people	24	45	12	5	9	4	52.0

[1] Includes living rent-free, living in a communal establishment and shared ownership.
Source: Census, 2001, England and Wales.

present trends might be that we should expect to find more of an ongoing convergence between ethnic groups as far as relationships between opportunities, tenure, and socio-economic status are concerned. Whereas low-income home ownership used to be seen as a persisting feature of minority ethnic experience, we might expect this to be eroded today if socio-economic position and access to wealth have become stronger predictors of tenure destinations. The impact of outward movement from established areas of minority ethnic settlement may not be solely a matter of middle-class success, but it does reflect to some extent the capacity of better-placed households to mobilise adequate resources, mirroring in part the trajectories of white groups. Meanwhile, most lower-income households – BME as well as white – have been facing common barriers implicit in rising house prices or mortgage costs, alongside a situation of limited social mobility and continuing economic disadvantage.

This picture would imply a re-acknowledgement of 'class' factors (or of relationships with labour markets and wealth) as key variables, but of course would remain cross-cut by the shared 'penalties' associated with being perceived as 'non-white' (Harrison et al., 2005, pp. 18–20), and complicated by distinctions between established and newer minorities that we mention again below.

Although it may be slow to take full effect in many places, there may also be some convergence as far as future housing needs of elders are concerned. Pressure for specific provision has been relatively low, reflecting youthful age profiles within minority groups overall. Not only will this eventually change across the established minority groups, but it is also difficult to predict how far patterns of extended family occupancy will be maintained into the future. It has seemed for some time that more caution may be needed with stereotypes about the housing roles played for South Asian elders by families and networks, although (as we noted above) strong commitments to elders continue to help shape households' housing options. A similar point about avoiding over-simple stereotypes applies when considering the emergent housing needs of women from these communities.

In order to make sense of the current position of minority ethnic groups within the UK housing market, it is often also important to distinguish between new migrants and more established minority ethnic groups. Accurate data on the current housing circumstances of asylum seekers, refugees, and new labour migrants settling in the UK are limited, although insights are provided by localised studies (see, for example, Bloch, 2002; Dwyer and Brown, 2004). Indications are that new migrants rely heavily upon the private rented and social housing sector, as well as friends and relatives. Evidence suggests that housing conditions of new migrants are often poor, that they often experience racist harassment in the deprived neighbourhoods in which they settle (or to which they are allocated by local authorities), and that they occupy a relatively weak marginal position when competing for decent affordable accommodation. The challenges facing people seeking asylum are dealt with more fully elsewhere in this book (see Chapter 3).

Meanwhile, the more established minority ethnic groups are generally faring better than a generation ago, and most (but not all) are better housed than new migrants. Although, as indicated above, their experiences may be dependent upon class, ethnicity, gender, generation, and locality, we have seen their patterns of settlement begin to change in quite significant ways. Inner-city clustering in poorer areas of housing is still a dominant feature of the pattern for many groups, but we are also seeing a clear trend towards suburbanisation. This is most pronounced for households of Indian heritage, but is also evident amongst all other established minority ethnic groups. While some minority ethnic households are locating in new areas of social housing, sometimes as a direct result of special schemes to support BME tenancies in traditionally 'white areas' (Simpson et al., 2007), others are buying into higher-status neighbourhoods as they acquire more wealth. The evidence suggests, however, that the transition from the inner city to the suburbs is not always easy, and that minority ethnic households may take longer to find a suitable property than white households and that they may experience harassment when settling in a new area (Phillips et al., 2007). Thus, established minorities still seem to share with newer arrivals a number of the negative effects of the penalties associated with being perceived as outside the white mainstream.

Insights from a European comparative perspective

Although comparative analysis has developed extensively in housing studies over the last 15 years, systematic cross-countries work on ethnicity and housing remains scarce, despite excellent exceptions (notably Özüekren and Van Kempen, 1997). In 2005, however, a major step in this field was taken by the European Union Monitoring Centre on Racism and Xenophobia (EUMC) as part of its *RAXEN* Project. EUMC activity has now passed to the European Union Agency for Fundamental Rights (FRA), which carries forward its role as a key player in independent and high quality research and information across the broader domain of ethnic relations and migration. The *RAXEN* project monitors racism, xenophobia, and anti-semitism, and in each EU state a national focal point produces information on relevant policy, legislation, and practice. In 2003 housing was added to the fields studied, with national housing reports produced for participating countries, and in 2004 updating material was generated. The EUMC then commissioned a review covering situations, practices, and performance in the 15 'old' member countries, building upon 30 reports submitted nationally. The resulting study (Harrison et al., 2006) provides the first systematic and comprehensive account of this field across the Union (as constituted prior to enlargement in 2004), and is, in effect, the first international analysis of racism and housing carried out on this scale.

Although there is a considerable diversity in minority ethnic experiences, outcomes, and strategies across Europe, minority ethnic housing disadvantage is widespread. New migrants and settled minorities generally appear to experience higher levels of homelessness, poorer quality housing conditions, poorer residential neighbourhoods (such as shanty towns), lack of dwelling amenities, and comparatively greater vulnerability and insecurity in housing status than 'mainstream' households. Very serious problems in particular places include lack of access to drinking water and toilets, higher levels of overcrowding than for other households, and exploitation through higher comparative rents and purchase prices. There is evidence of some improvement in patterns of housing conditions over time (although relative housing inequalities seem highly durable), but there are also numerous examples of very extreme conditions. The picture is particularly bleak for certain minority ethnic groups in Spain, Greece, and Italy; the national reports refer to a lack of the most basic facilities (such as drinking water or heating systems), squatting environments, or occupation of camps, abandoned industrial warehouses, or old apartment blocks awaiting demolition (see National Focus Point Reports: Spain, 2003, p. 24; Greece, 2003, p. 33; Italy, 2003, pp. 19–20). Squatting results partly from barriers to accessing rented housing, including high rents, price discrimination, and direct discrimination by landlords. Multiple problems may occur simultaneously for low-income households, with inadequate dwellings being accompanied by high costs, overcrowding, limited choice, insecurity, or poor neighbourhood amenities. There may also be poor mental and physical health, lower levels of educational attainment, restricted access to work, and lower income levels linked to poor housing conditions or locations.

The EUMC review points to the widespread incidence of unfair and discriminatory practices affecting housing markets, social rented housing allocation, and access to finance. Significantly, there is a recurrence from place to place of *key mechanisms* (such as denial of accommodation by private property owners) and *characteristic outcomes* (including limited choice for minorities, heavy dependence on social renting where this can be obtained, or poor quality accommodation). In several countries, separate approaches to the housing and settlement of asylum seekers complicate matters. People seeking asylum have become a focus for strategies that sometimes fail to meet what would be seen as necessary standards for other groups, and involve restrictive or disadvantaging settlement practices and options. Meanwhile, national indigenous minorities – such as Gypsy, Traveller, Roma, and Sinti populations – have also experienced persistent and systematic discrimination, reflected in a long history of housing deprivation and settlement marginalisation across Europe.

Not all migrant and minority ethnic households are in poor housing, and many overcome barriers to opportunity. We certainly should not see them as homogeneous or inactive victims of discrimination, supposedly unable to develop their own positive strategies, individually or collectively. Alongside progress by individual households, there have been some important collective initiatives towards self-management for groups of migrant origin, amongst which the history of the UK's BME Housing Associations seems to stand out for its scale and success (Harrison, 1995). Yet despite positive individual and collective progress, our comparative analysis confirms regularities and patterns of direct and indirect discrimination and disadvantage across housing domains, making it probable that migrant and minority ethnic households will be treated adversely by comparison with the 'native' or indigenous 'mainstream' in numerous contexts.

Policy and practice responses

There is considerable progress across Europe in the development of legislation addressing issues of discrimination and housing, affecting the UK alongside other states. European Directives 2000/43/EC and 2000/78/EC had been transposed into national legislation in most countries at the time of our review, despite some delays and limitations. National regulatory systems remain diverse, however, along with day-to-day implementation, while at the level of principles there is diversity in how ethnicity itself is approached. The UK's acceptance of ethnicity as a category is not by any means paralleled in all countries, and this affects policy approaches and data availability. Sometimes the preference may be for distinguishing simply between national citizens and 'foreigners' or 'immigrants'. Not surprisingly, governmental responses to racism in housing vary markedly between countries, with wide differences in commitment and in development of appropriate practices. Some national reports document resistance, hostility, and failure to address needs or the deprivation and discrimination suffered by minority ethnic groups.

It is important to appreciate that hostile or mixed official responses can be found in some of the most economically developed parts of the Union. For example, a key EU Directive had not been incorporated into Germany's national legislation by 2004, which apparently meant that there was no effective legal protection then against discrimination in the housing market and no national (Federal) system of ethnic monitoring in place (see National Focus Point Report, Germany, 2004, p. 37). National reporting also showed that evidence had been found of unchecked discriminatory practices in housing (such as quota systems working against 'non-German' households). The issue of discrimination in housing seemed to have been receiving less attention than questions about the integration of migrants (National Focus Point Report, Germany, 2003, pp. 10–11). There has certainly been urban planning and renewal activity in Germany, aiming amongst other things to support the integration of migrants into local communities, resolve intercultural conflicts, and tackle racism. These housing projects, however, often seek to benefit areas or populations in general (a feature of other countries too), rather than focusing explicitly on minority groups as such. As far as we could judge from the national reporting, an important feature of practice in Germany seemed to be a reliance on approaches that highlighted working to resolve differences, rather than according individuals or groups the rights and capacities to challenge discrimination and ill-treatment (and there seemed to be parallels elsewhere).

One crucial insight for UK audiences from reviewing policies across the EU is the discovery that Britain's national regulatory systems and mechanisms appear to be amongst the most complex and sophisticated as far as handling an equality and diversity agenda is concerned. Development of UK law and practices has been cumulative, involving many actors (for an outline linked to housing see Harrison et al., 2005, Chapter 3). Not only is the extent and depth of guidance impressive, but there has been a long tradition of trying to monitor in relation to ethnicity and performance, and to ensure a measure of compliance by organisations, as well as providing channels for individual redress. At the same time, the UK has had a particularly important history within the EU with respect to the inclusion of minority ethnic organisations in social rented housing provision (the BME-run housing associations). Unfortunately, there is a major weakness in regulation in the UK. Monitoring and regulatory policies are overwhelmingly focused on the public sector and voluntary or third sector bodies. While subject to the law, private companies are not generally expected to generate information on their performance comparable with the public sector, and are not likely to carry out systematic equality impact assessment of their policy developments. Furthermore, national processes of inspection (potentially a key ongoing development) focus on public and voluntary sector bodies rather than private sector ones.

Housing and integration

The idea of using housing schemes to promote social integration is frequently invoked in policy-making contexts across Europe. Integration, however, has many definitions and potential ambiguities. A neutral account would most likely conceptualise integration as being to some degree a two-way process, whereby minority groups and the majority population each tend to participate in processes of change and adaptation. Thus a distinction can be drawn between integration and assimilation, the latter generally being perceived as a one-directional process of migrant and minority ethnic acculturation and spatial dispersal. In fact, concepts of integration can become heavily politicised, with ideas about voluntary integration via housing becoming tangled up with more directive thinking about assimilation through social control.

Different countries' interpretations of integration reflect their varied histories, political discourses on immigration, citizenship and minority ethnic obligations, and different rights in relation to housing, welfare, and work. This manifests itself in differing levels of state control over the migrant settlement process, and varying degrees of housing market choice for both settled and new migrants. Countries such as Denmark, Finland, the Netherlands, and Germany, for example, appear to pursue policies designed to minimise cultural difference and promote minority ethnic dispersal, sometimes with the use of formal or unofficial settlement quotas to control migrant and minority ethnic clustering.

One politicised line of argument for seeking to limit minority ethnic residential segregation or 'ghetto' formation can be to stress associations (real or imagined) between minority groups' housing conditions in neighbourhoods, and their supposed involvements with crime, violence, and drug trafficking. In any event, new migrants such as asylum seekers and refugees are often particular targets of settlement and integration initiatives, with policies that sometimes appear very restrictive in pursuit of minority ethnic 'desegregation'. In one sense the UK might be seen as being at one pole in terms of the spectrum of conceptualisations of integration needs and strategies, given governmental commitments to multiculturalism. Yet even here the housing sector's 'race equality' and cultural diversity agenda sits somewhat uneasily alongside dispersal polices for asylum seekers, settlement control for Gypsies and Travellers, and the assimilationist and de-segregationist overtones of debates about community cohesion in the wake of ethnic disturbances in some cities with relatively high levels of minority ethnic segregation (Harrison et al., 2005; Phillips, 2006).

The settlement and integration of Gypsy, Traveller, Sinti or Roma people clearly present great challenges for policy-makers across Europe. The travelling population stands out as the most deprived and poorly treated minority ethnic group in the reports from the 15 European states. Although population numbers and sizes of encampments vary, these groups consistently experience xenophobic attitudes from the public (and often from officials as well), and suffer from a combination of neglect in terms of housing provision and control in terms of settlement. Their housing circumstances are typically highly segregated, deprived, and excluded from mainstream society. The picture for travelling people living in Southern European countries is particularly bleak. For example, although transit camps are provided for Roma across Italy, reporting indicates that these camps are located in remote, marginalised places, are usually overcrowded, and may not have drinkable water and electricity (National Focal Point Report, Italy, 2003, p. 11). Similarly, in Greece, nomadic Roma apparently often have no access to sanitary facilities, garbage disposal, sewage, water, or electricity, while some of their camps are situated in (or close to) landfill sites or heavily polluting factories. Encampments in Northern Europe are generally smaller than for Southern Europe, but reactions to Travellers or Roma often seem similarly negative (Harrison et al., 2006). Although proactive and supportive policies seem relatively rare, there are nonetheless examples from countries such as Finland, Ireland, and Sweden. Sustained commitment to such programmes, however, can be weak. Looking at the 15 EU countries as a whole, we suggest that official policies towards travelling people highlight the contradictory nature of state responses to such 'deviant' and marginal groups. On the one hand, there may be a push to assimilate them into preferred mainstream sedentary lifestyles and to restrict their independent collective practices (if necessary by destroying or

preventing their sites), and on the other, they are targets for exclusionary practices which may isolate their residences from those of the mainstream, while
dictating where they should settle and how.

As regards localised strategies in EU countries, it might be thought that
urban renewal would provide strong gains for minority households, and assist
their integration into the socio-economic mainstream, given the significance of
minority settlement in run-down districts. The benefits, however, often seem
uncertain or implicit rather than explicit. Programmes may focus on residents
in general in low-income districts, rather than on minority groups as such,
while physical reconstruction does not necessarily reflect strategies derived
from studying specific housing needs, and is sometimes a prelude to relocation
or dispersal that will not improve circumstances for minorities. A project may
specifically seek to eliminate housing where minority households live, rather
than address their welfare needs. In a worst-case scenario, an area might be
cleared of its residents under the banner of 'reducing segregation', but with
no effective benefits for displaced households. A more general criticism sometimes voiced is that area-focused strategies cannot solve wider problems of social
exclusion founded in the behaviours of institutions, the operation of labour
markets, and economic inequality. At the same time, a focus on an area may
build on assumptions that this is where the key problems are to be found,
implying that the answers lie in changing behaviour or lifestyles of poor people, or dispersing minorities and assimilating them elsewhere, rather than in
improving institutional performance or reducing discrimination. Furthermore,
tackling areas where minority populations are concentrated does little to alter
one key causative factor of segregation: the selective locational choices being
exercised by better-off 'mainstream' (especially white) households. Some of the
above criticisms have long been familiar amongst UK policy analysts.

A cross-national perspective: emerging themes

Racism and xenophobia are still potent forces shaping the housing and settlement outcomes of distinctive and negatively labelled minority ethnic groups
across a range of European countries. Poor housing conditions and lack of
market choices are amongst the most important manifestations of the frequent
social exclusion of these groups. Housing practices can also become mechanisms for reinforcing or creating such exclusion. Although there are important
political, economic, and cultural differences between countries, mediating in
processes of discrimination, similar mechanisms of housing discrimination and
disadvantage occur in differing countries. These mechanisms include denial of
accommodation by private property owners, imposition of restrictive conditions

shaping access into publicly supported accommodation, and harassment, abuse, or opposition from neighbours. Minorities' housing circumstances and settlement patterns are also affected by a number of general strategies for physical, social, or economic change, such as urban renewal, welfare system developments, changing housing subsidies, and so on. A shift away from provision of social renting (on which many depend) and towards privatisation or housing deregulation can disproportionately affect minority ethnic groups' housing opportunities. A shortage of affordable dwellings is often going to make progress difficult for many economically vulnerable minorities. In the UK we know that there are particular negative implications for younger low-income households, some newer migrants, female-headed households, and potentially elders, as well as for those facing problems of chronic illness and disability.

There is clearly an overlap between ethnicity and minority status on the one hand and socio-economic position on the other, and it may sometimes be difficult to disentangle the effects of racism from the effects of low incomes. This is important insofar as settlement patterns and general opportunities for advancement are concerned, where racism may reinforce exclusion based on socio-economic circumstances or vice versa. In the USA there is said to be a 'black tax' paid in housing by people regardless of economic position, and in the UK this type of experience has been summarised through the concept that people are likely to suffer an 'ethnic penalty' regardless of their socio-economic standing (Karn, 1997). Although neither of these terminologies is ideal, they do 'flag up' the need not to be diverted into assuming that the only issue is one of labour market positions, even though this is a vital factor in many European contexts. Nonetheless, we should not ignore the significance that socio-economic positioning has for households' housing pathways and destinations, particularly where housing costs are high and labour market options both insecure and poorly rewarded.

Finally – and this is a point that might be noted by UK politicians and policy-makers – our comparative work has revealed little evidence of any research capable of substantiating the assumed positive causative connection between policies encouraging ethnic residential dispersal on the one hand and social integration as an outcome on the other. This gap in evidence is particularly significant because the presumption of a link between social and spatial integration lies at the heart of some countries' official approaches to planned immigrant settlement. Integration policies need to be explicit and practical, and responsive to the diversity of households and their needs. In writing elsewhere, we have argued that what is required for the UK is *an inclusion and co-operation strategy*, rather than 'top-down' attempts to engineer social mixing amongst neighbours, or designs that over-optimistically seek to 'balance' and fix local population composition in some way. This inclusion and co-operation agenda

(Harrison et al., 2005, pp. 99–101) could build on processes of adaptation, advancement, and involvement that are regularly pursued by minorities and migrants themselves, while at the same time challenging the institutional barriers, resource problems, and racist practices that restrict choices. Putting UK experience and debates in a wider European context reinforces the case for a more sensitive approach to integration, and one that recognises peoples' own adaptation pathways as crucial variables, alongside the barriers that migrant and minority groups often face to participating in the societal mainstreams. This is not to suggest that multiculturalism should have no limits, but to argue for an open interaction that does not favour a crude assimilationism.

Suggested further readings

Harrison, M. with Phillips, D. (2003) *Housing and Black and Minority Ethnic Communities: Review of the Evidence Base*. London: Office of the Deputy Prime Minister.

Harrison, M., Phillips, D., Chahal, K., Hunt, L. and Perry, J. (2005) *Housing, 'Race' and Community Cohesion*. Coventry: CIH with HSA.

Phillips, D. (2006) 'Parallel Lives? Challenging Discourses of British Muslim Self-Segregation'. *Environment and Planning D: Society and Space* 24 (1): 25–40.

Ratcliffe, P. (2004) *Race, Ethnicity and Difference: Imagining the Inclusive Society*. Maidenhead: Open University Press.

Somerville, P. and Steele, A. (eds) (2002) *'Race', Housing and Social Exclusion*. London: Jessica Kingsley.

References

Bloch, A. (2002) *The Migration and Settlement of Refugees in Britain*. Basingstoke: Palgrave.

Cabinet Office (2000) *Minority Ethnic Issues in Social Exclusion and Neighbourhood Renewal: A Guide to the Work of the Social Exclusion Unit and the Policy Action Teams so far*. London: Crown Copyright.

Chahal, K. (2005) 'Racist Harassment and Anti-racist Strategies', in Harrison, M., Phillips, D., Chahal, C., Hunt, L. and Perry, J. *Housing, 'Race' and Community Cohesion*. Coventry: CIH with HSA, pp. 153–69.

Commission for Racial Equality [CRE] (1984) *Race and Council Housing in Hackney, Report of a Formal Investigation*. London: CRE.

CRE (1984a) *Abbey National Building Society, Report of a Formal Investigation*. London: CRE.

CRE (1985) *Walsall Metropolitan Borough Council: Practices and Policies of Housing Allocation, Report of a Formal Investigation*. London: CRE.

CRE (1985a) *Race and Mortgage Lending, Report of a Formal Investigation*. London: CRE.

CRE (1987) *Living in Terror: A Report on Racial Violence and Harassment in Housing*. London: CRE.

CRE (1988) *Homelessness and Discrimination, Report of a Formal Investigation into the London Borough of Tower Hamlets*. London: CRE.

CRE (1988a) *Racial Discrimination in a London Estate Agency, Report of a Formal Investigation.* London: CRE.

CRE (1990) *Racial Discrimination in an Oldham Estate Agency, Report of a Formal Investigation.* London: CRE.

CRE (1990a) *Sorry It's Gone.* London: CRE.

Dwyer, P. and Brown, D. (2004) *Meeting Basic Needs? Exploring the Welfare Strategies of Forced Migrants.* Summary of Findings from an ESRC-Funded study. Leeds: University of Leeds.

Harrison, M. (1995) *Housing, 'Race', Social Policy and Empowerment.* CRER Research in Ethnic Relations Series. Aldershot: Avebury.

Harrison, M. with Davis, C. (2001) *Housing, Social Policy and Difference: Disability, Ethnicity, Gender and Housing.* Bristol: Policy Press.

Harrison, M., Law, I. and Phillips, D. (2006) *Migrants, Minorities and Housing: Exclusion, Discrimination and Anti-discrimination in 15 Member States of the European Union.* Vienna: European Monitoring Centre on Racism and Xenophobia.

Harrison, M., Phillips, D., Chahal, K., Hunt, L. and Perry, J. (2005) *Housing, 'Race' and Community Cohesion.* Coventry: CIH with HSA.

Harrison, M. and Stevens, L. (1981) *Ethnic Minorities and the Availability of Mortgages*, Department of Social Policy and Administration, Social Policy Research Monograph 5. Leeds: University of Leeds.

Henderson, J. and Karn, V. (1987) *Race, Class and State Housing: Inequality and the Allocation of Public Housing in Britain.* Aldershot: Gower.

Home Office (2004) *Strength in Diversity: Towards a Community Cohesion and Race Equality Strategy.* London: Home Office Communication Directorate.

Julienne, L. (2001) *The Root to My Tree: Examining the Experience of Positive Action Training in Housing.* Ruislip: L8J Publications.

Karn, V. (ed.) (1997) *Ethnicity in the 1991 Census: Volume 4. Employment, Education and Housing among the Ethnic Minority Populations of Britain.* London: The Stationery Office.

Law, I., Davies, J., Phillips, D. and Harrison, M. (1996) *Equity and Difference: Racial and Ethnic Inequalities in Housing Needs and Housing Investment in Leeds.* 'Race' and Public Policy Research Unit. Leeds: University of Leeds.

National Focal Point, Germany (2003) *RAXEN Housing Report.* Vienna: EUMC.

National Focal Point, Germany (2004) *RAXEN National Report.* Vienna: EUMC.

National Focal Point, Greece (2003) *RAXEN Housing Report.* Vienna: EUMC.

National Focal Point, Italy (2003) *RAXEN Housing Report.* Vienna: EUMC.

National Focal Point, Spain (2003) *RAXEN Housing Report.* Vienna: EUMC.

Özüekren, S. and Van Kempen, R. (eds) (1997) *Turks in European Cities: Housing and Urban Segregation.* Utrecht: ERCOMER.

Phillips, D. (1986) *What price equality?*, GLC Housing Research and Policy Report No. 9. London: Greater London Council.

Phillips, D. (1998) 'Black Minority Ethnic Concentration, Segregation and Dispersal in Britain'. *Urban Studies* 35 (10): 1681–702.

Phillips, D. (2006) 'Parallel lives? Challenging Discourses of British Muslim Self-Segregation'. *Environment and Planning D: Society and Space* 24 (1): 25–40.

Phillips, D. and Harrison, M. (2005) 'Perspectives from the Grass Roots: A Bradford Case Study and Its Implications', in Harrison, M., Phillips, D., Chahal, C., Hunt, L. and Perry, J., *Housing, 'Race' and Community Cohesion.* Coventry: CIH with HSA, pp. 170–201.

Phillips, D., Davis, C. and Ratcliffe, P. (2007) 'British Asian Narratives of Urban Space'. *Transactions of the Institute of British Geographers* NS 32 (2): 217–34.

Ratcliffe, P. (1996) *'Race' and Housing in Bradford*. Bradford: Bradford Housing Forum.

Rees, P. and Butt, F. (2004) 'Ethnic Change and Diversity in England, 1981–2001'. *Area* 36: 174–86.

Sarre, P., Phillips, D. and Skellington, R. (1989) *Ethnic Minority Housing: Explanations and Policies*. Aldershot: Avebury.

Simpson, A. (1981) *Stacking the Decks: A Study of Race, Inequality and Council Housing in Nottingham*. Nottingham: Nottingham and District CRC.

Simpson, L., Phillips, D. and Ahmed, S. (2007) *Oldham and Rochdale: Race, Housing and Community Cohesion*, Report to the Oldham and Rochdale Housing Market Renewal (HMR) Programme.

CHAPTER 3

New Communities: Asylum Seekers and Dispersal

PATRICIA HYNES AND ROSEMARY SALES

Introduction

Refugees arriving in the UK to seek asylum encounter a battery of policies designed to deter them from entering the country and to ensure that their stay is both unpleasant and short. These measures include detention, deportation, compulsory dispersal and enforced destitution. This chapter focuses on compulsory dispersal, which was introduced in the *Immigration and Asylum Act, 1999*, and implemented from 2000. Dispersal involves sending people who have made a claim for asylum from London and the South East of England to other cities and larger towns. This forced movement often separates them from family and social networks, dispatching them to places to which they generally have no connection and where they often meet a hostile reception.

The introduction of dispersal was accompanied by the establishment of a centralised agency, the National Asylum Support Service (NASS), to administer the system. NASS slowly began a process of regionalisation before being officially disbanded in 2006 when the Borders and Immigration Agency (BIA) took over the running of asylum support. The BIA was renamed the UK Border Agency from April 2008 but compulsory dispersal continues.

Dispersal fundamentally changed the geography of settlement of those seeking asylum and the provision of accommodation and services (Hynes, 2006). Before then, most had remained in London while awaiting the outcome of their application since fellow nationals and community support networks and organisations were concentrated there (Carey-Wood et al., 1995). Recent initiatives to promote the integration of those granted refugee status have a strong regional dimension, with support conditional on retaining a 'local connection' in dispersal locations, further embedding regional patterns of settlement.

Compulsory dispersal involved a continuation of the punitive policies on asylum which had been implemented since the 1990s. It represented, however, a radical break with the principles underlying previous dispersal programmes.

These had involved groups who had already been recognised as refugees and thus had secure legal status. Access to mainstream financial and welfare support was a key principle of these programmes (Hale, 1993) and refugees were entitled to seek employment. Those in the current system must make individual claims for refugee status, becoming 'asylum seekers'.[1] Their status is thus insecure and their stay is expected to be temporary. The rate of success for asylum applications is low and the government has stated its determination to deport the majority of 'failed' asylum seekers with targets for removals introduced in 2002 (Somerville, 2006). Asylum seekers are excluded from mainstream services and the labour market and thus remain largely segregated from society.

Another key difference lies in the criteria for selecting dispersal locations. In earlier programmes, this was based on the availability of employment (Kushner and Knox, 1999) or secure accommodation (Carey-Wood et al., 1995). In the current programme, it has been based increasingly on the availability of temporary housing, which is generally concentrated in areas of economic deprivation.

The political context of the contemporary programme is also profoundly different. Groups of refugees arriving following highly publicised emergency situations, such as the Vietnamese 'boat people' (Duke, 1996) or Bosnians during the conflict in former Yugoslavia (Guild, 2000: 84), initially met a broadly sympathetic reception from the public and mainstream politicians. Recent political rhetoric and media coverage has been predominantly hostile (Lewis, 2005), suggesting that most asylum seekers are 'bogus'. Furthermore, the policies themselves, by identifying them as asylum seekers, have made them more visible and thus vulnerable to racism.

This chapter discusses the implementation of dispersal and its implications for social cohesion. It draws on research which examined the experiences of dispersed asylum seekers based on interviews with individuals as well as representatives of agencies providing service in London and three dispersal areas (Hynes, 2007). Fieldwork took place between November 2002 and February 2005, before the abolition of NASS. The process described, however, is similar in most respects to that under the new structures.

We begin by outlining the policy context and tensions between the restrictive asylum policy and the growing official concern over social cohesion. We then discuss the experience of individuals within the dispersal system, exploring the stages through which they pass between arrival and a decision on their claim. Finally, we discuss the implications of dispersal for social cohesion. We suggest that compulsory dispersal and the punitive way in which it has been implemented may undermine social cohesion through inhibiting asylum seekers from forming connections in the areas to which they have been involuntary relocated. Nevertheless, many resist being cast into limbo by these policies and engage in an active process of rebuilding a sense of identity and belonging.

The policy context

Asylum and immigration policy

The development of dispersal took place within the context of European policies, both at European Union (EU) level and in individual states, which focused mainly on deterrence. This has involved closure of borders and reducing the social rights of people seeking asylum. The coordination of EU immigration and asylum policy accelerated with preparations for the establishment of the European Single Market in 1992. The opening of borders within the EU raised concerns to protect the external borders from outsiders (Geddes, 2000). It coincided with increasing refugee movements following economic and political crises in many regions of the world, including the collapse of states in Eastern Europe. There was a fourfold increase in asylum applications between 1985 and 1992, from 159,176 to 674,056, to the 15 states which were then members of the EU (Levy, 1999).

EU asylum policy has involved both formal treaties and informal intergovernmental agreements developed outside EU structures. Many policy developments have originated in the Schengen Group, in which ministers from major EU states meet to develop policies on border control and security, and have subsequently been incorporated into EU law. For example, the 'one chance rule', which prohibits people from making asylum applications in more than one EU state, was included in the *Dublin Convention, 2000*. British governments have both implemented EU policy and developed their own initiatives, often going beyond the requirements of EU directives.

EU policy has been concerned mainly with border control while the treatment of asylum seekers has been left largely to individual states. There have been some moves to guarantee minimum conditions, for example a directive which allows them to take up employment if their asylum application has been outstanding for a year. Similarly, the 1951 Refugee Convention, which includes the internationally recognised definition of a refugee,[2] has been signed by all major refugee-receiving countries but its implementation, in relation to both the process by which applications are assessed and the support provided for applicants, is a matter for individual states.

Conditions for people seeking asylum therefore vary across European states but several have introduced dispersal. In Sweden dispersal began in 1985 and later developed into a 'Sweden-wide' strategy of compulsory dispersal (Hammar, 1993: 110; Andersson and Solid, 2003). Germany introduced a system of 'inter-Lander burden-sharing' in 1974, which was followed by legislation in 1982 including measures to reduce the social rights of asylum seekers. These policies were in line with proposals for 'burden sharing' at EU level put forward by individual states, including Germany and the UK (Thielemann, 2003) although subsequently rejected. The language of burden-sharing has, however, helped to frame the debate on asylum. It is highly ideological, presenting asylum seekers as inherently problematic and dependent and therefore without agency. Dispersal in Germany, as in Britain, was, however, as much about 'deterrence and control' as spreading costs (Boswell, 2003).

Britain had no domestic asylum legislation until the 1990s although the Refugee Convention was ratified in 1954. Following the increase in refugee numbers from the 1980s, a series of measures were initiated which have made their status more insecure and whittled away their rights (Sales, 2007; Schuster, 2004; Solomos, 2003). These have created a new legal and social category of 'asylum seeker' (Sales, 2002), increasingly distinguished from refugees. Since 1993, there have been six major Acts concerning immigration and asylum each of which has created a different system of support alongside previous arrangements, 'leaving a complex tangle of law, provision and regulation' (Mayor of London, 2004: 8).

The *Asylum and Immigration Appeals Act, 1993*, incorporated the Refugee Convention into immigration rules and created the process for dealing with asylum applications. The *Immigration and Asylum Act, 1996*, removed benefits from those making late asylum claims ('in country' applicants) and those appealing a decision. The High Court subsequently ruled that local authorities had a duty to provide 'in kind' support to destitute asylum seekers. They were given vouchers exchangeable at designated supermarkets, thus identifying them as asylum seekers. Another significant aspect of this policy was the shift in the cost of supporting asylum seekers from national to local authority budgets. They were concentrated in a few boroughs, mainly in London and the South East (Robinson et al., 2003), many with high levels of deprivation (Audit Commission, 2000a). The policy imposed strains on depleted housing stock and overstretched budgets and local authorities lobbied for dispersal to relieve the pressure.

A national system of compulsory dispersal system was introduced in the *Immigration and Asylum Act, 1999*. Dispersed asylum seekers were entitled to temporary accommodation on a no-choice basis and to social support. Those able to arrange their own accommodation could avoid dispersal by opting for Subsistence Only support. The government claimed that the new system met international obligations, since 'genuine' refugees would be prepared to undergo a temporary period of hardship until their claim was established:

> ... those who are genuinely fleeing persecution are looking for a safe and secure environment which offers a basic level of support while their applications are being considered. Such people will not be overly concerned about whether that support is provided in cash or in kind, nor about the location in which they are supported.

> (Home Office, 1999).

The primary aim of the policy, as outlined in official documents, was, however, to control entry and reduce incentives for 'economic migration' (Audit Commission, 2000b: 9). Dispersal thus became, with deportation and detention, one of the 'normalised essential instruments' of control (Bloch and Schuster, 2005: 491–512).

Social cohesion

Restrictive asylum policies have been pursued as part of increasingly selective 'managed migration' policies (Flynn, 2005) in which access to permanent residence and citizenship have become conditional on meeting more stringent tests. At the same time the government has become increasingly concerned that migrants or refugees deemed eligible to settle should integrate into British society. Social cohesion is the 'currently favoured shorthand' (Zetter et al., 2006: 4) to address these conflicting priorities. The concept has been defined in various ways but, according to one official report, includes a 'common vision and a sense of belonging for all communities' in which diversity is positively valued (ODPM, 2002, quoted in Temple and Moran, 2005: 5).

The development of the cohesion agenda took place in the context of political and economic changes which are widely seen as creating social fragmentation and dislocation. While the causes are multidimensional (for example, the decline of traditional employment, increased privatisation of welfare) they are widely attributed to the impact of globalisation. Immigration and ethnic diversity have been represented as a primary cause of this fragmentation in both official and popular discourse. As Castles (2000) argues, immigrants are the most visible sign of globalisation while its real causes are invisible and complex.

Official concern over social cohesion in Britain was given considerable impetus with the 'riots' in some cities in the North of England during the summer of 2001. The report which investigated these events (Cantle, 2001) claimed that Asian and white families were living 'parallel lives' with little meaningful interaction. Another crucial element was the 'war on terror' and in particular the London bombings of July 2005. These attacks have been interpreted by many people as evidence that some sections of the British Muslim population have loyalties which conflict with those of Britain (CRE, 2005: 10).

The promotion of social cohesion owes much to the concept of social capital most associated with the work of Robert Putnam (2000, 2007). Putnam defines social capital as 'social networks and the associated norms of reciprocity and trustworthiness' (2007: 137). He argues that social capital can produce benefits to those involved in networks and thus 'can help mitigate the insidious effects of socio-economic disadvantage' (2000: 319).

Reliance on social capital has been widely criticised as presenting an over-positive view of social networks and ignoring the power relations in which they operate and the processes of exclusion as well as inclusion which they involve (see, for example, Griffiths et al., 2005). Not all participation in local communities promotes cohesion, as the resurgence of extreme right racist groups in Britain demonstrates (Zetter et al., 2006: 10). Furthermore, the promotion of 'socially cohesive neighborhoods' through encouraging common values may be seen as a substitute for policies to tackle disadvantage (Cheong et al., 2007). It was not lack of understanding of British values that brought young British-born Asian men onto the streets during the summer of 2001. On the contrary, they were expressing frustration at what Young describes as their 'widespread cultural inclusion followed by structural exclusion' (Young, 2002: 15).

Compulsory dispersal embodies in extreme form the tensions between the agendas of rigid immigration control and social cohesion. By segregating asylum seekers from mainstream society they are prevented from building the connections on which social cohesion is based. Furthermore, the rhetoric which demonises them as 'undeserving' undermines the trust on which relationships might be built. Thus for asylum seekers, who experience institutional exclusion, social networks based on fellow nationals (Putnam's 'strong ties' and 'bonding' capital) may be a survival mechanism and reflect their exclusion from society rather than being the basis of participation.

Another tension within the social cohesion agenda lies between the promotion of shared values and the valuing of diversity. The developments discussed above have hastened the official retreat from multiculturalism and a renewed assimilationist agenda (Rattansi, 2002). Prominent in this has been the promotion of 'Britishness' with ceremonies to celebrate the acquisition of citizenship and the search for a common identity and a set of values which can be claimed as British (Goldsmith, 2008; Rogers and Muir, 2005). As Stevenson (2007: 3) argues, however, 'there are clearly potential tensions between the desire to celebrate common values and the notion of Britain as a nation that is welcoming and accommodating of a wide range of cultures and belief systems'.

The assimilationist agenda was evident in official justifications for dispersal which it was claimed would reduce racial tensions which might arise from 'visible' concentrations of ethnic minorities (Robinson et al., 2003: 164). This thinking represents outsiders as inherently problematic, requiring 'tolerance' from the 'host' society. The notion of British people as fundamentally 'tolerant' towards immigrants has been a consistent theme in official thinking (Holmes, 1988) and has underlied the notion that good race relations are dependent on rigid immigration controls (Sales, 2007). Introducing a new strategy on immigration in 2005, Tony Blair suggested that the British 'tradition [of] tolerance is under threat' (Home Office, 2005) from unwanted immigration. This negative perception of immigrants, of whom asylum seekers have become the main current target, impacts on all deemed outsiders, including those 'genuine' refugees who are later expected to integrate and become part of cohesive communities. We return to these issues below in the light of the discussion of the experience of dispersal.

The implementation of dispersal

In preparation for dispersal, in 1998 the Home Office invited local authorities to form consortia in order to bid for contracts with NASS to provide accommodation and support for asylum seekers. Although they varied across regions (Griffiths et al., 2005) these consortia were generally composed of representatives of local authorities, health authorities, housing providers and voluntary sector agencies including the major refugee agencies such as the Refugee Council. Their role was determined by central government and they had 'responsibility without ownership' of the policies they facilitated (Harrison, 2006).

Negotiations between NASS and regional consortia were long-drawn-out and often conflictual, whereas contracts with private providers were often negotiated faster. Some regions, such as the South West, relied solely on private accommodation in the early stages, a major departure from the local authority-led model which was originally envisaged (Zetter et al., 2002). An initial criterion for choosing dispersal locations was that they already had ethnic minority populations and some supporting infrastructure. It was also intended to 'cluster' asylum seekers into linguistic groups to facilitate better support. These criteria were soon abandoned as the availability of accommodation came to override all other criteria and as many as 80 different nationalities were sent to some dispersal locations. In line with the thinking about the dangers of concentrating ethnic minorities, the ratio of asylum seekers to the local population was to be a maximum of 200 in each dispersal location. This too proved difficult, as a representative from a regional consortium explained:

> So much depends on the local resources, the back-up support, the make-up of the host community, all those sorts of things. That figure 1 to 200 has sort of haunted the Home Office ever since.

The initial geography of dispersal was thus based largely on the availability of temporary housing, which implies low demand or unpopular accommodation (see Table 3.1). Dispersal to places where such accommodation was available ensured that asylum seekers were concentrated in areas with high levels of social exclusion. Nearly 80 per cent of the initial dispersal locations in England were in

Table 3.1 Regional distribution of asylum seekers in NASS/BIA accommodation by UK cluster areas, June 2001–2007

Region	June 2001	June 2002	June 2003	June 2004	June 2005	June 2006	June 2007
Yorkshire & Humberside	5,930	9,560	10,055	9,555	8,000	6,610	7,745
North West	5,870	9,500	9,755	7,325	6,155	4,655	6,810
North East	4,060	5,750	5,475	4,620	3,620	2,925	3,310
West Midlands	3,610	9,340	9,600	7,820	5,530	4,020	5,685
East Midlands	1,490	4,054	4,165	2,850	2,210	2,055	2,220
Greater London	620	2,230	2,845	2,035	1,225	1,190	1,545
South West	480	815	1,095	1,255	920	995	1,135
South Central/South East	360	1,040	1,290	940	610	545	460
East of England	210	520	570	670	540	490	465
England total	**22,620***	**42,805***	**44,850***	**37,070***	**28,810***	**23,490***	**29,385***
Northern Ireland		90	165	110	120	155	190
Scotland		5,040	5,885	5,580	5,640	4,730	5,230
Wales		1,150	2,130	2,375	2,285	2,335	2,475
UK total		**49,085***	**53,050***	**45,135***	**36,855***	**30,710***	**37,280***

* total includes 'disbenefited cases'.[3]
Source: Home Office.[4]

the 88 most multiply deprived districts identified by the Social Exclusion Unit in 2000 (see Map 3.1). These concentrations remained relatively fixed over time since contracts were awarded for periods of between three and five years, while later dispersal areas tended to follow this same pattern (see, for example, Atfield et al., 2007). These areas were often historically associated with immigrants and 'chosen because of their unpopularity'[5] and thus offered limited infrastructure. The focus on cheap accommodation also meant that asylum seekers were highly concentrated in some areas, increasing their visibility. In practice, then, dispersal brought concentrations of asylum seekers to particular locations. A Home Office report suggested that emerging 'ghettos' of asylum seekers and refugees in deprived areas hindered their 'future integration into communities' once granted refugee status (Home Office, 2005: 7). Another service provider summed up the connections:

It was the more deprived areas that had available public sector housing. Councils saw that as an ideal opportunity of actually utilizing that vacant housing, getting some income and whole streets suddenly became asylum seeker areas. You are halfway to disaster.

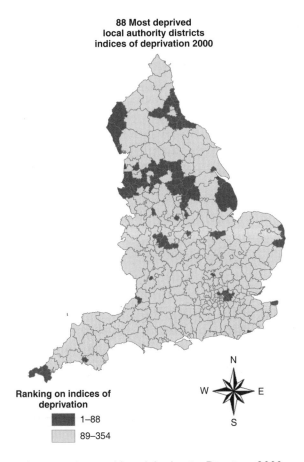

**88 Most deprived
local authority districts
indices of deprivation 2000**

**Ranking on indices of
deprivation**

■ 1–88
▢ 89–354

Map 3.1 Eighty eight most deprived Local Authority Districts, 2000.
Source: Department of the Environment, Transport and the Regions, Indices of Deprivation 2000.

Asylum seekers opting for 'subsistence only' (SO) support were heavily concentrated in Greater London. This reflects the availability of family and wider social networks since this group were dependent on others to provide accommodation. This difference between where asylum seekers chose to go voluntarily and where they were compulsorily relocated underlines the way in which dispersal cut people off from support networks.

In the early years of dispersal, asylum seekers were required to apply to the Home Office to have their application for refugee status assessed and separately to NASS for financial assistance and support with accommodation. In 2006 a 'New Asylum Model' was introduced which involved 'segmenting' asylum claims into different categories according to their perceived 'credibility' with different procedures for assessing their claims. This involved greater control over asylum seekers during the process of status determination to enable them to be arrested if their asylum application failed. Detention on arrival became more common and those detained had their applications heard through fast-track procedures.

After NASS was abolished and its functions taken over by the Borders and Immigration Agency, support was claimed in the same way, with accommodation on a no-choice basis. The system was changed again in 2007 when the asylum claim and the social support were brought together under a single 'case owner' responsible for every aspect of the contact between the Home Office and the asylum seeker.[6]

The following section discusses the experience of asylum seekers within the dispersal system using interviews carried out during the NASS period. While the 'NASS system' looms large in these accounts, the fundamental nature of the programme, and particularly its punitive and compulsory character, remains.

The experience of dispersal

> We have our roots in our hands. We carry them from place to place. Then we put them down and have to pull them out again. You are waiting for life for years. You have no rights to define what you do (Iranian refugee in dispersal area, July 2003).

A case worker, describing the dispersal process, said, 'This is where the suffering begins', suggesting that for refugees seeking asylum, arrival in Britain is often associated with pain rather than with regaining a sense of security. Suspicion and mistrust were fundamental to the process, and for many arriving alone with little knowledge of the system, this was an unexpected element of their experience. Faisal[7] from Sudan described his initial reaction:

> It is very difficult. You don't know what the process is .... You can't do anything, because you don't understand the system. ... Before they listened to my case they warned me that if they didn't believe me they would send me back. ... They give you the feeling that they are suspicious of you and don't even listen to your story.

Involuntary dispersal meant that asylum seekers lost control over where they lived and what they could do. They become subject to rules made by other people which they have no option but to obey. As David from Zimbabwe put it,

> I was taken over by NASS. I was funded by NASS now. This is where you wait to be dispersed to whatever area they give you. I am not trying to bite the hand that feeds me.

The system was complex and asylum seekers often had difficulty in distinguishing between the different functions of the Home Office since both the asylum interview and the application for support involved similar questions. They also tended to see all those who they had to deal with as part of the 'NASS system' and were not always able to distinguish between representatives of refugee agencies who assist with completing application forms and immigration officers who decide on their claim. Confusion was compounded by the pressure to apply as soon as possible after arrival since failure could harm their asylum claim and lead them to be deemed ineligible for support. Dispersal involved a number of distinct stages which we discuss below.

Emergency accommodation

Initially, there was a period in emergency accommodation pending dispersal until Induction Centres were phased in from 2004. Although it was planned that this would last for only seven to ten days, it could be much longer and the accommodation was basic. Single people and even families were often placed in shared accommodation, as Saida from Lebanon describes:

> They put us together with singles, about four singles. And no one knows how to clean or to take care of themselves. There was only one shower for all of us. The singles would sit in the sitting room, drink and watch television. We cannot keep him [the baby] in the small room we had.

Her baby had an accident on the day of her arrival and was taken to hospital. The family was left completely alone, not knowing how to get back to their accommodation.

> Nobody came to get us from NASS.... We didn't know where we were. We had no money. We didn't know our address because we arrived during the night.

This period of waiting was marked by frustration, boredom and uncertainty. It was impossible to put down roots since friends could be dispersed to different locations. Adults made few attempts to access education or other services because of the feeling of temporariness they experienced. David from Zimbabwe Commented,

> The question of education did not come into it before dispersal, because of the uncertainty of the length of time you were going to stay there. You never knew. If I was to start college or school one day, I might be dispersed the next day.

Dispersal became a lottery as people waited to find out where they would be sent. David recalled this period:

> Every morning at 9 o'clock, somebody would come in from NASS, and pin up names, lists of names on the walls. . . . I spent September, October, November, December, until the 6th of December. During that time, every day I looked. The rest of the day you go back to your room and just wait.

His name finally appeared next to Lincoln, a town he had never been to or even heard of. He was given a train timetable and told to find his own way:

> Nobody knew I was coming. I did not have an address. It was the middle of winter, 6th of December. I had run out of money on my mobile phone. I had to find a police station. It was very difficult. A black man stuck in the county, a country environment like this in Lincoln. I had put on a very nice summer suit to arrive there. I must have looked a sight.

David had attempted to adopt a 'strategy of invisibility' (Malkki, 1995) by arriving smartly dressed in this new city, but found that he was highly visible in the new location.

Dispersal

Lack of choice over the location or type of accommodation added to the difficulties for asylum seekers in regaining control over their lives. They retained the stigmatised identity of 'asylum seeker' which David had attempted to shake off and remained subject to strict monitoring and required to report regularly to police stations. Other agencies were involved in the system of control. Landlords had to report to the Home Office any absence of more than a few days as well as any form of anti-social behaviour. Felicia from the Congo described how her private landlord interfered in her life:

> I didn't like him because he came in my house anytime he wants. I had no privacy! In my house! Every time I go to school he went into the house to check everything. One day I was in the toilet. I knew my children were in school – British schools – so I took a shower. I was alone in my house. I only had a small towel around me and he was there!

Although allegations of poor standards were widespread, complaints to NASS tended to be met with disbelief or indifference. In Leicester, participants living in the International Hotel reported lack of hot water, poor food and windows which had been painted over, but, as Duran from Kosovo commented, 'They don't accept our problems, they don't believe us.'

The coincidence between dispersal and deprived areas compounded feelings of exclusion which were felt not merely in material deprivation. Many participants mentioned problems in obtaining bank accounts, loans, credit cards and mobile phones as a result of living in areas with 'bad' postcodes. Ali from Libya complained about the poor reputation of the area to which he was sent:

> These are very bad areas. You see people lying in the street, drunks. Very bad. ... police always come to our neighbours.

Access to services was limited and uneven. One participant in Bristol, who had been tortured in his country of origin, was refused registration with a GP because he had a temporary address. Other research has suggested that dispersed asylum seekers experience barriers to health and education (BMA, 2004; Rutter, 2003). Dispersal can be dangerous for people with particular health needs. The National Aids Trust (2006), for example, found serious concerns about the health of asylum seekers with HIV. Separation from community structures also makes it difficult to gain help such as interpretation, exacerbating isolation and depression. Asylum seekers are forced to rely on fellow nationals, who are already experiencing severe exclusion themselves, for practical and emotional support (Griffiths et al., 2005).

Frequent and unexpected relocation, which was an integral part of the dispersal process, compounded the sense of limbo, making it difficult to begin to put down roots and entrenching social exclusion. It inhibited the rebuilding of social trust as developing social contacts in the dispersal location – whether based on ordinary day-to-day encounters or involving deeper relationships – were broken. Relocation could take place within the same region or even to a totally different region. The experience of Felicia, who was moved from the

West Midlands to the South West, illustrates the disruptive impact on the lives of both adults and children.

> Sometimes they tell you, you have two weeks and you must move. . . . It is not good for me or for the children because my child, she missed her technology exam because it was the middle [of the term]. She had nearly finished her programme and since we came here she hasn't gone to school. . . . If you say no they stop the money so you must.

The status determination decision

A positive decision can be a cause for celebration and the point when refugees can start rebuilding their lives. It also marks a recognition of a refugee's 'victim-hood' although the process of acknowledging the loss that this has entailed may take many more years. The decision also brings immediate practical difficulties. Those granted refugee status must leave dispersal accommodation within 28 days and start negotiating with a new set of agencies. Although they are entitled to access policy initiatives aimed at promoting integration, links between these structures and the dispersal system were poor and gaining information was difficult. Integration programmes are locally based so people lose casework support and accommodation if they move. In applying for social housing they are restricted to the dispersal area where they are deemed to have a 'local connection' but are no longer considered in 'priority need' of public housing unless they can prove, for example, medical need. Many felt adrift once again at this 'move on' stage, as Pierre from Burundi commented:

> NASS services are really awful. Once you have got your refugee status, they cut everything and you are almost paralysed.

In recognition of the problems in transition between asylum and refugee status, new pilot projects – the Strategic Upgrade of National Refugee Integration Services (SUNRISE) – were announced in 2005 to administer the process. SUNRISE has had, however, little impact on the availability of housing, particularly for single refugees. Refugee community organisations continue to fill gaps in services, securing temporary accommodation for those whom formal agencies are unable to assist.

A negative decision clearly creates even more difficulties. They face eviction after only seven days and only emergency support is available. They also acquire a new label, 'failed asylum seeker'. Many go underground, becoming undocumented, in order to escape deportation. For Rashid from Sudan the decision crushed his attempts to rebuild his life:

You start getting on well in your life, you make friends, you talk about different topics ... you start having hope that you can be part of the society in a way. Suddenly you get a letter killing all the hope, it changes your life completely and you have to start thinking about the problem of immigration and police.

Dispersal – policy-imposed liminality

For participants in the study the main experience of dispersal was loss of control over their lives, creating a sense of liminality, or limbo. This was intensified by the lack of choice over where they lived and the frequent relocation. They found it difficult to know who they could trust, were treated with suspicion and were continually called upon to answer questions and to repeat their story. Mistrust was intensified by a process which rendered them powerless, forced to wait passively for decisions to be made by others, decisions which may appear random. Refugees must constantly demonstrate their vulnerability (Baines, 2004) to be accepted as 'genuine' and to gain access to material support. The creation of an unwanted patron disadvantaged client relationship, in which the imperative is not to offend those with power over their lives, undermines autonomy and dignity. Service providers, particularly those from voluntary agencies, may find it difficult to establish boundaries around the support they offer (East, 2008).

The NASS system undermined individuals' attempts to rebuild a sense of self. The 'one size fits all' character of the process meant that individual histories and characteristics were subsumed under the label 'asylum seeker'. The implementation of dispersal meant that they retained this stigmatised identity in the areas to which they were relocated.

Some asylum seekers attempt to regain some control by resisting the demands imposed by the system, adopting mistrust of officialdom as a survival strategy. Given their vulnerable legal status, direct confrontation may not be possible but informal resistance takes a number of forms. For many within the dispersal system, this involved what the Home Office called a 'failure to travel' to dispersal locations. A private accommodation provider commented:

They usually don't bother to get on the coach if they don't want to go. A lot of them don't arrive when we go to meet them at the coach station.

Others, like David, 'opt out' of the NASS system. He left his NASS accommodation before permission to work was revoked and took up employment:

I said this is useless. There was no reason to live off public money. I didn't feel good. So, I left NASS and stayed with a couple of my friends. And then eventually I became independent.

More direct and well-publicised forms of resistance have taken place in dispersal locations. These include extreme acts such as stitching up eyes and mouths to symbolise that the system denied them a voice. Kurdish asylum seekers organised a hunger strike in Liverpool in 2004.[8] Another set himself alight in the office of Refugee Action in Manchester after being refused refugee status. Unable to find a specialist solicitor and, with no permanent accommodation, he had been unable to access a GP in order to obtain a medical report to support his appeal.[9]

Many refugees in the study resisted the dehumanising impact of the system by investing in a future in the UK even though their status was insecure. They learned the language, made friends from the 'settled' population and participated in volunteering schemes when unable to take up paid employment. In spite of the obstacles placed in their way, they started to develop the skills and networks which could enable them to build a new life.

Dispersal and social cohesion

The study, like other research, suggested that dispersal has complex implications for social cohesion in dispersal areas. On the one hand, the forced movement of people to places where they have no connection, and where they are visibly outsiders, may generate tensions. Dispersal has produced widespread conflict and racism, including violence and even murder, which have led to several dispersal locations being suspended or ceased. On the other hand, it may provide opportunities for the kind of everyday interaction which can reduce hostility and build positive relations. Significantly, a report by the Institute for Public Policy Research (IPPR) found that negative attitudes towards asylum seekers were based on ignorance, and concern was often in areas where there were 'few or no asylum seekers' and where little meaningful interaction has taken place (Lewis, 2005: 1).

The experience is complicated by regional variations in the structure, management and implementation of dispersal (Griffiths et al., 2005). A study for the Refugee Council found significant differences in support services, ethnic diversity and refugee communities in different dispersal areas (Atfield et al., 2007: 15) which impact on the ability of refugees to participate and move towards some form of integration.

Many of the negative aspects of the current programme lie in its coercive and compulsory character. The policy context has problematised the whole nature of asylum, contributing to negative public attitudes. As Temple and Moran (2005: 4) argue, the starting point of meaningful and lasting relationships between communities can be built only when all have a say about the terms on which they relate to each other. In contrast, dispersal has often involved the sudden arrival of groups of newcomers to areas which had previously been relatively ethnically homogeneous. This made them highly visible, a visibility increased by the removal in 2002 of the 'concession' which had allowed asylum seekers to apply to take up employment after six months. With no work and no money to spend, they had little choice but to just 'hang around'. Enforced idleness revealed their dependence on benefit (Boswell, 2001), reinforcing perceptions of asylum seekers as a 'burden'.

These perceptions were not countered by the preparation of local populations for the arrival of asylum seekers. Local communities were given neither the information nor the resources to facilitate their reception (Zetter et al., 2006: 7). As one interviewee from a refugee agency complained:

Nobody tells them [the local residents of a dispersal location] that it is only temporary. No one is telling them that if the person living there gets a negative asylum decision they will lose all this. They either have to go underground, or they will get deported.

Problems are exacerbated by the concentration of dispersal in deprived areas. While it was claimed that dispersal would reduce social exclusion through decreasing competition for scarce resources (Robinson et al., 2003; Zetter et al., 2002), the choice of locations has meant that services may be overstretched and local populations resentful and liable to seek scapegoats. A MORI poll for the Commission on Integration and Cohesion (2007) found that more than half the people interviewed (56 per cent) feel that some groups get unfair priority from public services and that 'the groups most often named spontaneously were asylum seekers, refugees or immigrants.' One woman working with a voluntary agency described the problem in her city:

People who are at the very margins of society, have low income, have got high unemployment, they have got problems in their community – they see houses completely kitted out with all new stuff and then they see asylum seekers moving in, so they are up in arms that this has been provided, they are getting all this free.

Compulsory dispersal has undermined trust, which is an essential component of community engagement, participation and cohesion. The refugee experience is in itself one of breakdown of trust (Colson, 2003; Daniel and Knudsen,

1995; Hynes, 2003; Robinson et al., 2003; Voutira and Harrell-Bond, 1995). Refugees lose trust in both individuals and institutions responsible for their persecution, and mistrust is often replicated in the process of seeking asylum. The system requires them to answer questions, to retell their story and to justify their presence. This has led many to reject any involvement with organisations seen as linked to the Home Office, including refugee agencies, once their case is decided (Hynes, 2007; Sepulveda, 2006). Furthermore, the dispersal system generates suspicion between asylum seekers and populations in dispersal areas.

While the rhetoric of social cohesion is based on building connections between people, asylum policy is based on divorcing people from society and from shared experience. The racism inherent in immigration policy and practice is rarely addressed in 'community'-based initiatives, including those concerning social cohesion (Craig, 2007). Immigration policy treats asylum seekers as temporary residents who are not expected to integrate and become part of 'cohesive' communities.

The study found that the maintenance and recreation of social networks were essential for asylum seekers in developing a sense of belonging and avoiding extreme isolation. Dispersal, however, ruptures close ties by separating them from community networks which may provide support in the process of engaging with the new society. As networks become scattered across different cities, official policy controls mobility and thus the ability to retain these contacts. At the same time, they are prevented from developing bridging capital in the dispersal location which could link them to others. Their economic situation forces them to rely on others in the same marginalised position, and as Zetter et al. (2006: 11) suggest, they internalise social capital to fill the chasm left by the withdrawal of state support and, rather than leading to greater participation, 'may generate social capital as the currency of exclusion' with bonding capital 'an end state, rather than a stage in a dynamic process of bridging and linking' (*ibid*: 18).

Even 'genuine' refugees must endure dispersal and the experience of this period of limbo, in which they are physically within a particular place but not permitted to be part of a local 'community', cannot merely be wiped out once refugee status is granted. The research evidence suggests that they are not, as official policy claims, 'unconcerned' at their treatment and that the needs of refugees and of asylum seekers cannot be separated (Temple and Moran, 2005: 8). Prohibited from taking up employment and with obstacles placed in the way of learning the language, they experience the local 'community' as unwelcoming and distant. The negative effect of this period may thus be not merely to postpone, but to hinder, the building of connections.

Compulsory dispersal has been experienced in predominantly negative terms by asylum seekers. The policy has increased racial tensions in many dispersal areas and the racialisation of asylum has produced a broader impact on community relations. Lewis (2005: 36) found a widespread assumption in some areas that any non-white or obviously non-British person is an asylum seeker and this hostility has served to legitimise the expression of racist attitudes.

Although other forms of racism are becoming socially and legally unacceptable, there is 'no social sanction against expressing extremely prejudiced and racist views about asylum seekers' (Lewis, 2005: 44–5). This has given opportunities for the mobilisation of racist organisations in some dispersal areas.

In spite of these effects, many refugees are choosing to remain in the dispersal locations once they have been granted secure status. Although initially unwilling to move to these areas, many have set up home and plan to stay permanently. Some of those in the study who were dispersed to Leicester found conditions difficult but they also described themselves as comfortable there. Some described the 'multicultural' character of the city as making them feel at home, a multiculturalism which their own presence contributes to.

Vertovec (2006) rightly points out that it would be naive to suggest that simply by virtue of living near to each other people from different communities will overcome differences and tensions. The recent examples of ethnic conflict in Rwanda and Bosnia point to the dangers of this view. Real engagement, however, through local institutions, as well as individual relationships, offers the possibility of breaking down the divisions which immigration policy produces. Schools provide one of the best environments where people from diverse backgrounds can engage in a common, and familiar, purpose. It is no accident that many campaigns to protect 'failed asylum seekers' from deportation have been waged by children and teachers coming together to protest at the removal of friends and pupils. Dispersal has generated positive responses from many communities, including those who may have had no previous contact with refugees, providing opportunities for groups and individuals to work together to mobilise practical and political support (Atfield et al., 2007; East, 2008).

Conclusions

The contemporary dispersal programme is part of an overall policy of deterrence in which the majority of asylum seekers were seen as 'bogus' and thus as having no legitimate right to remain in the country. Destitute asylum seekers are dispersed without regard to their human experiences, skills and resources, becoming effectively dehistoricised. Segregated, stigmatised and socially excluded, asylum seekers move through a process characterised by continuous waiting, austere living conditions and a lack of control over their own lives. Denying them the opportunity to begin the process of resettlement, the dispersal system ensures that they remain in a situation of liminality. Arguably, it is these experiences, more than violence, flight and exile and other aspects of the 'refugee experience', that distinguish them from other migrants.

Furthermore, the dispersal programme has intensified hostility towards asylum seekers, a hostility which is often extended to all 'outsiders'. This policy, and the wider policy agenda on asylum, does not therefore provide a sound basis for promoting cohesion.

In spite of these obstacles there are signs that refugees are starting to rebuild their lives, even in the dispersal areas to which they had been involuntary located and where many choose to remain once refugee status is granted. While some local residents may be initially, or remain, hostile, others work hard to build connections through formal channels and voluntary and campaigning agencies. These activities directly or indirectly challenge the legislation which renders asylum seekers powerless and places them outside local communities. Thus some form of 'integration' is occurring in spite of asylum policy and the barrage of restrictions which it imposes.

Notes

1. 'Asylum seeker' has become a pejorative term in popular discourse and some prefer to avoid the term (see, for example, Temple and Moran, 2005). For brevity we use the term here to denote those with the legal status of asylum seeker – that is, awaiting the outcome of an application for asylum – for whom dispersal was introduced.
2. The 1951 United Nations Convention Relating to the Status of Refugees (the '1951 Refugee Convention') defined a refugee as someone who '... owing to a well-founded fear of being persecuted for reasons of race, religion, nationality, membership of a particular social group or political opinion, is outside the country of his nationality and is unable or, owing to such fear, is unwilling to avail himself of the protection of that country; or who, not having a nationality and being outside the country of his former habitual residence ... is unable or, owing to such fear, is unwilling to return to it'. The 1967 Bellagio Protocol Relating to the Status of Refugees removed the geographical and temporal limits of the 1951 Refugee Convention.
3. 'Disbenefited' cases refer to those cases previously supported by Local Authorities or the Department for Work and Pensions (DWP), which were then supported by the NASS after it began operating in 2000. They subsequently received a refusal for asylum but appealed. NASS was responsible for supporting appeal cases from September 2000. They are allowed to stay in their previous accommodation so will not all be in dispersal areas and can be distributed widely throughout each region.
4. Figures for June 2001 provided by email from Home Office.
5. ICAR (2003), Mapping the UK, section on Leicester city – viewed on 23 June 2003 at http://www.icar.org.uk/? lid=1052.
6. For more details of the current process, see UK Border Agency, http://www.ukba. homeoffice.gov.uk/asylum/process.
7. The names of individuals have been changed.

8.   Interview with representative of RCO, London, August 2004.
9.   *Open Verdict on Asylum Seeker Who Slept in a Wheelie Bin*, Manchester Committee to
     Defend Asylum Seekers, viewed on 25 October 2004 at http://www.asylumpolicy.info/
     notsuicideverdict.htm.

Suggested further readings

Bloch, A. and Schuster, L. (2005) 'At the Extremes of Exclusion: Deportation, Detention and
    Dispersal'. *Ethnic and Racial Studies* 28 (3): 491–512.
Griffiths, D., Sigona, N. and Zetter, R. (2005) *Refugee Community Organizations and Dispersal:
    Networks, Resources and Social Capital*. Bristol: Policy Press.
Robinson, V., Andersson, R. and Musterd, S. (2003) *Spreading the 'Burden'? A Review of Policies
    to Disperse Asylum Seekers and Refugees*. Bristol: Policy Press.
Sales, R. (2007) *Understanding Immigration and Refugee Policy*. Bristol: Policy Press.

References

Andersson, R. and Solid, D. (2003) 'Dispersal Policies in Sweden' in Robinson, V. (ed.)
    Spreading the 'Burden'? A Review of Policies to Disperse Asylum Seekers and Refugees. Bristol:
    Policy Press.
Atfield, G., Brahmbhatt, K. and O'Toole, T. (2007) *Refugees' Experiences of Integration*. Refugee
    Council and University of Birmingham.
Audit Commission (2000a) *Another Country: Implementing Dispersal under the Immigration and
    Asylum Act 1999*. London: Audit Commission.
Audit Commission (2000b) *A New City: Supporting Asylum Seekers and Refugees in London*.
    London: Audit Commission.
Baines, E. (2004) *Vulnerable Bodies: Gender, the UN and the Global Refugee Crisis*. Aldershot:
    Ashgate.
Boswell, C. (2001) *Spreading the Costs of Asylum Seekers: A Critical Assessment of Dispersal
    Policies in Germany and the UK*. London: Anglo-German Foundation for the Study of
    Industrial Society.
Boswell, C. (2003) 'Burden-Sharing in the European Union: Lessons from the German and
    UK Experience'. *Journal of Refugee Studies* 16 (3): 316–35.
British Medical Association (BMA) (2004) *Asylum Seekers and Their Health*. London: BMA.
Cantle, T. (2001) *Community cohesion*, Report of the Independent Review Team chaired by Ted
    Cantle. London: Home Office.
Carey-Wood, J., Duke, K., Karn, V. and Marshall, T. (1995) *The Settlement of Refugees in Britain*.
    London: HMSO.
Castles, S. (2000) *Ethnicity and Globalization*. London: Sage.
Cheong, P., Edwards, R., Goulbourne, H. and Solomos, J. (2007) 'Immigration, Social
    Cohesion and Social Capital: A Critical Review'. *Critical Social Policy* 27 (1): 24–49.
Colson, E. (2003) 'Forced Migration and the Anthropological Response'. *Journal of Refugee
    Studies* 16 (1): 1–18.
Commission for Racial Equality (2005) *Citizenship and Belonging: What is Britishness?* London: CRE.
Commission on Integration and Cohesion (2007) *Our Shared Future*. London: CIC.

Craig, G. (2007) ' "Cunning, Unprincipled, Loathsome": The Racist Tail Wags the Welfare Dog'. *Journal of Social Policy* 36 (4): 605–23.

Daniel, E. V. and Knudsen, J. C. (eds) (1995) *Mistrusting Refugees*. Berkeley: University of California Press.

Duke, K. (1996) 'The Resettlement Experiences of Refugees in the UK: Main Findings from an Interview Study'. *New Community* 22 (3): 461–78.

East, L. (2008) *Asylum seekers at the limits of Hospitality*. Unpublished PhD Thesis, University of Lancaster.

Flynn, D. (2005) 'New Borders, New Management: The Dilemmas of Modern Immigration Policies'. *Ethnic and Racial Studies* 28 (3): 463–90.

Geddes, A. (2000) *Immigration and European Integration: Towards Fortress Europe?* Manchester: Manchester University Press.

Goldsmith, Lord (2008) *Citizenship: Our Common Bond*. London: Ministry of Justice.

Guild, E. (2000) 'The United Kingdom: Kosovar Albanian refugees' in van Selm, J. (ed.) *Kosovo's Refugees in the European Union*. London: Pinter.

Hale, S. (1993) 'The Reception and Resettlement of Vietnamese Refugees in Britain' in Robinson, V. (ed.) *The International Refugee Crisis: British and Canadian Responses*. Basingstoke: Macmillan.

Hammar, T. (1993) 'The "Sweden-wide Strategy" of Refugee Dispersal' in Black, R. and Robinson, V. (eds) *Geography and Refugees: Patterns and Processes of Change*. London: Belhaven Press.

Harrison, J. (2006) *Boundary Strategies: Statecraft and Imagined Identities*. Unpublished PhD Thesis, Department of Sociology, University of Leicester.

Holmes, C. (1988) *John Bull's Island: Immigration and British Society, 1871–1971*. Basingstoke: Macmillan.

Home Office (1999) *Asylum Seekers Support: An Information Document Setting Out Proposals for the New Support Scheme for Asylum Seekers in Genuine Need and Inviting Expressions of Interest from Potential Support Providers*. London: HMSO Immigration and Nationality Directorate.

Home Office (2005) *Controlling Our Borders: Making Migration Work for Britain. Five Year Strategy for Asylum and Immigration*. London: Home Office.

Hynes, T. (2003) *The Issue of 'Trust' or 'Mistrust' in Research with Refugees: Choices Caveats and Considerations for Researchers*, New Issues in Refugee Research, Working Paper No. 98, Evaluation and Policy Analysis Unit, UNHCR, Geneva.

Hynes, P. (2007) *Dispersal of Asylum Seekers and Processes of Social Exclusion in England*. Unpublished PhD Thesis, Middlesex University.

Hynes, P. (2006) *The Compulsory Dispersal of Asylum Seekers and Processes of Social Exclusion*, Summary of Findings, Middlesex University and ESRC, Swindon.

Kushner, T. and Knox, K. (1999) *Refugees in an Age of Genocide*. London: Frank Cass.

Levy, C. (1999) 'European Asylum and Refugee Policy After the Treaty of Amsterdam: The Birth of a New Regime?' in Bloch, A. and Levy, C. (eds) *Refugees, Citizenship and Social Policy in Europe*. Basingstoke: Macmillan.

Lewis, M. (2005) *Asylum: Understanding Public Attitudes*. London: IPPR.

Malkki, L. (1995), *Purity and Exile*. Chicago: University of Chicago Press.

Mayor of London (2004) *Safe and Sound: Asylum Seekers in Temporary Accommodation*. London: GLA.

National Aids Trust (2006) *Dispersal of Asylum Seekers Living with HIV*. London: National Aids Trust.

Putnam, R. D. (2000) *Bowling Alone: The Collapse and Renewal of American Community*. New York: Simon and Schuster.

Putnam, R. D. (2007) 'E Pluribus unum': Diversity and Community in the Twenty-first Century. The 2006 Johan Skytte prize lecture.' *Scandinavian Political Studies* 30 (2): 137–74.

Rattansi, A. (2002) 'Who's British?' in *Cohesion, Community and Citizenship: Proceedings of a Runnymede Conference*. London: Runnymede Trust.

Rogers, B. and Muir, R. (2005) *The Power of Belonging: Identity, Citizenship and Community Cohesion*. London: IPPR Executive Summary.

Rutter, J. (2003) *Working with Refugee Children*. York: Joseph Rowntree Foundation.

Sales, R. (2002) 'The Deserving and the Undeserving? Refugees, Asylum Seekers and Welfare in Britain.' *Critical Social Policy* 22 (3): 456–78.

Schuster, L. (2004) *The Exclusion of Asylum Seekers in Europe*. Working Paper No. 1, Centre on Migration, Policy and Society (COMPAS), University of Oxford.

Sepulveda, L. (2006) *Refugees, New Arrivals and Enterprise: Their Contribution and Constraints*, Draft report of early results prepared for Small Business Service, Department of Trade and Industry, London.

Solomos, J. (2003) *Race and Racism in Britain*, 3rd Edition. Basingstoke: Palgrave Macmillan.

Somerville, W. (2006) 'Success and Failure under Labour: Problems of Priorities and Performance in Migration Policy.' *JCWI Immigration Rights Series*. London: JCWI http://www.jcwi.org.uk/archives

Stevenson, W. (2007) 'Preface' in Johnson, N. (ed.) *Britishness: Towards a Progressive Citizenship*. London: Smith Institute.

Temple, B. and Moran, R. (2005) *Learning to Live Together: Developing Communities with Dispersed Refugee People Seeking Asylum*. York: Joseph Rowntree Foundation.

Thielemann, E. R. (2003) 'Between Interests and Norms: Explaining Burden-Sharing in the European Union.' *Journal of Refugee Studies* 16 (3): 223–35.

Young, J. (2002) 'To these Wet and Windy Shores: Recent Immigration Policy in the UK', Paper Presented at the Common Study Programme in Critical Criminology, University of Athens, April.

Vertovec, S. (2006) 'The emergence of super-diversity in Britain', Centre on Migration, Policy and Society (COMPAS) Working Paper 25.

Voutira, E. and Harrell-Bond, B. E. (1995) 'In Search of the Locus of Trust: The Social World of the Refugee Camp' in Daniel, E. V. and Knudsen, J. C. (eds) *Mistrusting Refugees*. Berkeley: University of California Press.

Zetter, R., Pearl, M., Griffiths, D., Allender, P., Cairncross, L. and Robinson, V. (2002) *Dispersal: Facilitating effectiveness and efficiency – Final Report*, Home Office Research Paper. London: Home Office.

Zetter, R. et al. (2006) *Immigration, Social Cohesion and Social Capital: What are the Links?* York: Joseph Rowntree Foundation.

CHAPTER 4

The Continuing Significance of 'Race': Racism, Anti-racist Politics and Labour Markets

SATNAM VIRDEE

Introduction

The sociological research programme of class analysis has from its outset been a debate with the ghost of Marx. Post-war British sociologists, focusing on two related and often contentious debates about class consciousness and imagery made it one of their primary tasks to investigate and identify those factors that helped to explain why the British working class had not played its historically designated role as the agent of radical social transformation, and thereby become, as Marx had predicted, the gravedigger of capitalist society. Seeing consciousness as the intermediary between structural position and social action or what some termed the 'S-C-A approach' (Pahl 1989), the sociological consensus that emerged was that the 'class position of workers did not generate a clear and coherent class-consciousness' (Devine and Savage 2005: 6); instead, it was asserted that workers were driven by a form of instrumental collectivism that sought to improve conditions strictly within the parameters of the existing social order (Marshall et al. 1988). Thinking they had finally laid the ghost of Marx to rest, neo-Weberian class analysts have in more recent years shifted their attention away from the study of class formation (and the exploration of class in its totality) towards the much narrower remit of mapping the class structure and measuring the extent of social mobility and class-based inequality in late capitalist society (Marshall 1997).

This chapter represents an attempt to unsettle this current consensus, which weighs heavily on the sociological community and stifles further research and intellectual advancement in the area of class analysis. It does so by noting that a particularly striking but rarely commented upon feature of the golden age of British stratification research between the 1950s and the 1980s was its complete neglect of the impact of racism on the class structure, working-class consciousness and working-class politics. From the black-coated and affluent worker studies of the 1950s and 1960s to the international comparative studies of class structure carried out during the 1980s, one is hard-pressed to find any sustained attention given to questions of how racism might affect and inform the core research questions and agenda of the sociological analysis of class.

In part, this neglect was a product of the long-standing attachment of the vast majority of the British sociological community to a paradigm that associated the concept and therefore the study of society narrowly with that of the nation. This in turn led to the social construction of migrants as 'outsiders' or as 'not British' within the discipline itself such that any studies of these social groups and the questions they raised were never properly integrated into the research agendas of mainstream sociology, including the sociological analysis of class. Instead, the study of migrants tended to be marginalised, leading it to become the specialist preserve of a small group of sociologists and anthropologists working in what came to be known as the sociology of 'race relations'.

This chapter makes an explicit case for integrating the theoretical and empirical insights of racism studies with the sociological research programme on class to see what additional analytical insights can be gained about patterns of class formation since the 1950s. Specifically, it is contended that integrating racism as a key structuring variable of the sociological class analysis programme may help to understand both the allure of reformist politics for the ('white') working class and their attachment to elements of privatism, instrumental collectivism and a fatalistic acceptance of structured inequality.

An immediate practical problem one is confronted with at this stage is how can these objectives be achieved if neo-Weberian class analysts, due to their nationalist prejudices, failed to collect data on these issues in the 1960s and 1970s? Whilst mainstream sociology, including those working within the area of class analysis, may have failed to collect data on migrants, the State certainly did not. Partly as a consequence of the 1958 racist riots in Nottingham and Notting Hill, London, previously localised manifestations of racist expression mutated onto the national political scene, contributing to its racialisation. By 1962, the Conservative government had taken the step of introducing a racist immigration policy; racist in the sense that its intention was to restrict migration to Britain on the basis of a colour-coded selection process (Miles and Phizacklea 1984). However, accompanying the rise of State racism was the simultaneous concern amongst other often-competing fractions of the capitalist and political elite that those migrants (and their British-born children) who were already legally resident in Britain be accorded fair and equal treatment under the law. It was a Labour government that enacted the 1965 and the 1968 Race Relations Acts, which outlawed the most blatant manifestations of racist behaviour in public places and established the Community Relations Commission (CRC) to help enforce the new laws.

Lest there be any impression that associates Labour governments as being more progressive on matters of 'race' and immigration than Conservative governments, one need note only that it was a Labour government, under pressure from the adverse public reaction generated at the arrival of a small number of Ugandan Asians, that enacted the 1968 Immigration Act, which further restricted migration from what was then called the 'New Commonwealth' countries. This bipartisanship built around the State strategy of control and integration was neatly encapsulated by Roy Hattersley (a former Home Office minister) in his formulation: 'Integration without control is impossible, but control without integration is indefensible' (cited in Solomos 1993: 84).

It was as part of this twin-track strategy of control and integration that the British State began to collect data by 'racial' and then ethnic origin on a range of matters, including levels of crime, victimisation, demographic change and migration patterns. And it was against this political backdrop that a liberal think tank called Political Economic Planning (PEP) – a forerunner of today's Policy Studies Institute (PSI) – was commissioned in 1965 to undertake a study that would map the extent and nature of racist discrimination in Britain (Daniel 1968).

Whilst the government class schema employed by the study has been criticised by sociologists for its lack of theoretical grounding, most have also acknowledged that it bears a striking resemblance to the neo-Weberian Goldthorpe schema and its arrangement of occupations (see Crompton 1993: 59; Marshall et al. 1988). More significantly still, since the review of Government Social Classifications undertaken by the Economic and Social Research Council (ESRC) during the 1990s, the two class schemes have converged explicitly with the decision to adopt the Goldthorpe schema as the basis for the new official class schema – NS-SEC (Rose and Pevalin 2005: 15). Hence, the data presented in this chapter outlining the historical and contemporary class position of Britain's racialised minorities have, implicitly until the 1980s and explicitly thereafter, been informed and constructed by a neo-Weberian understanding of class.

Neo-Weberian analyses of racialised minority employment patterns: 1966–present

In one of the first studies of its kind in Britain, Daniel (1968) found that whilst the one-million-strong migrant population of mainly Caribbeans, Indians and

Pakistanis had occupied a diverse range of class positions in their countries of origin, they had undergone a profound process of proletarianisation on their arrival to Britain. For example, 71 per cent of agricultural labourers and peasant farmers had been transformed into an industrial working class centred on manufacturing industry. Whilst difficult to infer that this represented a form of downward social mobility for this particular segment of the migrant population, such a conclusion is far easier to sustain for those who had worked as white-collar employees prior to migration, 72 per cent of whom found themselves forced into manufacturing industry (Daniel 1968: 60). Such a process of largely undifferentiating proletarianisation of the migrant labour force, irrespective of their diverse class origins, was further demonstrated by Daniel's finding that

> Half the people who formerly held clerical, administrative or professional positions are now employed as wholly unskilled manual workers, largely general labourers or cleaners in factories. Ninety per cent of them are employed in manual work of one kind or another. Only 7 per cent remain in white-collar jobs of any kind and there is no certainty that these are at the level of either their previous employment or their qualifications and abilities.
>
> (Daniel 1968: 61)

Daniel (1968) went on to establish the causes of such proletarianisation by conducting research with employers and staff at employment bureaux. He found that 'a very substantial proportion of coloured people claim experience of discrimination, ... their claims are largely justified and ... it is the most able ones [i.e. white-collar workers] that experience most discrimination' (Daniel 1968: 82). This path-breaking study demonstrated conclusively that in 1960s Britain racist discrimination ranged from the 'massive to the substantial' (Daniel 1968: 209) with an informal colour bar in operation which whilst 'more covert and insidious than that operated in some other societies with different legal status for people of different colours, ... [was] none the less effective, and perhaps even more distressing, for that' (Daniel 1968: 217).

Since the 1960s, however, occupational data derived from the 2nd, 3rd and 4th PSI surveys (Brown 1982; Modood et al. 1997; Smith 1977) has consistently demonstrated a steady change in the employment position of Britain's racialised minorities, although this change has been more marked for some racialised minority groups than others. Drawing on the data analysis of the Labour Force Survey (LFS) carried out by Heath and Cheung (2006), an outline of the position of racialised minorities in the contemporary occupational class structure of Britain is presented here.

Half a century after the initial wave of mass migration from the Indian
sub-continent and the Caribbean, some racialised minority groups, in particular men and women of Pakistani and Bangladeshi descent, continue to suffer
severe disadvantage even prior to entering the labour market. Whilst men of
Indian, Caribbean (including those identified as mixed 'black'), African and
Chinese descent had similar rates of labour force participation to 'whites' (ranging between 74 per cent and 84.6 per cent), men of Pakistani and Bangladeshi
descent had significantly lower rates of labour force participation (68.7 per cent
and 61.8 per cent respectively) largely as a result of the large numbers reporting
long-term illness, sickness or disability (Heath and Cheung 2006: 81).

In the case of women, rates of labour force participation stratified into three
clusters with 'white' and Caribbean (including those of 'black' mixed origin)
women having the highest rates of labour force participation (between 74.8
per cent and 68 per cent). This group was followed closely by that of women
of Indian, African and Chinese descent who had labour force participation rates
ranging from 62.7 per cent to 57.8 per cent. However, it was women of Pakistani
and Bangladeshi descent who had the lowest rates of labour force participation
(28.7 per cent and 18.4 per cent) – this time as a result of large proportions
reporting ill-health or domestic responsibilities such as looking after the home
(Heath and Cheung 2006: 82).

The disadvantage facing those of Bangladeshi and Pakistani descent (and, to a
lesser extent, men and women of Caribbean and African descent), is further reinforced when considering their rates of economic activity, (that is, those who are
in employment (e.g. employees and self-employed) and those who are actively
seeking work (e.g. unemployed)). Table 4.1 shows that men of Chinese, 'white'
and Indian descent had the lowest rates of unemployment (ranging from 4.3
per cent to 6.2 per cent), whereas rates of unemployment for men of Pakistani,
'black' African, 'black' Caribbean (including those identified as 'black' mixed)
and Bangladeshi men were between two and three times greater (12.9 per cent to
17.3 per cent). Similarly, Table 4.2 shows that whilst women of 'white', Chinese
and Indian origin had the lowest rates of unemployment (between 4.1 per cent
and 6.9 per cent), rates of unemployment amongst women of Caribbean (including 'black' mixed), African, Bangladeshi and Pakistani women were between
two and three times higher (10.8 per cent to 15.1 per cent) (Heath and Cheung
2006: 81–2).

It has long been established that racialised minority groups have high rates
of self-employment (Smith 1977). Today, the highest rates of self-employment
are to be found amongst men of Pakistani and Chinese descent (25 per cent). On
the other hand, rates of self-employment amongst those men defined as 'black'
mixed, 'white', Bangladeshi and Indian are significantly lower at between one
in seven and one in six men, with the lowest rates of self-employment amongst

Table 4.1 Patterns of employment and unemployment – men (row percentages)

	Employed full-time	Employed part-time	Self-employed full-time	Self-employed part-time	Unemployed	N = Total sample size
Black African	64.2	14.3	6.8	0.7	13.9	961
Black Caribbean	64.6	9.0	9.9	1.5	15.1	1,025
Black Mixed	59.4	9.7	12.9	0.9	17.0	317
Indian	67.0	9.0	16.6	1.1	6.2	2,202
Pakistani	46.3	12.7	25.2	2.9	12.9	1,181
Bangladeshi	47.1	20.1	15.5	0.0	17.3	399
Chinese	59.8	11.0	23.1	1.9	4.3	419
British, other whites	73.2	6.6	13.9	1.5	4.8	124,013

Source: Labour Force Survey 2001–2004 in Heath and Cheung 2006.

Table 4.2 Patterns of employment and unemployment – women (row percentages)

	Employed full-time	Employed part-time	Self-employed full-time	Self-employed part-time	Unemployed	N = Total sample size
Black African	59.7	26.0	2.0	0.7	11.6	915
Black Caribbean	62.0	24.9	1.7	0.6	10.8	1,134
Black Mixed	50.6	33.2	1.4	3.5	11.3	347
Indian	55.0	30.5	4.5	3.1	6.9	1,701
Pakistani	42.1	35.5	4.7	2.7	15.1	484
Bangladeshi	48.7	33.3	0.9	4.3	12.8	117
Chinese	49.3	31.4	9.2	4.6	5.5	348
British, other whites	51.2	38.2	3.3	3.2	4.1	98,136

Source: Labour Force Survey 2001–2004 in Heath and Cheung 2006.

'black' African and 'black' Caribbean men (between one in twelve and one in ten). Whilst women of 'white' and racialised minority descent tended to have lower rates of self-employment than men (about one in twenty), Chinese women did have rates of self-employment comparable to men (one in seven).

Turning now to employment levels, the highest rates of employment (excluding self-employment) are to be found amongst 'white', 'black' African, Indian and 'black' Caribbean men (between 79.8 per cent and 73.6 per cent). However, 'black' mixed, Bangladeshi and particularly Pakistani men have significantly lower rates of employment (ranging from 67.2 per cent to 59 per cent); even those Pakistanis and Bangladeshis who are in work tend to be in part-time work. Whilst women overall have higher rates of employment than men, a much greater proportion of women's employment is part-time work (between a quarter and a third of all employment). Nevertheless, rates of employment are similar across women of all social groups (around 80 per cent).

Assessing the occupational attainment of those who are employees only, it was found that men of Chinese, Indian, 'white', 'black' mixed and 'black' African descent had similar proportions in the managerial and professional occupations (46 per cent to 38.81 per cent) (Table 4.3). However, men of 'black' Caribbean, Pakistani and particularly Bangladeshi descent were significantly under-represented in these occupations (30.8 per cent to 17.8 per cent). Instead, Heath and Cheung's analysis demonstrates that men of Bangladeshi descent (50.2 per cent) and, to a lesser extent, men of 'black' Caribbean and 'black' African descent (36.5 per cent to 35.6 per cent) were over-represented in less skilled working-class work compared with Chinese, Indian and 'white' men (18.2 per cent to 24.5 per cent) (Heath and Cheung 2006).

Table 4.3 Occupational attainment – men

	High and low professional, managerial (%)	Semi-routine and routine (%)
Black African	38.8	35.6
Black Caribbean	30.8	36.5
Black Mixed	41.1	28.8
Indian	45.3	23.7
Pakistani	27.9	29.7
Bangladeshi	17.8	50.2
Chinese	46.0	18.2
British, other whites	41.8	24.5

Source: Labour Force Survey 2001–2004 in Heath and Cheung 2006.

Table 4.4 Occupational attainment – women

	High and low professional, managerial (%)	Semi-routine and routine (%)
Black African	43.0	33.2
Black Caribbean	39.4	31.9
Black Mixed	45.2	28.1
Indian	37.0	31.2
Pakistani	30.0	39.0
Bangladeshi	20.7	52.9
Chinese	41.6	26.7
British, other whites	37.0	31.1

Source: Labour Force Survey 2001–2004 in Heath and Cheung 2006.

The representation of women in the occupational structure is rather different to that of men with women of 'black' mixed, 'black' African, 'white', 'black' Caribbean, Indian and Chinese descent having significantly higher proportions in managerial and professional occupations (45.2 per cent and 37 per cent) than Pakistani and Bangladeshi women (between 30 per cent and 20.7 per cent) (Table 4.4). Instead, the latter groups found themselves heavily over-represented in less skilled working-class work (52.9 per cent and 39 per cent).

As would be expected, those groups with better occupational profiles – Indians, 'whites' and the Chinese – also had the highest hourly earnings (Heath and Cheung 2006: 17). Conversely, particularly striking was that 45 per cent of Bangladeshi men and 15 per cent of Pakistani men aged over 22 were earning below the national minimum wage compared with only 4 per cent of 'white' men. On the other hand, there were relatively few differences in the proportions of women earning less than the minimum wage (11 per cent of 'white' women compared with 12 per cent of Pakistani and Bangladeshi women) (Heath and Cheung 2006: 18).

In drawing together these empirical results, Heath and Cheung (2006: 18) conclude that

> Overall, we find that at the beginning of the twenty-first century, a number of ethnic minority groups, notably Pakistani, Bangladeshi, black Caribbean and black African men continue to experience higher unemployment rates, greater concentrations in routine and semi-routine work and lower hourly earnings than do members of the comparison group of British and other whites. Women from these groups also have higher unemployment rates

than the comparison group although, for those in work, average hourly earnings tend to be as high or higher than those of white women. The situation of Pakistani and even more so of Bangladeshi groups is a particular cause for concern. They have notably high proportions of men who are economically inactive (largely because of long-term sickness and disability) as well as unemployment rates of well over ten percent. Bangladeshi men who are actually in work are disproportionately concentrated in semi-routine and routine work.

Neo-Weberian explanations of upward social mobility and continuing disadvantage in the labour market: a critique

Arising from this mapping of the major trends in racialised minority employment, neo-Weberians have sought answers to two principal questions. First, what factors help to account for the upward social mobility experienced by racialised minorities since the mid-1960s, especially amongst those of Indian and Chinese descent. And, second, how can the continuing disadvantage faced by racialised minorities be understood, especially amongst those of Pakistani and Bangladeshi descent?

Modood (1997), employing a conventional version of human capital theory, contends that key to understanding patterns of upward social mobility has been the acquisition of human capital, in particular educational qualifications or, following Bourdieu and Passeron (1990), what I prefer to call certified cultural capital. According to Modood, it is this certified cultural capital that has enabled racialised minorities to compete more successfully for jobs that were previously closed to them: 'The growing influence of qualifications on employment is … one of the factors in the reduction of racial disadvantage. An increase in educational achievement does not guarantee socio-economic equality, but it seems to be a pre-requisite' (Modood 1997: 347).

However, this type of argument is predicated on an understanding that racialised minorities didn't have this form of cultural capital to enter skilled, white-collar jobs in the 1960s and 1970s. Yet data from the 1st and 2nd PSI national surveys (Daniel 1968; Smith 1977) directly contradicts this assumption with Smith's observation as early as the mid-1970s that there 'are a substantial proportion [amongst racialized minority groups] who are qualified for professional or white collar jobs' (Smith 1977: 58), yet despite this 'Asians and West Indians with academic qualifications lag far behind "whites" with equivalent qualifications in getting white collar, professional or management jobs' (Smith 1977: 76). In fact, the studies found not only that a substantial proportion of racialised minorities had the relevant qualifications, but also that they had the necessary work experience in their countries of origin.

In the light of this evidence, other neo-Weberians like Heath (2003: 27), whilst continuing to claim that 'Human capital levels are a key determinant of labour market success', have refined Modood's argument by claiming it was the acquisition of certified *British* cultural capital that was key to propelling racialised minorities into better employment positions. In fact, this 'modification' to the main argument represents a tacit acknowledgement that during the 1960s and 1970s migrants did have the necessary qualifications to access the salariat but that their qualifications were not portable because they had been gained abroad: 'when they did have qualifications, they were often foreign ones that might not be recognized as having equal standing with British qualifications' (Heath and Yu 2003: 2). Heath goes on to identify Indians and the Chinese as 'model minorities' who have successfully pursued this strategy of British cultural capital acquisition such that they are now 'on average doing well and often out-performing whites in schools and in the labour market' (Heath 2003: 4), leading him to conclude that 'there are no insuperable barriers to successful economic and social integration' (Heath 2003: 4)

However, there are a number of cultural assumptions implicit within Heath's argument that require further interrogation, especially the attempted naturalisation of employer preference for British qualifications over equivalent qualifications gained abroad. What Heath fails to consider is how racism articulated with such nationalist preferences in structuring the labour markets of the 1960s and 1970s. The arrival of 'non-white' migrants from the Indian sub-continent and the Caribbean in the 1950s and 1960s triggered a racist reaction amongst much of the 'white' British population such that blackness and Britishness came to be reproduced as mutually exclusive categories, as neatly captured in Gilroy's 1987 book *There Ain't No Black in the Union Jack*. According to the rules of this 'new racism', Britain was re-imagined as a 'white' nation. This ideological work accomplished by employers and workers in tandem allowed them to legitimise the systematic exclusion of 'non-white' migrants from the more skilled jobs available in the Britain of the time, regardless of whether they had the requisite cultural capital to undertake the job. This association between whiteness and Britishness meant that those who had been remade as 'non-whites' found their certified cultural capital delegitimised and therefore worthless in the labour market of 1960s and 1970s Britain. The effect of this racialising nationalism was that many migrant workers who had been white-collar employees in their countries of origin were simply proletarianised:

Half the people who formerly held clerical, administrative or professional positions are now employed as wholly unskilled manual labourers, largely general labourers or cleaners in factories. Ninety per cent of them are employed in manual work of one kind or another. Only 7 per cent remain in white collar jobs of any kind and there is no certainty that these are at the level of either their previous employment or their qualifications.

(Daniel 1968: 61)

Whilst Modood and Heath focused on the individual characteristics of racialised minorities, especially the volume and quality of certified cultural capital acquired as the primary driver of alleged upward social mobility, other neo-Weberian analysts of class like Iganski and Payne (1996) have focused on the demand for certain kinds of labour. For them, key to the changing class position of racialised minority groups has been the expansion of non-manual work: 'the growth in opportunities for more desirable jobs increases the upward mobility chances of everybody, including those born at the bottom of the heap' (Iganski and Payne 1996: 130) such that 'more members of each group now have more desirable occupations' (Iganski and Payne 1996: 118). However, *ceteris paribus*, this would mean that a greater proportion of both racialised minorities and 'whites' would be in better jobs. This doesn't explain why racialised disadvantage – that is, the *relative* position of racialised minorities to 'whites' – has actually declined (something which all social scientists are agreed upon), implying that racialised minorities had secured white-collar jobs at a greater rate than 'whites'.

To their credit, Iganski and Payne (1996: 130) recognise the flaw in their initial argument by subsequently claiming that the convergence in occupational profiles was facilitated by the use of formal recruitment procedures that were more bureaucratic and credentialist and which therefore restricted the possibility of employers engaging in racist discriminatory practices. However, this just leads them toward the same dead-end that Heath and Modood find themselves in. Their suggestion that non-manual employers are less likely to discriminate because of the use of more formal and credentialist recruitment criteria is just not tenable; otherwise, why did we not witness the appointment of suitably qualified 'non-white' workers in the 1960s and 1970s as shown above? Again, like the explanations for alleged upward social mobility advanced by Heath and Modood, Iganski and Payne's ultimately fails to account for the social change they have identified.

Let's turn now to how neo-Weberians have attempted to answer the second question, namely how can the continuing disadvantage faced by racialised minorities be understood? Employing multiple regression, Heath and Cheung (2006: 35) found that 'even after like-for-like analysis, all ethnic minority groups are disadvantaged relative to Whites in comparable circumstances' with just £9 of the £1,126 wage gap between 'blacks' and 'whites' accounted for by variables such as age, education, family structure and recency of migration. With their theoretical modelling failing to identify the primary sources of disadvantage,

Heath and his collaborators are forced to introduce the concept of ethnic penalty to account for the gap between 'whites' and 'non-whites'. Ethnic penalty is defined by Heath and McMahon (1995: 1) as 'all the sources of disadvantage that might lead to an ethnic group to fare less well in the labour market than do similarly qualified Whites' and includes such factors as the degree of assimilation, cultural and religious factors, business opportunities, government infrastructure, quality and location of housing, levels of access to social capital and racism.

Heath, unlike Modood, doesn't make the mistake of claiming that racism has declined. Indeed, he concedes that whilst such statistical analysis cannot uncover the relative weight of racist discrimination in understanding continuing levels of disadvantage and 'despite significant improvements, there is evidence that within some workplaces, racial discrimination still exists' (Heath 2003: 38). Nevertheless, one is left to conclude that the numerous research reports, funded so generously by multiple government departments, including the Cabinet Office, seem only to have yielded a negative result, namely that all those factors that successive governments and academics like Heath believed might be important in determining the labour market chances of racialised minority groups actually have little impact. These studies in practice have served, both in the political and in the academic communities, to deflect attention, research and resources away from the main sources of continuing racialised minority disadvantage – racism and the restructuring of the British economy under neo-liberalism. It is no coincidence that national studies measuring the extent of racist discrimination have not been funded since the mid-1980s – the same time frame in which the State and its agencies began to invest heavily in funding the multilevel modelling studies of Heath, Modood and their collaborators.

The analysis offered by Heath and his associates has contributed to an underestimation of racism in the following ways. First, as has been shown above, by naturalising the employer preference of British qualifications, Heath neglects how, during the 1960s and 1970s, such nationalist preferences articulated with racism to exclude suitably qualified 'non-whites' from white-collar jobs. Second, by attempting to isolate and measure the so-called 'independent effect' of factors such as certified cultural capital on racialised minority employment patterns, Heath and his collaborators fail to consider how racism may be interacting with this variable to determine the volume and quality of certified cultural capital acquired. There is now ample quantitative and qualitative evidence collected over a considerable time frame across a range of countries which demonstrates unequivocally how societal-wide racist representations are drawn upon by schoolteachers and children to structure the lives of racialised minority children at school, including influencing the quality of certified cultural capital they leave school with (Mac an Ghaill 1988). Racism is an indivisible component of variables like cultural capital and class and cannot be conceptually distinguished or separated out as Heath, Modood and others attempt to do using multiple regression. It is not just that there is a reciprocal interaction between them but rather that over time they come to take on a form of non-separability. This means asking different sorts of questions such as to what extent is class racialised or in what ways is the acquisition of certified cultural capital shaped by processes of racialisation? Further, any consideration of the influence of such variables must be undertaken by embedding them in the social contexts from which they derive not by abstracting them from their real-world settings.

Third and finally, this mistaken underestimation of the diverse and multiple ways in which racism shapes and compounds the structural location of racialised minorities is accentuated by their introduction of the concept of ethnic penalty. The focus on religion, culture and the degree of assimilation amongst other factors when evaluating the relative weight of the ethnic penalty shifts the sociological gaze away from racism and external, constraining forces and towards what will inevitably be interpreted as 'problematic' norms, values and patterns of behaviour amongst the minorities themselves. This merely serves to reify the problem and results in a gross underestimation of the multifarious ways in which racism shapes the employment patterns of racialised minorities. Simultaneously, it creates a political space for those right-wing interest groups, social movements and individuals who wish to use the alleged improvement in the employment position of some racialised minority groups (e.g. Indians) to divert political attention away from the significance of racism in understanding the continuing disadvantage faced by other racialised minority groups (e.g. Pakistanis) and towards explanations that focus on the alleged cultural deficiencies or shortcomings of these groups (e.g. attachment to anti-modernist forms of religious belief, sexism, etc.). Hence, the relative success of the quintessential model minorities of British society (e.g. Indians) in securing entry into white-collar and professional work is juxtaposed with the failings of the quintessential problematic minorities of British society (e.g. Pakistanis), resulting in the further racialisation of social relations between what various publics perceive as 'good pakis' and 'bad pakis'.

The mapping of such problematic scenarios and the contribution that academics may have made to their more likely realisation is not mere idle speculation. This form of racist reasoning is already widely prevalent in the US, where authors like Charles Murray (1994) have contended that the poor economic position of the African American 'underclass' is the result of changes in family patterns and styles of parenting rather than a product of economic and social change. In the current political climate where anti-Muslim racism has become so respectable amongst large swathes of the population in England as a result of both global and national factors, it would not require much effort on the part of the right-wing media and political commentators to advance arguments that claim the primary reason why Pakistanis have failed to advance in socio-economic terms is not racism (otherwise, how would one explain the successful performance of Indians and African Asians who are also 'non-white'?) but their own failure to 'get a decent education' or their attachment to the norms and values associated with a 'problematic' religion.

Another striking feature of the neo-Weberian approach of Heath, Modood and others is the almost complete absence of collective actors and political struggle in the labour market. Instead, the only actors appear to be individuals – employees and employers, the former trading their certified cultural capital on a free market and finding themselves positioned within the appropriate segment of the labour market. Any assessment of the rich and diverse forms of contentious politics, social movements and interest groups that exist in most workplaces – be they advocating forms of racist exclusionary practice or trying to combat it – is entirely removed from consideration in their conceptual frame to analyse racialised minority employment patterns.

In summary, whilst these neo-Weberian explanations for changing racialised minority employment patterns represent a welcome advance from the 'race-blind' scholarship of Goldthorpe, Lockwood and so much of post-war British class analysis, it nevertheless remains the case that these explanations remain flawed, manifesting errors and oversights which render them hugely problematic. Consequently, in the remainder of the chapter, the philosophical foundations of an alternative theoretical explanation are outlined and the additional explanatory power this frame provides in understanding the changing patterns of racialised minority employment is empirically demonstrated.

Holism and moving beyond methodological individualism

Many of the failings of neo-Weberian class analysis stem from their adoption of a methodological individualist standpoint. One of the strongest advocates of methodological individualism, Max Weber, proclaimed that

> Interpretative sociology considers the individual ... and his action as the basic unit, as its 'atom' – if the disputable comparison may be permitted. In this approach, the individual is also the upper limit and the sole carrier of meaningful conduct.... In general, for sociology, such concepts as 'state', 'association,' 'feudalism,' and the like, designate certain categories of human interaction. Hence, it is the task of sociology to reduce these

concepts to 'understandable' action, that is, without exception, to the actions of participating individual men.

(Weber cited in Gerth and Mills 1993: 55)

Hence, from the perspective of methodological individualism, broad society-wide developments can only be understood as the aggregation of decisions by individuals. It is an approach that construes individual elements as self-contained and self-determining and combining arithmetically to form groups such that the knowledge of things consists of reducing complexity to simple separate elements. In this sense, it precludes the possibility of social collectivities making decisions and insists that social sciences must ground their theories in individual action. What is perhaps ironic about such a standpoint is how Weber's successors have been far more consistent practitioners of it than Weber was himself. Indeed, Gerth and Mills (1993: 57) observe how it would have been difficult for Weber to have produced his most profound works such as *The Protestant Ethic and the Spirit of Capitalism* and *General Economic History* had he worked within the limits of his own narrowly conceived standpoint:

Were one to accept Weber's methodological reflections on his own work at their face value, one would not find a systematic justification for his analysis of such phenomena as stratification or capitalism. Taken literally, the 'method of understanding' would hardly allow for Weber's use of structural explanations, for this type of explanation attempts to account for the motivation of systems of action by their functions as going concerns rather than by the subjective intentions of the individuals who act them out.

What this reveals is that Weber himself did in fact have a clear understanding of the individual being located in a particular kind of society (e.g. capitalism) characterised by certain forms of social relations. By grounding the subsequent analysis in the counter-philosophical perspective of holism, I hope to avoid the errors and silences associated with neo-Weberian explanations and move towards a more nuanced understanding of the relationship between racism, anti-racism and collective action in shaping labour market outcomes. Holism is a perspective that suggests the best way to study the behaviour of human beings in societies is to treat it as a whole and study it at the level of principles governing the behaviour of the whole system and not at the level of its component parts. It is a perspective that construes elements as part of a total system of relations that constitute them and insists that knowledge of things requires an understanding of elements as complex, multifaceted entities that are dialectically related to other things.

A necessary first step is to re-embed individuals within a historically concrete reading of the capitalist social formation. For, as Mandel (1989) quite rightly notes, 'Individuals "in general", divorced from the social conditions in which they are embedded, are as unreal, abstract and metaphysical (mythical, pure products of imagination) as "history" is in general and in the abstract.' In turn, this twin process of embedding and historicising helps to direct our sociological gaze towards those already existing 'social forces and institutions which have a logic of their own, separate and apart from that of any individuals who compose them – irrespective of whether that logic operates *a priori* or *a posteriori* to that of personal motivations' (Mandel 1989).

In contrast to the neo-Weberians for whom the individual is the basic unit of decision-making and the primary social actor, Mandel draws our attention to how societies are already structured by collective social forces and institutions locked in oppositional conflict who through force of circumstance socialise individuals such that they come to fashion themselves in ways that facilitate their identification with particular types of social collectivities – collectivities that themselves aren't real in any way but are themselves the temporary product of previous waves of political struggles and social conflict. In contrast to methodological individualism which conceives of individuals as independent entities with self-containing properties, holism therefore assumes that individuals are inextricably bound to one another in a form of interdependence, of reciprocally interacting relationships, often in opposition to other groups of individuals.

Within historical capitalism, the most prominent of these collective social forces have been constructed along the axis of nations, classes, 'races' and genders. Each of these social collectivities has established institutions, interest groups and social movements to protect and advance what they have framed as their material and ideological interests, often in opposition to, and in conflict with, other social groups (e.g. trades unions versus employers). Against this backdrop, social change can no longer be interpreted as the product of individual decision-making but of a complex interaction between structural constraints and human agency. Mandel (1989) observes how

> Human beings are characterized by a great many conflicting drives, passions, interests, goals, motives, etc. Which one of them (or which precise combination of them) will ultimately determine given forms of social actions or behaviours (as opposed to 'purely' personal ones) ... will largely depend upon the pressure of prevailing social circumstances, mediated through clashes between social groups ... and their relative force. When these circumstances change, behaviour changes without necessarily any change in the individual's 'total personality.'

This of course is not to deny the role of the individual in history but to recognise that any individual decision is always and everywhere a constrained choice. Mandel's concept of parametric determinism allows one to grasp the real place of human action in the way the historical process unfolds and the way the outcome of social crises is decided:

> Men and women make their own history. The outcome of their actions is not mechanically predetermined. Most, if not all, historical crises have several possible outcomes, not innumerable fortuitous or arbitrary ones; that is why we use the expression 'parametric determinism' indicating several possibilities within a given set of parameters.

Even with such broad-brush schematic theorizing, the social world is unmasked as far more complex than that portrayed by the neo-Weberian analysts of class and ethnicity. One can discern the presence of group formation and collective actors, conflict and struggle and a dynamic and fluid representation of society marked by inequality and domination. Analytically, such a conception contrasts favourably with that of the neo-Weberian ideal-type nationally bounded labour market abstracted from history and political conflict where individual decision-making units sell their certified cultural capital to individual employers in a static, ideology- and conflict-free society.

Lest individuals think this is a divide between Marxist and Weberian ontologies, there are also traditions within historical materialism like that of analytical Marxism, including such notables as G. A. Cohen, John Roemer and Jon Elster, who also adopt the standpoint of methodological individualism:

> The elementary unit of social life is the individual human action.... To explain social institutions and social change is to show how they arise as the result of the actions and interaction of individuals.
>
> (Elster 1989: 13)

However, embracing the perspective of methodological individualism implies the rejection of holism and dismissal of dialectics as 'hegelian metaphysics'. Conversely, it is contended that both are central with the latter constituting the essence of Marx's method (Hook 2002; Ollman 2003). Only with dialectics can real contradictions be grasped; that is, the contradictory character of the movement of nature, of history and of the cognition process itself. It is what gives historical materialism a fluidity and dynamism and the capacity to capture social change in a manner entirely absent from the formalistic Marxism of Elster. By rejecting the materialist dialectic, methodological individualists – both neo-Weberians and analytical Marxists alike – impede their own understanding of the mediating role of social forces between individuals and the social environment they are embedded in. Human historical progress is not linear but contradictory – diachronic not synchronic.

Understanding social change in labour markets: the significance of the restructuring of the capitalist economy, racism and anti-racist politics

In this final substantive section of the chapter, an alternative explanation for understanding both the changing employment patterns of racialised minorities and their continuing disadvantage in the labour market is presented. Specifically, two questions are answered: first, how this change took place and, secondly, whether it is suggestive of upward social mobility? By re-embedding an analysis of changing racialised minority employment patterns within a historically concrete reading of the capitalist social formation, the neo-Weberian claim that entry into self-employment was a primary driver of upward social mobility, especially for South Asian men, is brought into serious question. Whilst I concur with the neo-Weberian claim that the survey data reveals a four-fold increase in Asian male self-employment between 1974 and 1994 (Modood 1997), my contention is that much of this increase ought to be interpreted not as an indication of upward social mobility but racialised minority working-class adjustment to the twin pressures of a rapidly de-industrialising British economy and continuing racist exclusion from the wider labour market.

Since the self-employed are allocated across two strata in the neo-Weberian schema, let's begin by focusing on class IIIm of Registrar General's Social Classes (RGSC) made up of skilled manual workers. Much of the growth in self-employment in this class represents working-class accommodation to the shift from a Fordist regime of accumulation to a flexible regime of accumulation. Employment in the Fordist regime of accumulation was traditionally built on a tripartite consensus of employers, organised labour and the State and was characterised by relatively secure, unionised, assembly-line jobs in manufacturing (Harvey 1993). However, by the early 1970s, the rising price of oil coupled with growing competition from the East, especially Japan, forced fractions of the British capitalist elite to launch an offensive against the post-war welfare settlement, leading to major conflict with sections of organised labour. By the mid-1980s, led by a combative Thatcher in Britain and Reagan in the US, organised labour had been defeated thereby cementing the new regime of accumulation. This regime, that we continue to live under today, has come to be characterised by, among other things, increased flexibility in the workforce, continuing attempts to lower production costs through downsizing the numbers of permanent employees and the increased use of part-time, temporary and sub-contracted labour whose terms and conditions are characterised by low wages and few benefits (Ackers et al. 1995).

The employment profile in Britain was transformed with three million jobs lost in manufacturing industry between 1971 and 1988 (Crompton 1993: 82). Significantly, this process of industrial restructuring and rising unemployment did not impact equally on the 'black' and 'white' working class; instead, as a consequence of the post-Second World War racist discriminatory practices that had forced racialised minorities into the most vulnerable jobs in manufactur-ing (as discussed above), the results of the employer offensive of the 1970s and 1980s impacted disproportionately on racialised minorities, and some racialised minority groups in particular (Brown 1982).

It is against this backdrop of the deep structural transformation of the cap-italist world economy, including within Britain, that the constrained choices facing racialised minority communities – between a life of long-term unemploy-ment and precarious employment in the new service sector characterised in the main by poor terms and conditions of employment – must be understood. If we take Pakistani taxi drivers – a significant component of the racialised minor-ity self-employed in RGSC IIIm – it would be difficult to sustain an argument that these individuals experienced any genuine and meaningful upward social mobility as Modood (1997) claims. Instead, their movement from 'textile mills to taxi ranks' (Kalra 2000) was motivated by the need to accommodate to the devastation of the textile industry in the North West (where they were heavily concentrated), which forced unemployment up from 6 per cent in the mid-1970s to 29 per cent in the early 1980s (Brown 1982). Unable to secure alternative man-ual employment and white-collar local state employment due to racism (Cantle 2001), large numbers of Pakistani men were faced with an unenviable choice of long-term unemployment or driving mini-cabs and taxis. Hence, this shift in the occupational position of Pakistani men over the past three decades ought to be interpreted as a desperate attempt to accommodate to the ravages wrought by the introduction of a flexible regime of accumulation and continuing racist exclusion from those parts of the labour market unaffected by such transforma-tions and certainly not as evidence of upward social mobility as Modood claims. Many of the South Asian workers who are currently self-employed have moved from low-paid, relatively secure employment in the manufacturing industry to low-paid, insecure employment in the service sector.

An important second category of South Asian self-employed are found in the occupational strata made up of managerial and technical occupations. Typical of Asian self-employment in this occupational class are small family-run busi-nesses like grocery shops, newsagents and off-licences (Modood 1997: 101) – the classic petty-bourgeoisie of small property owners 'who make their living primarily by the exercise of their own labour with their self-owned means of production or other property' (Draper 1978: 288). Objectively, the shift into this class does represent a change in their relationship to the means of production. However, as with the archetype Asian taxi driver, much of this movement into the petty-bourgeoisie seems to have been driven by economic recession and a lack of opportunities in the wider labour market (McEvoy et al. 1982). Despite these inauspicious motivating circumstances, a significant proportion of this social layer have nevertheless made a success of their businesses (as measured by turnover and numbers of staff employed) such that they are now firmly part of the British petty-bourgeoisie (Metcalf et al. 1996).

This discussion about the different types of South Asian self-employment suggests that the overwhelming majority of the South Asian self-employed have not experienced any upward social mobility. Apart from a small minority of mainly Indian and African Asian entrepreneurs that bifurcated into the petty-bourgeoisie, for the vast majority, entry into self-employment represented a working-class strategy to negotiate the threat of unemployment created by the destruction of manufacturing employment and the advent of the neo-liberal economy.

A second component of the upward social mobility thesis advanced by neo-Weberian class analysts has been the increasing representation of racialised minorities in non-manual occupations, especially junior white-collar work (Modood 1997). As shown earlier in the chapter, in spite of having the appropriate certified cultural capital and the necessary work experience, South Asians and Caribbeans found non-manual occupational jobs closed to them due to the operation of a racializing nationalism. Yet, by the 1980s, the neo-Weberian evidence clearly suggests that this was no longer the case and that growing numbers of racialised minority men and women were employed in this occupational class. This then raises the important question of why didn't employers of non-manual labour exclude racialised workers to the same extent as they had in the 1960s and 1970s?

The argument advanced by some neo-Weberians like Modood (1997), although not Heath (2003), that the changes are the direct result of the declining significance of racism – 'The qualifications, job levels and earnings spread in 1994 are roughly what one would have predicted from the spread of qualifications in 1974, *if racial exclusion was relaxed*' (Modood 1997: 347 emphasis added) – can be rejected. If racism had declined, surely such a momentous transformation would require some elaboration as to exactly how it had come to pass, particularly since Modood's argument is predicated on such an assumption. Yet, he ventures nothing more on this crucial question. It is possible to speculate that racism may have declined due to the introduction of anti-racist legislation, especially the 1965, 1968 and 1976 Race Relations Acts. However, this argument has also been rejected on the grounds that discrimination testing found 'no evidence during the 1980s to suggest that the extent of discrimination fell at all' (Brown 1992: 60) such that for some (e.g. Solomos 1987: 50) this legislation has acted as a cloak to mask continuing discrimination: 'the weight of existing evidence would seem to support the thesis that race relations policies have functioned largely at the symbolic level since 1965'.

In contrast, the argument advanced in this chapter is that the growing representation of racialised minorities in non-manual work was the outcome of complex interactions between the changing political opportunity structure of 1980s England and the formation of an anti-racist social movement. The American political scientist Ira Katznelson (1997: 51) suggests that to understand social change one should focus on those 'moments when system creating choices are made.... Such intervals of indeterminacy are times when the boundary conditions of politics are renegotiated and reset.' The early 1980s were exactly such a 'moment' when it comes to understanding the transformation in the employment position of racialised minorities. Of decisive importance was the reaction of the central and local state to the urban unrest of 1980 and 1981. Although research suggests that the participants comprised both 'black' and 'white' youths (Gilroy 1987), two mutually antagonistic sets of social forces ensured that racism or, more precisely, 'race', came to dominate public policy debate about the main causes of the unrest.

On the one hand, anti-racists insisted that the root causes of the unrest lay in the systematic destruction of the lives of racialised minority communities through the operation of racist discriminatory practices and state (mainly police) harassment, which had served to create a 'racially-defined subproletariat' (Sivanandan 1990). On the other hand, much of the tabloid press forcefully denied that the unrest was the result of racism and instead attempted to criminalise the unrest by representing it as the product of a 'black' criminal underbelly within society (Gilroy 1987; Solomos 1988).

It was amidst this highly charged political atmosphere that the results of the Scarman Inquiry into the urban unrest were published in November 1981 (Scarman 1981). The Report advanced a series of recommendations including the need to introduce measures to combat 'racial disadvantage' in employment. However, apart from giving qualified support to the findings contained in the Report (see Raison 1984: 244–57), the right-wing Conservative administration remained averse to introducing even minor reforms because of its disagreement with the materialist explanation of the unrest advanced by the Scarman Inquiry (Ball and Solomos 1990).

At this juncture, one may have expected key workplace institutions like employers and trade unions to exclude racialised minority workers from the remaining areas of employment stability, especially non-manual state employment as they had in the 1960s and 1970s (Smith 1977). However, such a scenario failed to materialise in large part because the political climate in 1980s England was radically different to that which prevailed during the 1960s, where there was an absence of anti-racist activism (Virdee 2000). For instance, when considering trade unions, although rank-and-file working class militancy had subsided since its high point in the mid-1970s, union activists that had led the industrial unrest remained in positions of leadership such that by the early 1980s, they were to some extent, to the left of their membership over a range of issues, including the need to combat racism (Virdee 2000).

An anti-racist social movement comprising a coalition of 'white' trade union activists, 'black' activists in the community and left-wing councillors angered by the politics of the Labour Party in power ensured that the recommendations of the Scarman Report were forced onto the local state public policy agenda, especially in Labour-controlled local authorities in the Greater London area (where nearly half the 'black' and Asian racialised population was spatially located) (Owen 1992). As Ouseley (cited in Solomos 1993: 104) makes clear, the unrest and resulting mobilisations 'forced local authorities to respond to the demands ... for action on racial discrimination in employment'. The resultant action, including the introduction of, amongst other things, equal opportunity policies, was instrumental in helping to force open intermediate non-manual work in the local state to an unprecedented extent (see Ouseley 1990; Solomos 1993) such that by the mid-1990s large numbers of racialised minorities, especially Caribbean men and women, were heavily dependent on such employment (Modood 1997: 109–10).

Whilst some scepticism was expressed about whether such gains could be maintained in the long run, subsequent research confirms that these events marked a major turning point in terms of understanding the changing employment profile of racialised minority workers. The reasons why these gains were consolidated are complex. Of primary importance was the new influx of 'non-white' workers into non-manual state employment and the organisational strategies they pursued; in particular, the establishment of 'black' members groups within the local government trade union, the National and Local Government Officers Association (NALGO). The philosophy underpinning the creation of these groups was that self-organisation constructed around a racialised 'black' identity was a necessary and essential condition for ensuring the effective tackling of racism at work:

As black trade unionists we must force the union to recognise the vital role it must play in fighting against exploitation and for equal rights. The 1980s, however, have been witness to an increased urgency for consolidation and action on equality. The black perspective is vital in the analysis, the policies and action of NALGO, and is the only thing which can hope to change the structures and services of the unions so that black people are no longer an itch on someone's back but the very spine of solidarity, the first principle of trade unionism . . . it is not self-organisation for the sake of being separate. It is to ensure exactly the opposite that black issues and rights are addressed by the trade unions to which we belong in a way acceptable to black members. As black trade unionists we believe in the principles of solidarity and support but these can never happen if the union works only for some.

> (Karen Chouhan, Secretary, National Black Members Coordinating Committee (NBMCC), cited in NBMCC 1986: 6)

Throughout the 1980s and 1990s, these workplace groups acted as a powerful interest group within NALGO, forcing its leadership to maintain 'racial equality', including the effective implementation of equal opportunity policies, as a priority item when negotiating with employers. Hence, it was political struggle – in particular, anti-racist activism around a racialised 'black' identity – that opened up intermediate non-manual work during the 1980s and not the acquisition of cultural capital and the declining significance of racism as Modood claims. It was only after such political action had removed some of the worst discriminatory practices in the local state labour market and forced employers to consider racialised minorities as potential employees that those with the necessary certified cultural capital were able to enter intermediate non-manual work in ever-increasing numbers.

Significantly, this process of self-organisation in trade unions around a racialised 'black' identity was replicated across much of the public sector such that by the mid-1980s other large public sector employers such as the Civil Service and the National Health Service (NHS) had followed suit and introduced equal opportunity and anti-discriminatory policies designed to encourage the recruitment and selection of racialised workers for administrative and clerical work (Beishon et al. 1995).

Summing up these events, it was political struggle – first outside the workplace, then within the workplace, especially within sympathetic trade unions and left-leaning Labour councils – that enabled racialised minority workers to penetrate and ultimately consolidate their position in non-manual state work and alter the long-term position of some racialised groups in the employment structure in England. What is truly remarkable and testament to the successful struggle waged by racialised minority activists (and their 'white' allies) is that this transformation took place in an era of rising neo-liberalism, a period that many althusserian marxists predicted would spell disaster for racialised minorities. In fact, the total number of racialised minorities employed in intermediate non-manual work, especially in the local and national state, increased dramatically in an era when the overall numbers employed in this type of work actually declined (Brown 2001: 16).

However, as with the case of the growth of Asian self-employment, caution needs to be exercised in drawing conclusions that associate the increasing representation of racialised minorities in non-manual work with a rise in upward social mobility. If the social change effected by anti-racist protest is grounded in a historically concrete analysis of the social formation it reveals a bitter irony. Non-manual state employment was forced open to 'non-whites', especially 'non-white' women, at a historical conjuncture when such work was increasingly being characterised by growing routinisation and deskilling (Crompton and Jones 1984; see also the collection of papers in Hyman and Price 1983). Such an argument helps to reinforce the overall scepticism of this chapter towards liberal and neo-Weberian claims that equate entry into non-manual state employment with upward social mobility. Instead, it would be more appropriate to speak of the growing representation of 'non-whites', especially 'non-white' women, in the 'new' state working class (Fairbrother 1989).

This discussion of the opening up of intermediate non-manual work in the state sector coupled with the earlier observations on Asian male self-employment helps us to understand the extent and nature of the change in racialised minority employment in recent years. The term 'change' is used purposively in that whilst I concur with the neo-Weberians that social change has taken place, I disagree strongly with their explanations of how such change has taken place and whether such change represents evidence of upward social mobility. Apart from the small class fraction of self-employed that has consolidated its move into the petty-bourgeoisie, much of the change described in this chapter represents what Erik Olin Wright refers to as shifts in class position *not* class relations. Amidst this transformation of the nature and type of working-class work in the 'new economy' there is clear evidence that one of the impacts of contentious anti-racist politics in the workplace has been the greater integration of the racialised minority and 'white' working class, especially within state sector employment. Since this is the area of work that remains most strongly unionised in British society today, any future conflagrations of class conflict are likely to be multicultural events.

Diversity in patterns of racialised minority employment today

I now move on to discuss the important question of why some racialised minority groups and genders were better able to take advantage of these opportunities than other groups. To answer this requires the unravelling of the complex relationship between the spatial distribution of different racialised minorities, anti-racist activism, relative levels of cultural capital (including the occupational status of migrants in their countries of origin) and the operation of racist discriminatory practices.

Over the past three decades or so, individuals of Indian and African Asian descent have witnessed a substantial transformation in their employment profile. Initially, a significant proportion, including those with high educational qualifications, were proletarianised due to the widespread operation of a colour-coded racism and reduced to working in semi-skilled and unskilled manual work. This situation was made worse in the 1970s with the shift to a more flexible regime of accumulation which left many Indians and African Asians unemployed or forced them into self-employment. Whilst much of this self-employment can be characterised as workers attempting to negotiate the adverse changes wrought by economic restructuring, a significant minority of the Indian and African Asian self-employed were able to achieve a degree of upward social mobility and cement their position in the petty-bourgeoisie in England.

In large part, this can be explained by the interaction of two factors. First, a history of entrepreneurship – in particular, involvement as 'middleman minorities' in the former African colonies of Uganda, Kenya and Tanzania – enabled a greater proportion of African Asians (and Indians) to benefit from access to knowledge specific to the business they themselves would eventually come to own in England (Parmar 1982: 236–75; Metcalf et al. 1996: 34). Second, many of the businesses owned by Indians and African Asians were located in the South East and Greater London, the main areas of economic growth in the 1980s and early 1990s (Owen and Green 1992). These factors were crucial to understanding the creation of a significant and thriving Indian and African Asian petty-bourgeoisie in the South East of England. The employment profile of Indians and African Asians was further transformed by the anti-racist activism that forced open non-manual work in the state sector, especially local government and, subsequently, the Civil Service and the NHS. With state employers forced to consider 'non-white' applicants, the relatively high levels of cultural capital held by mainly British-born Indians and African Asians, especially Asian women, ensured they were able to move smoothly into intermediate non-manual work.

The complex interplay of these factors that had worked to alter and to some extent improve the employment profile of Indians and African Asians worked to the detriment of those of Pakistani descent. Whilst many Pakistani men were forced into self-employment as a result of a lack of opportunities in the wider labour market, unlike many of those of Indian and African Asian descent, few Pakistanis were able to achieve any degree of meaningful change in their material circumstances. Principally, this was due to two main reasons.

First, with their predominantly peasant-class origins at the point of migration to Britain, relatively few had any history of involvement in self-employment, which meant they lacked the experience and technical knowledge crucial to securing the long-term success of the business. As a result, few Pakistanis actually consolidated their status within the petty-bourgeoisie. Second, the anti-racist activism that did so much to open up non-manual state employment in the South East of England, especially within the Greater London area, was too weak to achieve this objective in areas of the North and North West of England where the large majority of Pakistanis were spatially concentrated (Cantle 2001). Hence, what proved to be an important safety valve for many of the British-born racialised minority communities in the South of England was largely absent in the North, where Pakistanis lived. With little in the way of relatively secure state employment to cushion the impact of economic restructuring, many British-born Pakistanis faced a depressing future of long-term unemployment, working as mini-cab drivers or trapped in declining manufacturing industries.

Turning to the employment structure of Caribbeans, it is clear that whilst it is not as favourable as that of Indians and African Asians, it is rather better than that of Pakistanis. The primary reason is that the population is spatially concentrated in precisely those areas like Greater London where anti-racist activism had its greatest impact in forcing open first non-manual work in the local state followed quickly by employment in the Civil Service and the NHS. It is clear that had it not been for the success of such anti-racist activism which contributed to substantial proportions of Caribbean men and women being employed by the state, their economic position may actually have been as bad, if not worse, than that of many Pakistanis in the North of England.

Finally, the Bangladeshi population is the sole racialised minority group in contemporary England that remains disproportionately concentrated in semi-skilled and unskilled manual work. Despite their overwhelming geographical concentration in the area of greatest economic growth in the South of England, especially Greater London, their relatively lower level of cultural capital acquisition meant that they were left competing with 'white' workers for the remaining skilled manual working-class jobs left in this region. Unfortunately, continuing racism in this sector meant they were largely excluded from such jobs. Consequently, a large proportion have been forced to adopt an alternative strategy of survival, which has meant relying heavily on the resources of their own community with almost half the Bangladeshi men working in catering and restaurants (Modood 1997) and a large proportion of Bangladeshi women involved in homeworking (Phizacklea and Wolkowitz 1995).

Conclusions

Whilst recognising the important empirical contribution that neo-Weberian class analysts have made in identifying and mapping the changing position of racialised minorities in the labour market, this chapter has identified a number of important weaknesses regarding their explanation for such social change. At the root of these difficulties has lain their attachment to a form of methodological individualism which has contributed to an intellectually impoverished vision of social change with atomised individuals carrying different volumes of certified cultural capital at its heart. Such an approach has also been mortally hamstrung by its neglect of collective actors in the workplace, especially the ways in which different social collectivities may advance workplace struggles against racism (often in opposition to other collective actors). Further, their gross underestimation of the continuing significance of racism in structuring the life chances of racialised minorities has opened up a political space for reactionary individuals, social movements and political parties to advance arguments that locate any continuing disadvantage at the door of racialised minorities themselves.

It is against this backdrop that a case has been advanced for a paradigm shift, away from a neo-Weberian approach grounded in methodological individualism towards an agent-centred materialist approach grounded in holism. Through the introduction of group formation and collective actors, conflict and struggle within a dynamic and fluid conception of society rooted in domination and inequality, I have tried to demonstrate concretely the greater analytical and explanatory power of such a perspective in understanding social change in the labour market.

The term 'social change' is used deliberately in that the conceptual approach adopted in this chapter has led to the conclusion that the extent of upward social mobility has been greatly exaggerated by neo-Weberians. Rather, much of the movement into self-employment by Asians represented a working-class strategy to negotiate the threat of unemployment created by the shift from a Fordist to a flexible regime of accumulation. Even much of the racialised minority shift into non-manual or white-collar work driven by the power of anti-racist politics built around a 'black' identity occurred in the context of the growing deskilling, routinisation, and therefore proletarianisation of such work such that it becomes more appropriate to speak of their growing representation in the state working class. Consequently, it would be a mistake to equate such social change with a change in their objective position in class relations. Instead, the vast majority remain working class, albeit members of a very different working class to that of the 1960s, with a small minority entering the petty-bourgeoisie and bourgeoisie.

Such an analysis seeks in no way to diminish the fact that changes in the patterns of racialised minority employment have taken place at a different rate for different groups, merely that such change is not the result of the differential volume of certified cultural capital held by each individual (and therefore, in the aggregate, each racialised minority group), but rather the outcome of a complex interaction between the spatial distribution of different racialised minorities, anti-racist activism, relative levels of certified cultural capital and the continuing operation of racist discriminatory practices.

It is precisely the uneven impact of this social change on different racialised minority groups and the resulting representation of racialised minorities across a far broader range of industries and occupations that has in part contributed to the diminishing of a public space for an autonomous anti-racist politics constructed around a black identity. On the one hand, the relative success of black anti-racist politics in forcing open local and central state work in the Greater London and West Midlands conurbations has increasingly bound the fortunes of this fraction of the racialised minority working class (mainly those of Caribbean and Indian descent) to those of its fellow 'white' workers and their trade unions. On the other hand, the failure of an anti-racist black politics (due in large part to the presence of an unreconstructed old left less interested in anti-racist politics than the new left) to achieve a similar breakthrough in areas of the North West where those of Pakistani descent were overwhelmingly located forced them into self-employment and a resulting disillusionment with black politics.

Hence, already economically marginalised and increasingly subject to forms of racism which placed a growing emphasis on the negative signification of their religious beliefs, many within the Pakistani community have drawn on their faith as an ideological resource to combat racism, lending contemporary anti-racism a distinctively religious flavour as witnessed since the 'Rushdie Affair'.

Against this backdrop, the prospects for the development of an inclusive, anti-racist politics built around a 'black' identity look increasingly forlorn; instead, anti-racist politics (where they exist at all today) increasingly manifest a fragmented form characterised by a greatly diminished utopian vision. Any political struggles to counter the continuing significance of racism in structuring the life chances of Britain's racialised minorities are much the poorer for that.

Acknowledgements

I would like to thank Stephen Ashe, Alice Bloch, John Solomos and Louise Virdee for their helpful comments on previous drafts of this chapter.

Suggested further readings

Heath, A. (2003) *Ethnic Minorities and the Labour Market: Final Report*. London: Cabinet Office.

Heath, A. and Cheung, S. I. (2006) *Ethnic Penalties in the Labour Market: Employers and Discrimination*. London: Department for Work and Pensions Research Report 341.

Loury, G., Modood, T. and Teles, S. M. (2005) *Ethnicity, Social Mobility and Public Policy*. Cambridge: Cambridge University Press.

Wilson, W. J. (1978) *The Declining Significance of Race*. Chicago: Chicago University Press.

Wilson, W. J. (1997) *When Work Disappears*. London: Vintage.

References

Ackers, P., Smith, C. and Smith, P. (1995) *The New Workplace and Trade Unions*. London: Routledge.

Ball, W. and Solomos, J. (1990) 'Racial Equality and Local Politics' in Ball, W. and Solomos, J. (eds) *Race and Local Politics*. Basingstoke: Macmillan.

Beishon, S., Virdee, S. and Hagell, A. (1995) *Nursing in a Multi-Ethnic NHS*. London: Policy Studies Institute.

Bourdieu, P. and Passeron, J. C. (1990) *Reproduction in Education, Society and Culture*. London: Sage.

Brown, C. (1982) *Black and White Britain*. London: Heinemann Policy Studies Institute.

Brown, C. (1992) ' "Same Difference": The persistence of racial disadvantage in the British employment market' in Braham, P., Rattansi, A., and Skellington, R. (eds) *Racism and AntiRacism*. London: Sage.

Brown, K. (2001) *British Asians Today: A Statistical Profile*. London: Centre for Social Markets.

Cantle, T. (2001) *Community Cohesion*. London: Home Office.

Crompton, R. (1993) *Class and Stratification*. Cambridge: Polity Press.

Crompton, R. and Jones, G. (1984) *White-Collar Proletariat: Deskilling and Gender in the Clerical Labour Process*. Basingstoke: Macmillan.

Daniel, W. W. (1968) *Racial Discrimination in England*. London: Penguin.

Devine, F. and Savage, M. (2005) 'The Cultural Turn, Sociology and Class Analysis' in Devine, F., Savage, M., Scott, J. and Crompton, R. (eds) *Rethinking Class: Culture, Identities and Lifestyle*. Basingstoke: Palgrave.

Draper, H. (1978) *Karl Marx's Theory of Revolution: The Politics of Social Classes Vol. II*. New York: Monthly Review Press.

Elster, J. (1989) *Nuts and Bolts for the Social Sciences*. Cambridge: Cambridge University Press.

Fairbrother, P. (1989) 'State Workers: Class Position and Collective Action' in Duncan, G. (ed.) *Democracy and the Capitalist State*. Cambridge: Cambridge University Press.

Gerth, H. and Mills, C. W. (1993) *From Max Weber*. London: Routledge.

Gilroy, P. (1987) *There Ain't No Black in the Union Jack*. London: Heinemann.

Harvey, D. (1993) *The Condition of Postmodernity*. Oxford: Blackwell.

Heath, A. (2003) *Ethnic Minorities and the Labour Market: Final Report*. London: Cabinet Office.

Heath, A. and Cheung, S. I. (2006) *Ethnic Penalties in the Labour Market: Employers and Discrimination*. London: Department for Work and Pensions Research Report 341.

Heath, A. and Yu, S. (2003) *Explaining Ethnic Minority Disadvantage*. Oxford: Department of Sociology, University of Oxford.

Heath, A. and McMahon, D. (1995) 'Education and Occupational Attainments: The Impact of Ethnic Origins' in Karn, V. (ed.) *Ethnicity in the 1991 Census, Volume 4, Education, Employment and Housing*. London: HMSO.

Hook, S. (2002) *Towards the Understanding of Karl Marx*. New York: Prometheus Books.

Hyman, R. and Price, R. (1983) *The New Working Class?* Basingstoke: Macmillan.

Kalra, V. (2000) *From Textile Mills to Taxi Ranks*. Aldershot: Avebury.

Katznelson, I. (1997) 'Working-class Formation and American Exceptionalism, Yet Again' in Halpern, R. and Morris, J. (eds) *American Exceptionalism?* Basingstoke: Macmillan.

Iganski, P. and Payne, G. (1996) 'Declining Racial Disadvantage in the British Labour Market'. *Ethnic and Racial Studies* 19 (1): 113–33.

Mac an Ghaill, M. (1988) *Young, Gifted and Black: Student–Teacher Relations in the Schooling of Black Youth*. Milton Keynes: Open University Press.

McEvoy, D., Jones, T. P., Cater, J. and Aldrich, H. (1982) 'Asian Immigrant Businesses in British Cities' Paper presented to *The British Association for the Advancement of Science Annual Meeting*, September.

Mandel, E. (1989) 'How to Make No Sense of Marx' in Ware, R., and Neilson, K. (eds) *Analysing Marxism. Canadian Journal of Philosophy Supplementary* 15: 105–32.

Marshall, G. (1997) *Repositioning Class*. London: Sage.

Marshall, G., Rose, D., Newby, H. and Vogler, C. (1988) *Social Class in Modern Britain*. London: Hutchinson Education.

Metcalf, H., Modood, T. and Virdee, S. (1996) *Asian Self-employment: The Interaction of Culture and Economics in England*. London: Policy Studies Institute.

Miles, R. and Phizacklea, A. (1984) *White Man's Country*. London: Pluto Press.

Modood, T., Berthoud, R., Lakey, J., Nazroo, J., Smooth, P., Virdee, S. and Beishon, S. (1997) *Diversity and Disadvantage: Ethnic minorities in Britain*. London: Policy Studies Institute.

Murray, C. (1994) *Losing Ground*. New York. Basic Books.

National Black Members Coordinating Committee (NBMCC) (1986) *Proceedings of the First National Black Members Conference*. London: NBMCC.

Ollman, B. (2003) *Dance of the Dialectic: Steps in Marx's Method*. Urbana: University of Illinois Press.

Ouseley, H. (1990) 'Resisting Institutional Change' in Ball, W. and Solomos, J. (eds) *Race and Local Politics*. Basingstoke: Macmillan.

Owen, D. (1992) *Ethnic Minorities in Great Britain: Settlement Patterns. 1991 Census Statistical Paper No. 1*. Coventry: CRER, University of Warwick.

Owen, D. and Green, A. (1992) 'Labour Market Experiences and Change Among Ethnic Groups in Great Britain'. *New Community* 19 (1): 7–29.

Pahl, R. (1989) 'Is the Emperor Naked?' *International Journal of Urban and Regional Research* 13: 711–20.

Parmar, P. (1982) 'Gender, Race and Class: Asian Women in Resistance' in CCCS *The Empire Strikes Back*. London: Hutchinson.

Phizacklea, A. and Wolkowitz, C. (1995) *Homeworking Women*. London: Sage.

Raison, T. (1984) 'The View from the Government' in Benyon, J. (ed.) *Scarman and After*. Oxford: Pergamon Press.

Rose, D. and Pevalin, D. (2001) *The National Statistics Socio-economic Classification: Unifying Official and Sociological Approaches to the Conceptualisation and Measurement of Social Class*. Institute for Social and Economic Research, Colchester: University of Essex.

Scarman, Lord. (1981) *The Brixton Disorders 10–12 April 1981: Report of an Inquiry by the Rt. Hon. The Lord Scarman OBE*. London: HMSO.

Sivanandan, A. (1990) *Communities of Resistance*. London: Verso.

Solomos, J. (1987) 'The Politics of Anti-discrimination Legislation: Planned Social Reform or Symbolic Politics? in Jenkins, R. and Solomos, J. (eds) *Racism and Equal Opportunity Policies in the 1980s*. Cambridge: Cambridge University Press.

Solomos, J. (1988) *Black Youth, Racism and the State*. Cambridge: Cambridge University Press.

Solomos, J. (1993) *Race and Racism in Britain*. Basingstoke: Macmillan.

Smith, D. J. (1977) *Racial Disadvantage in England*. London: Penguin.

Virdee, S. (2000) 'A Marxist Critique of Black Radical Theories of Trade-union Racism'. *Sociology* 34 (3): 545–65.

CHAPTER 5

Community Cohesion and National Security: Rethinking Policing and Race

EUGENE MCLAUGHLIN

Introduction

The police are the institution mandated by society to deal with social conflict. Consequently, it is inevitable that police officers will, on occasions, have problematic relationships with certain individuals and sections of the population. Citizens can come into contact with the police either as suspects, victims, witnesses, bystanders or as members of various community consultative groups. Contact with police officers is primarily generated by members of the public in response to criminal victimisation or calls for assistance whilst other contacts are officer-initiated. The police also act as the gatekeepers to the criminal justice system. Routine police work provides the prosecutorial, judicial and penal systems with a range of reluctant customers to judge, sentence and punish. The criminal justice agenda regarding the 'who, why, when and why' of criminality is effectively defined by the police. In many jurisdictions a persistent allegation is that policing and therefore the criminal justice system is contaminated with pervasive, systemic racial and ethnic bias. This racialised bias, it is claimed, subjects particular minority groups to inappropriate, disproportionate and unfair treatment at every level of contact with the police; for example, surveillance, stops and searches, arrests, detention and the decisions of the criminal justice system – prosecutions, sentencing, parole and probation. Equally significantly, there are also complaints of an unequal police response to ethnic and racial minorities as victims of crime and work-based discrimination against ethnic and racial minority personnel in terms of recruitment, retention and career progression. It is worth noting from the outset that serious data gaps preclude a comprehensive analysis of the changing impact of race and ethnicity on policing and criminal justice.

This chapter provides an overview of the current redefinition of the parameters of 21st-century UK police-race/ethnic relations. The contemporary policing environment has been radically altered and complicated by three racially sensitive operational pressure points, namely

- street crime and gang culture
- new forms of criminality associated with recent surges in migration and
- the threat posed by Islamist terrorism.

Context: from 'institutional racism' to 'social cohesion' and national security

The enquiry into the racist murder of Stephen Lawrence chaired by Sir William Macpherson was a devastating indictment of the Metropolitan Police force. His report, which was published in 1999, concluded that key parts of the unsuccessful murder investigation could only be explained by the presence of 'institutional racism', defined as 'the collective failure of an organisation to provide an appropriate and professional service to people because of their colour, culture or ethnic origin' (Macpherson, 1999, p. 6.34).

The Macpherson Report noted the 'inescapable evidence' of a breakdown in trust between the police and criminal justice system and the ethnic minority communities, which related to evidence of over-representation at each stage of the criminal justice process – as suspects, defendants and prisoners. At the same time, as the Stephen Lawrence case had demonstrated, there was considerable disquiet about the experience of ethnic minorities as victims of crime. The Report concluded that the police and criminal justice system needed to demonstrate procedural fairness to generate trust and confidence within minority ethnic communities, 'who undoubtedly perceive themselves to be discriminated against by "the system". Just as justice needs to be "seen to be done" so fairness must be "seen to be demonstrated" in order to generate trust.'

The extensive reform programme initiated in the aftermath of the Macpherson Report should have been able to stand as the basis for a new settlement on vexed issues of policing, race and ethnicity (see, for example, Metropolitan Police, 2000) (see Box 5.1).

Box 5.1   Post-Macpherson policing reforms

- an 'anti-racist' policing philosophy that would allow the police to be 'a part of' rather than 'apart from' the community

- making racism a sackable offence in the police
- prioritisation of the policing of racist crime
- re-examination of the use of 'stop and search' powers
- recruiting a representative workforce that visibly reflects the diversity of multi-ethnic Britain.

'Stop and search' powers had first been identified as a source of friction by the Scarman Report on the 1981 riots and Lord Gifford's report on the 1985 riots (Scarman, 1981). In 1981, the Metropolitan Police launched 'Operation Swamp' in an attempt to deal with a surge in street crime in South London. Police officers used 'SUS' laws to stop and search large numbers of young black men on the streets of Brixton. The intensity of the resultant conflictual street encounters sparked sustained rioting in London and elsewhere. Although Lord Scarman's report on the rioting rejected claims of 'institutionalized racism' in the police, he expressed concern about both racial stereotyping within the rank-and-file police culture and the criminality of a minority of young black men. His recommendation of tighter control over the use of stop and search powers was included in the 1984 Police and Criminal Evidence Act. Nevertheless complaints about the racist use of stop and search resurfaced in the aftermath of the 1985 riots and periodically during the rest of the 1980s and 1990s.

The Macpherson Report, although it concentrated on improving the police response to racist violence, could not avoid addressing this contentious issue. The Report accepted that the power was necessarily required for the prevention and detection of crime. However, because 'stop and search' was a gateway into the criminal justice system, the police had to ensure that it was used fairly and effectively. In future, police officers would be required to make a record of all 'stops' and 'stops and searches' – including non-statutory or the so-called 'voluntary' stops. The record would include the reason for the stop, the outcome and the self-defined racial/ethnic identity of the person stopped. A copy of the record would be given to the individual stopped. Stop and search records would be monitored and analysed by the police and government and be published (see Macpherson, 1999, pp. 61–3).

And, with regard to 'stop and search', an immediate effect of the Macpherson recommendation was official Home Office acceptance that black, Asian and ethnic minority groups were significantly more likely than white people to be stopped and searched by police officers. Police researchers focused on trying to understand the reasons for 'disproportionality', defined as the 'extent to which police powers are used against different groups of people in proportion the demographic profile of the population' (Home Office, 2005, p. 32). Particular interest was paid to the decision-making processes of officers and to identifying the grounds for 'reasonable suspicion' that most commonly led police officers to conduct a stop and search. The critical task was to improve both the effectiveness and the legitimacy of 'stop and search' by shifting from stereotypical (or categorical) to intelligence-led suspicion. As a result, the debate on racial and ethnic disproportionality regarding 'stop and search' practices is much more complicated and nuanced (see Delsol and Shiner, 2006; Fitzgerald, 1999; Fitzgerald et al., 2002; Havis and Best, 2004; Home Office, 2005; Metropolitan Police Authority, 2004; Miller et al., 2000; Waddington et al., 2004). In the immediate aftermath of the Macpherson Report, there was a notable decline in the use of the power. In London, stop and search fell from 180,000 in 1999/2000 to 169,000 the following year, and nationally, the number of 'stop and searches' fell by 21 per cent.

Unlike Lord Scarman's report, the Macpherson Report was sociologically narrow in its focus. As I have argued elsewhere, because its reference point was a racist murder that took place in 1993, it could not provide an informed overview of the rapidly changing nature of race relations and community dynamics (see McLaughlin, 2007). Macpherson's conclusions and recommendations were still being digested by the police and government when serious riots between white and Asian youths broke out in several northern English towns. Race riots between young Pakistani/Bangladeshi Muslim and white youths in Bradford in April 2001 were followed by rioting in Oldham and Leeds in May and Burnley in June, and violence raged again in Bradford in July. Official reports on the riots identified serious communal tensions and divisions (Cantle, 2001; Clarke, 2001; Denham, 2001; Ritchie, 2001; see also Ouseley, 2001).

The Cantle Report (2001) concluded that in many parts of England polarised communities 'operate on the basis of a series of parallel lives. These lives often do not seem to touch at any point, let alone overlap and promote any meaningful interchanges (Cantle Report, 2001, p. 9). According to Cantle, government initiatives had fostered 'enclavisation' and a perception of unfairness in the allocation of public resources in virtually every section of the localities. Without opportunities and spaces to cultivate commonalities, suspicions, resentments, mythologies and racist attitudes had increased, allowing ill-liberal communities to close in on themselves. Communal divisions and fears were feeding into extremist ideologies. The lack of cross-cultural contact at neighbourhood level was compounded by the absence of a shared notion of Britishness and little attachment to national identity. Of concern were the difficulties Muslims found in reconciling their strong sense of religious identity with the looser identity requirements of a multicultural secular society. A report on Bradford's troubles chaired by Lord Ouseley also described a fractured city with deep-rooted mistrust between and ignorance of different communities. The reviews of the Oldham and Burnley riots reached broadly similar conclusions, calling for policies that actively promoted civic integration and community cohesion.

The Cantle Report's 'community cohesion' perspective changed the terms of debate on race and ethnic relations in significant ways (see Home Office, 2001, 2004; Cantle, 2005; for a counter-perspective see Amin, 2003; Burnett, 2007; Joppke, 2004; Kundnani, 2001). This led, for example, to an explicit questioning of the role Britain's model of 'multiculturalism' had played in licensing ethnically based 'ghetto mentalities' and disunity:

> Multi-culturalism ... has not simply entrenched the divisions created by racism, but made cross cultural interaction more difficult by encouraging people to assert their cultural differences. And in areas where there was both a sharp division between Asian and white communities, and where both communities suffered disproportionately from unemployment and social deprivation, the two groups began to view the problems through the lens of cultural and racial differences, blaming each other for their problems. The inevitable result was the riots.
>
> (Malik, 2002)

Trevor Phillips, the then chair of the Commission for Racial Equality (CRE), reinforced this post-multiculturalism perspective with a subsequent warning, in September 2005, that British society was 'sleepwalking' towards US style segregation, which was producing volatile racial and cultural antagonisms and voluntary 'no-go' areas (Phillips, 2005). For him, the government must prioritise policies to create 'resilient communities' premised upon liberal democratic values and mechanisms to integrate migrants into a stronger notion of Britishness. In August 2006 the government established a 'Commission on Integration and Cohesion' to provide an honest analysis of the dynamics that were transforming local communities. The Commission shared the concerns of Cantle et al. and added that as Britain became more diverse as a result of new migration and residential patterns – resultant from (a) 'super-diversity', (b) multiple identities and (c) transnationalism – maintaining an integrated, cohesive society would be extremely challenging (see Commission on Integration and Cohesion, 2007; Worley, 2005).

The community cohesion agenda has reflected itself in the debate about race, ethnicity and policing in complicated ways. The Cantle Report, and indeed the other riot reports, had remarkably little to say about policing philosophy and practice. This is surprising as what they were effectively dealing with was a form of 'slow rioting' (see King and Waddington, 2004). The reports supported visible, proactive neighbourhood-based policing that focused on both petty crime and rooting out serious drug-related crime from certain localities. This policing model would be better able to understand and respond to emerging community tensions. The 'community cohesion' agenda overlapped with both community safety initiatives and an emergent 'reassurance' neighbourhood policing strategy geared towards addressing high levels of criminal victimisation and fear of crime (see ACPO, 2001; Home Office, 2004a).

However, the policing and social cohesion landscape, as I noted in the introduction, is now further complicated by three operational policing responsibilities related to evidence of further social division and fragmentation:

- street crime and violent gang culture
- criminality associated with new patterns of migration and
- the threat of home-grown Islamic terrorism.

Policing and race I: street crime and gang culture

Post Macpherson there has been increasing anxiety within black communities about the seemingly entrenched criminal behaviour by a cohort of young black men and 'black-on-black' crime. This highly sensitive issue was reignited in November 2000 when a young Nigerian boy, Damilola Taylor, was murdered in north Peckham, London. A heated debate took place about the brutalisation of everyday life, fearful public spaces and various initiatives against anti-social behaviour and an alarming rise in levels of violent street crime in certain neighbourhoods (see HMIC, 2003a; Curran et al., 2005).

> Mike Best, the editor of the influential *The Voice* newspaper, declared that an inadequate police response to significant rises in gun crime and a cycle of deadly street violence meant that black communities were living in fear. This could only be contained by community support for stop and search as a highly visible operational policing tactic. This was against a backdrop of a rapid rise in street crime in autumn 2001 and 21 'black on black' gun murders, 67 attempted murders and a further 80 shootings resulting in minor injury or criminal damage (*BBC News*, 4 March 2002). Best received support from Sir John Stevens, the then Commissioner of the Metropolitan Police and Trevor Phillips, the then chair of the CRE. Phillips argued that it was time to marginalise 'the small minority in our community' who wanted to downplay 'the threat posed by black criminals. More importantly, it emphasises that the mainstream of the black community is deeply concerned about the spate of arbitrary and violent crime which is disfiguring our cities – and by the way, bearing down more heavily on us than anyone else' (*BBC News*, 5 March 2002). Sir Ian Blair, the Deputy Commissioner of the Metropolitan Police,

tried to prise open the race and street crime debate further in November 2002 when he asked the community to address the fact that according to police statistics two thirds of muggings in London were carried out by those described by victims as Afro-Caribbean (see also HMIC, 2003b).

Whilst recognising the extreme sensitivities around the debate, Lee Jasper (2002), the then policing advisor to the Mayor of London, argued that the strains associated with long-term structural racial inequality was producing a generation of young black men who have found alternative validation and support among peers whose creed is 'live rich, live fast and don't give a damn about society'. At its most basic this is manifested in a street 'gangsta' or 'ghetto fabulous' iconography played out in school playgrounds. But at its most extreme it is about an underground criminal economy founded on guns and drugs and now spilling over into the mainstream. Black neighbourhoods have become free trade zones for every kind of drug and illegal contraband, including guns. The black community is left paralysed by fear that it will not be taken seriously or protected by the police if it informs on violent drug dealers prepared to kill at the drop of a hat.

Jasper renewed his support for 'Operation Trident', which had been established by the Metropolitan Police in March 1998 in response to 'black-on-black' gun crime in Lambeth and Brent. The initial 'Operation Trident' focus continued to be on the disorganised criminality associated with 'Yardie' gangsters from Jamaica. The police focus subsequently changed when it was established that much of the gang violence was being perpetuated by 'homeboys' – young black British men. There was a major outcry about the fatal shootings of Birmingham girls Latisha Shakespeare and Charlene Ellis in January 2003; 7-year-old Toni-Ann Byfield on September 2003 so that she could not identify her father's killer; and 14-year-old Danielle Beacon in October 2004 in Nottingham.

In 2007/2008 the surge in teen-on-teen killings continued: by September 2008 the toll in London reached 26, the same number as for the whole of 2007. This compared with 17 in 2006, 16 in 2004 and 2005 and 15 in 2003 (*The Times*, 15 September 2008). The debate concentrated, once more, on the ruthlessness and recklessness of a younger generation of prolific offenders attached to a proliferating number of street gangs. A particular issue was the fact that it was seemingly acceptable within black youth culture to participate in street crime, engage in 'postcode warfare' and use violence to enforce respect, threaten and intimidate. This led to renewed calls for tougher knife and gun laws and strategies to dissuade youngsters from becoming involved in gangs, guns, anti-social behaviour and/or violent crime, and prevent the development of inter-gang rivalry. There was also extensive discussion about the infiltration of guns into certain communities, the criminogenic situational factors propelling young black men into a criminal lifestyle glamourised by 'gangsta rap' and ragga artists, and the links with alienation, social exclusion and violence (Hales et al., 2006; Young et al., 2007).

The then Prime Minister Tony Blair intervened in dramatic fashion in April 2007 supporting those who argued that 'political correctness' could not be allowed to stifle debate and action on a small group of young black men who were not abiding by 'the same code of conduct as the rest of us'. In respect of knife and gun crime, 'the black community – the vast majority of whom in these communities are decent, law abiding people horrified at what is happening – need to be mobilised in denunciation of this gang culture that is killing young black kids. But we won't stop this by pretending it isn't young black kids doing it.'

During a subsequent 'Q&A' session Blair said, 'Economic inequality is a factor and we should deal with that, but I don't think it's the thing that is producing the most violent expression of this social alienation. I think that has to do with the fact that particular youngsters are being brought up in a setting that has no rules, no discipline, no proper framework around them' (*Guardian*, 12 April 2007). Blair's statement contradicted Home Office minister Lady Scotland, who one month earlier had told a Home Affairs Select Committee that there was no evidence that street crime issue was 'solely or disproportionately an issue for young black men'. She was concerned not to perpetuate stereotypical images of young black males being deemed to be responsible for street crime and violence.

Blair argued for

- tougher enforcement of the supposed mandatory five-year sentences for possession of illegal firearms;
- lowering the age from 21 to 18 for this mandatory sentence; and
- penalties for gang membership and extra police powers to carry out surveillance on the homes of suspected gun holders.

Blair received support from various black community representatives, including Keith Jarrett, the then president of the National Black Police Association, who called for an escalation of the use of 'stop and search' tactics to combat knife and gun crime in black communities. The available research confirms that knife and gun crime is not unique to young black men but it also provides stark evidence that it can have a disproportionate effect on black communities. Consequently, the police have been re-mandated to deploy stop and search tactics and mobile weapon scanners and search wands to target teen gang members. Such 'in your face' street encounters, if not targeted and carefully handled, run the serious risk of not only generating complaints of harassment but increasing community tensions and distrust of the police as well as criminalising a generation of young people. It is worth noting that before this latest development, the latest government statistics indicated that during 2006–7, the police recorded 955,000 stop and searches under Section 1 of the Police and Criminal Evidence Act 1984 and other legislation. This was an increase of nearly 9 per cent on 2005/6, and was the highest figure since 1998/9. Of the searches carried out in 2006/7, 15.9 per cent were of black people, 8.1 per cent were Asian people and 1.5 per cent were people of 'Other' ethnic origin. Relative to the general population, black people were seven times more likely to be stopped and searched under these powers than white people; Asian people were twice as likely to be stopped and searched than white people. Relative to the general population, black people were 3.6 times more likely to be arrested than white people. Box 5.2 shows the measures taken to tackle youth street crime in London.

Box 5.2 Measures to tackle youth street crime in London

Operation Blunt: Metropolitan Police initiative to identify and arrest teenagers carrying knives

Project Dedalus: segregating first-time offenders from 'hardened' repeat offenders in youth offending institutions

Project Brodie: police working with educational welfare officers to target school truants

Project Titan: positive role models

Educational Support, Sports and Music Initiatives

Policing and race II: new migration, new crime concerns

For the most part, chief police officers have been careful not to get drawn into politically heated debates on the social impact of the latest waves of immigration that concerned the 'Commission on Integration and Cohesion'. ACPO is aware of how easy it is for the tabloid press and extremist right-wing political parties to seize upon criminality amongst new migrants, particularly refugees and asylum seekers in order to fuel xenophobic fears. There is particular political sensitivity regarding the lack of reliable data on the numbers of

- individuals who enter the UK illegally by land, sea and air, including airport transit zones, often with the aid of forged documents or with the help of organised criminal networks;

- individuals who enter legally with a valid visa or under a visa-free regime, but who 'overstay' or change the purpose of stay without Home Office approval; and
- 'failed' asylum seekers who are not removed after a final negative decision.

In a remarkably frank comment in 2006, David Roberts of the Immigration and Nationality Directorate admitted that he had not got the 'faintest idea' of how many illegal immigrants were there in the UK. The lack of accurate data is compounded by public confusion regarding UK-born minorities, settled migrants, current legal migrants, asylum seekers and illegal immigrants.

However, there are indications of increased exasperation regarding the operational challenges posed by the rapidly changing ethnic profile of cities, towns and neighbourhoods. The primary police complaint is that government predictions about the scale and pace of immigration have turned out to be unreliable as a basis for operational planning needs. In 2005, an estimated 565,000 migrants arrived to live in the UK for at least a year. The UK population also increased by 375,000 in 2005 – the largest annual rise in numbers since 1962 – with net migration into the UK from abroad being the main factor in population growth. Unacknowledged levels of illegal immigration and unanticipated migrant 'surges', most notably from Eastern Europe, have altered local circumstances. An HMIC (2003a) report acknowledged the adverse side effects of the chaotic dispersal of sizeable numbers of asylum seekers, including

- lack of knowledge of UK's criminal justice system;
- the practical demands of responding to numerous cultures and languages;
- negative perceptions and mistrust of the police because of experiences in countries of origin;
- the rise in racist and xenophobic sentiments associated with the housing of refugees and asylum seekers in areas of existing social deprivation;
- criminality within asylum and new immigrant communities including links to transnational crime networks; and
- criminal victimisation of asylum seekers.

The need to develop strategies to respond to the exacerbation of existing social fractures and new forms of serious and organised crime was addressed by Chief Constable Matthew Baggot in 2004 and Chief Constable Chris Fox, President of Association of Chief Police Officers (ACPO), in May 2005:

At this stage it is pertinent to articulate the growing complexity and breadth of the challenges facing policing, all of which directly influence social cohesion. It would be true to say that global problems now affect every street corner in a way that was unimaginable only several years ago. The impact of the Iraq war and events in Afghanistan, for example, led to a rise in heroin price on the streets of Leicester of 30%. This in turn resulted in a corresponding rise in burglary as addicts sought the means to finance the increased costs for their fix. The implications of global terrorism do not need stating. Similarly, societal changes have resulted in the greater polarisation of differing groups and neighbourhoods, leading in turn to great changes in both the context and nature of crime. It would be a mistake to limit social cohesion to issues of race and culture, as vulnerability and fragmentation are much more complex issues. Indeed, even the term 'community' is now questionable as even small geographic areas contain a rich variety of multi-faceted interests, associations and backgrounds.

(Baggott, 2004)

Mass migration has brought with it a whole new range and a whole new type of crime, from the Nigerian fraudster, to the eastern European who deals in drugs and prostitution to the Jamaican concentration on drug dealing. Add to that the home grown criminals and we have a whole different family of people who are competing to be in the organized crime world. My personal view is that this is a small island. We have some very, very intensely-populated areas and I think we have to be careful just how we let the mix develop. It's healthy that we've got lots of different people, but if you go into some of the cities, looking at the north, Bradford simmers, Blackburn simmers. It doesn't take much to disturb the balance, and I think we've got to be very careful to make sure that we're not overwhelming our current infrastructure.

(Chris Fox, *Observer*, 18 May 2005)

The police admit that they are on a steep learning curve regarding the local consequences of global flows of illegal commodities and services; for example, human trafficking, 'black market' exploitation and extortion, benefit fraud, money laundering, narcotics and firearms trafficking, the sex trade, racketeering and counterfeiting. In addition, the involvement of young refugees and asylum seekers in street criminality is generating unpredictable forms of gang warfare in hyper-diverse neighbourhoods. The police now also have to respond to illegal 'third world' cultural practices such as forced marriages, 'honour killings', female circumcision as well as domestic violence. All of this is taking place within a policy environment where resource-strapped local authorities are unable or incapable of fulfilling obligations to asylum seekers and new migrants, and there is political debate about the scale and nature of illegal, undocumented immigration. One notable manifestation is the record number of foreign prisoners being held in British prisons. Ministry of Justice figures indicate that in 2008, 949 out of 4,505 women and 10,559 out of 78,789 men in prison were foreigners. They come from 173 countries, with the largest numbers emanating from Nigeria, Jamaica, Poland and Vietnam (*The Times*, 1 August 2008).

Policing and race III: home-grown Islamist terrorism

Policing, and the criminal justice system, is now having to adapt to the long-term threat of home-grown Islamist terrorism. Conceptually, the use of the category 'Asian' to refer to people who were not categorised as 'black' meant that Muslims in Britain were, by and large, invisible. The Salman Rushdie affair and 9/11 did place British Muslims under the spotlight of public attention. Between 2001 and 2004 it was assumed that the main Islamist terrorist threat to the UK emanated from foreign terrorists, particularly those from North Africa (see, for example, Home Office, 2004, 2006; House of Commons Home Affairs Committee, 2005). There was also police and security services knowledge of pockets of support for Al Qaeda amongst British Muslims, communities harbouring possible 'sleeper cells' consisting of individuals who had trained in camps in Afghanistan and Pakistan and those British Muslims who had been killed or detained by the US military in various parts of the world. However, various incidents in the UK and elsewhere heightened internal security consciousness and clarified official perceptions of the risk and threat posed by home-based radical Islamists. The suicide terror attacks on London's transport system on 7 July 2005 by four British-born Muslims, the martyr videos left by the bombers, the failed attacks of 21 July 2005, the killing of Jean Charles de Menezes by counter-terror police, subsequent terrorist 'red alerts', police raids and court cases have altered debates regarding the balance between national security and individual liberties in an open society in a fundamental manner.

The exceptional nature of the home-grown Islamist terrorist threat has been spelt out by the police and security services. For example, in the immediate aftermath of the 7/7 bombings, Sir John Stevens, the former Commissioner of the Metropolitan Police, stated that at least eight major terror attacks had been prevented since 2001. He also announced that, according to police and security services estimates, since the mid-1990s, approximately 3,000 British-born and British-based Muslims had been in contact with Al Qaeda in Afghanistan and Pakistan (*Times*, 11 July 2005). The nature of the terrorist risk was described in detail by Eliza Manningham Buller, the then head of M15, in November 2006. She warned that the UK security services and the police were 'working to contend with some 200 groupings or networks, totalling over 1,600 identified individuals (and there will be many we don't know) who are actively engaged in plotting, or facilitating, terrorist acts here and overseas'. She said that the security services were also alarmed by the scale and speed of the radicalisation: 'If the opinion polls conducted in the UK since July 2005 are only broadly accurate, over 100,000 of our citizens consider that the July 2005 attacks in London were justified.... More and more people are moving from passive sympathy towards active terrorism through being radicalised or indoctrinated by friends, families, in organised training events here and overseas, by images on television, through chat rooms and websites on the Internet' (*Times*, 10 November 2006).

This assessment was made after the life imprisonment of Dhiren Barot for planning terrorist attacks in the UK and US, including the use of a so-called 'dirty bomb'. The MI5 analysis was amplified by the prime minister, government ministers and Deputy Assistant Commissioner Peter Clarke (2007) with the latter arguing that the police 'are often working at the very limits of our capacities and capabilities' and struggling *to understand the precise nature of the terrorist threat that is unfolding* (italics added). By April 2008 Jacqui Smith, the Home Secretary, reconfirmed that the police and the security forces were monitoring 2,000 individuals, 200 networks and 30 active terrorist conspiracies.

The nature of the threat has inevitably focused government attention on the UK's Muslim communities. An assortment of cross-cutting 'soft' and 'hard' policing strategies are being rolled out under the auspices of the CONTEST strategy (Home Office, 2005; Nagshbandi, 2006). The favoured strategy is to work with 'mainstream Islam' to undermine extremist ideologies, identify and support individuals who are vulnerable to recruitment, increase the capacity of communities to resist violent extremists, and understand real and perceived grievances:

> The government intends to challenge the ideology of violent extremism behind the acts of terrorism. And whatever the outcome of the debate, the government's approach to dealing with terrorism will be widespread. Already governmental agencies are working closely with Muslim groups, with anti-extremism counsellors in prisons, and with schools in at-risk neighbourhoods, giving them tools and training for dealing with extremism. They are also working closely with the internet technology industry – as they have on issues like paedophilia – to identify how and where terrorist recruiters are working online to groom young people as future terrorists. Obviously Muslim communities are most at risk when the propagandists of violent extremism spread their messages of violence, so there is a critical role in the government's efforts for Muslim organisations, institutions and civic groups. Already, many Muslim groups are engaged in the effort, and the Home Secretary credited them with many unsung achievements so far, 'often done without a fanfare of publicity, but with quiet determination and great conviction.' And it is 'quiet determination' that will ultimately prevail.
>
> (Home Secretary Jacki Smith, 2008)

With increasing numbers of terrorists and sympathisers being convicted there is also increased concern – given the increasing number of Muslim prisoners – about the spread of extremist ideologies in prisons.

Muslim communities have also been advised that, given the nature of the threat, 'hard edged' security measures are unavoidable. The counter-terrorist legal framework has been modernised via the Anti-Terrorism, Crime and Security Act 2001, the Prevention of Terrorism Act 2005 and Terrorism Act 2006. Accompanying a doubling of resourcing since 9/11, the state has reorganised its counter-terrorism capabilities. This includes the fusing of the Metropolitan Police Special Branch and Anti-Terrorism Branch into a Counter-Terrorism Command, the establishment of a regional network of Counter-Terrorism Units and Regional Intelligence Cells and the allied regionalisation of M15. Equally significantly, in May 2007, the functions formerly housed within the Home Office were split between the Home Office and a new Ministry of Justice. The Home Office is now free to concentrate on terrorism, crime, border controls and immigration matters. Included in the Home Office is an Office for Security and Counter-Terrorism, which is linked to a new Downing Street Committee on Security and Terrorism. Because of the difficulty in mapping and anticipating the motives and actions of home-grown Islamist terrorists and their support networks there has been an intensification of intelligence gathering to generate both advance warnings and evidence. Because terrorism is no longer defined by the territorial boundaries of the nation state, domestic intelligence hubs are now networked with border security and immigration controls and emergent transnational policing and security arrangements.

In addition, there are operations to locate and disrupt terrorist activities and prosecute terrorists and their supporters. Section 44 of the Terrorism Act 2000 gives police the power, within a specific geographical area and during a specified period, to search people and vehicles for items that could be used in committing a terrorist act. It is under this law that police can conduct random searches in the public transport system. Unlike with other stop and search powers, they do not need reasonable suspicion to do it. According to the police these powers help to deter and disrupt terrorist reconnaissance of potential targets, ensuring that it is risky to carry or use explosives and weapons. Officers have been warned not to stereotype as terrorists come from a wide variety of backgrounds and may attempt to change their behaviour to disguise their criminal intents and blend into their surroundings. However, it is also acknowledged that there will be circumstances 'where it is appropriate for officers to take account of a person's ethnic origin in selecting persons to be stopped in response to a specific terrorist threat (for example, some international terrorist groups are associated with particular ethnic identities)'.

In 2002/3 there was a 300 per cent increase in the number of Asians stopped and searched under Section 44 of Terrorism Act compared to the previous year (744 to 2989). The total number of Section 44 stops increased by 150 per cent (8550 to 21577). The '300 per cent' increase became a headline statistic. However, the police stressed that the proportion of Asian stops was 16 per cent of the total, and given that 80 per cent of the stops were in London, where the Asian population is 13 per cent, and took place in parts of London with large Asian populations, there is no statistical evidence of indiscriminate targeting of Asians. A Home Affairs Committee subsequently concluded that although stop and search is fraught with difficulty, there was no evidence of discriminatory racial profiling.

There seems to be a division of opinion within the police regarding the use of counter-terrorism powers. Various statements have been made to the effect that it is unfortunate but inevitable that in certain locations at certain times young British Muslim men will be targeted more heavily than other groups. However, the police are aware of the damage that the allegation of Islamphobic policing could do to community relations. Intensive surveillance and intelligence gathering and terrorist incidents are also leading to high-profile arrests and counter-terrorism raids in Muslim neighbourhoods and high-profile court proceedings. Armed Metropolitan Police officers raided two houses in Forest Gate, East London, in June 2006 during which one man was shot and wounded. Mohammed Abdul Kahan and Abul Koyair were arrested during the search for a chemical bomb but were released without charge after officers found no device in the properties. This incident further fractured relations between the police and Muslims with the latter angry at what were defined as heavy-handed and counterproductive police tactics (see IPCC, 2007). The total cost of this unsuccessful anti-terrorist operation was £2 million, with the two men being awarded £60,000 in compensation. The Metropolitan Police subsequently suggested that it would consider sharing intelligence and information with security-vetted representatives of Muslim communities before launching anti-terror operations. The police hope this strategy can provide assurance that police action is proportionate and justified.

Perhaps most controversially, the police have developed an operational methodology that is deemed to be appropriate and proportionate to the nature of the risk posed by suicide terrorism. 'Operation Kratos' was designed to cover all contingencies relating to suicide bomb attacks, including the use of lethal force tactics to immobilise suicide bombers without detonating explosives. It was adopted as national policy by ACPO in January 2003, the year that the two British Muslims were involved in a bomb attack on Tel Aviv. The fatal shooting on 22 July 2005 of Jean Charles de Menezes, a 27-year-old Brazilian electrician who was mistaken for a suicide bomber, gave the operational logics of 'Operation

Kratos' dramatic public form. This incident initiated a heated debate about the impact of a 'shoot-to-kill' policy on community confidence and the fact that armed police officers and covert surveillance operatives were working with a profile of what a potential suicide bomber looked like and how he/she would behave in particular contexts. ACPO subsequently defended its tactics to deal with the threat posed by suicide bombers as 'fit for purpose'. This was subsequently confirmed by the Independent Police Complaints Commission report on the circumstances surrounding the shooting of Jean Charles de Menezes (see IPCC, 2007). A final point to note before leaving this section is that Muslims working for the police, security services and military are now being subjected to security checks and monitoring. This of course has serious implications for simultaneous attempts to recruit more Muslim officers who are deemed to be essential in community cohesion and counter-terrorism work.

Conclusion

To summarise the main arguments of this chapter, operational policing is being stretched across the contradictory demands and expectations of community cohesion and national security. There has been post-Macpherson acceptance that 21st-century policing will have to respond to a range of perplexing community tensions and conflicts and social problems; and ever-increasing public expectations, ranging from low level incivilities and anti-social behaviour through to violent crime, globally organised crime flows and new terrorist threats. As British conurbations become evermore diverse, drawing in more people from different cultural, religious and racial and ethnic backgrounds, the police need to be embedded within multi-pluralist neighbourhoods. Effective police-work depends on being able to legitimately gather information and intelligence; encourage the reporting of crime; identify developing crime trends as well as community tensions and potential flashpoints; and intervene using coercive force if necessary. However, as has been noted throughout this chapter, we are witnessing highly sensitive discussions about the links between race, ethnicity and crime along with tensions associated with new forms of immigration and asylum settlement. And perhaps most significantly, policing is being reshaped by the long-term repercussions of an evolving home-grown Islamic terrorist threat. This is likely to have wide-ranging, unpredictable implications for police-race/ethnic relations and it is inevitable that there will continue to be complaints about Islamophobic policing practices. What is also likely to complicate matters, as a leaked report from the Home Office in September 2008 warned, is that any significant deterioration in macroeconomic conditions could have a significant impact on the three operational pressure points discussed in this chapter (see *Guardian*, 1 September 2008). An increase in xenophobia and support for far right political parties; a possible increase in support for radical Islamist groups from Muslims who experience racism and unemployment; an increase in public hostility to migrants as the job market tightens; and a rise in acquisitive forms of crime – street robbery, burglary and so on. Any economic downturn will, of course, also affect the resources available for expenditure on the police and the criminal justice.

Suggested further readings

Commission on Integration and Cohesion (2007) *Our Shared Future*. London: Commission on Integration and Cohesion.

Kundnani, A. (2001) 'From Oldham to Bradford: The Violence of the Violated'. *Race and Class* 43 (2): 105–31.

Macpherson, W. Sir. (1999) *The Stephen Lawrence Inquiry: Report of an Inquiry by Sir William Macpherson of Cluny*. London: Home Office.

Waddington, P., Stenson, K. and Don, D. (2004) 'In Proportion: Race and Police Stop and Search'. *British Journal of Criminology* 44 (6): 889–914.

Worley, C. (2005) "It's Not About Race. It's About Community": New Labour and community cohesion'. *Critical Social Policy* 25 (4): 483–96.

References

Amin, A. (2003) 'Unruly Strangers?: 2001 Riots in Britain'. *International Journal of Urban and Regional Research* 27 (2): 460–63.

Association of Chief Police Officers (2001) *Re-Assurance: A Proposal for Police Reform*. London: ACPO.

Baggott, M. (2004) *Policing and Social Cohesion: ACPO Submission to Commons ODPM Select Committee Enquiry into Social Cohesion*. London: ACPO.

Burnett, J. (2007) 'Britain's "Civilising Project": Community Cohesion and Core Values'. *Policy and Politics* 35 (2): 353–57.

Cantle, T. (2001) *Community Cohesion: A Report of the Independent Review Team*. London: Home Office.

Cantle, T. (2005) *Community Cohesion: A New Framework for Race and Diversity*. Basingstoke: Palgrave Macmillan.

Clarke, P. (2007) 'Learning from Experience: Counter Terrorism in the UK since 9/11', 1st Colin Crampton Memorial Lecture. London: Policy Exchange.

Clarke, T. (2001) *Burnley Speaks, Who Listens: Report of the Burnley Task Force*. Burnley: Burnley Borough Council.

Commission on Integration and Cohesion (2007) *Our Shared Future*. London: Commission on Integration and Cohesion.

Curran, K., Dale, M., Edmunds, M., Hough, M., Millie, A. and Wagstaff, M. (2005) *Street Crime in London: Deterrence, Disruption and Displacement*. London: Government Office for London.

Delsol, R. and Shiner, M. (2006) 'Regulating Stop and Search: A Challenge for the Police and Community Relations in England and Wales'. *Critical Criminologist* 14 (3): 241–63.

Denham, J. (2001) *Building Cohesive Communities: A Report of the Ministerial Group on Public Order and Community Cohesion*. London: Home Office.

FitzGerald, M. (1999) *Stop and Search: Final Report*. London: Metropolitan Police, http//www.met.police.uk

FitzGerald, M., Hough, M., Joseph, I. and Quereshi, T. (2002) *Policing For London*. Cullompton: Willan.

Hales, G., Lewis, C. and Silverstone, D. (2006) *Gun Crime: The Market in and Use of Illegal Guns*. London: Home Office RDS Directorate, Study 298.

Havis, S. and Best, D. (2004) *Stop and Search Complaints 2000–2001*. London: Police Complaints Authority.

Her Majesty's Inspectorate of Constabulary (2003a) *Diversity Matters*. London: Home Office.

Her Majesty's Inspectorate of Constabulary (2003b) *Streets Ahead: A Joint Inspection of the Street Crime Initiative*. London: Home Office.

Home Office (2001) *Building Cohesive Communities: A Report of the Ministerial Group on Public Order and Community Cohesion*. London: Home Office.

Home Office (2004) *Strength in Diversity: Towards a Community Cohesion Strategy*. London: Home Office.

Home Office (2004a) *Counter-Terrorism Powers: Reconciling Security and Liberty in an Open Society (Discussion Paper)*. Cm 6147 London: Home Office.

Home Office (2005) *Improving Equality, Strengthening Society: The Government's Strategy to Increase Racial Equality and Community Cohesion*. London: Home Office.

Home Office (2005) *Preventing Extremism Together: Report from Working Groups*. London: Home Office.

House of Commons Home Affairs Committee (2005) *Terrorism and Community Relations*, 6th Report of Session 2004–5, Vol 1. London: Stationary Office.

Independent Police Complaints Commission (2007) *Forest Gate Report*. London: IPCC.

Jasper, L. (2002) 'Breaking out of the Black "gangsta" Ghetto'. *Observer* 17 February.

Joppke, C. (2004) 'The Retreat of Multiculturalism in the Liberal State'. *British Journal of Sociology* 55 (2): 237–57.

King, M. and Waddington, D. (2004) 'Copycat disorders and changing relationships between police public order strategy and practice – a critical analysis of Burnley riot'. *Policing and Society* 14 (2):118–37.

Kundnani, A. (2001) 'From Oldham to Bradford: The Violence of the Violated'. *Race and Class* 43 (2): 105–31.

Macpherson, W. Sir (1999) *The Stephen Lawrence Inquiry: Report of an Inquiry by Sir William Macpherson of Cluny*. London: Home Office.

McLaughlin, E. (2007) 'Diversity or Anarchy? The Post Macpherson Blues' in Rowe, M. (ed.) *Policing Post Macpherson*. Cullompton: Willan.

Malik, K. (2002) 'Against Multiculturalism'. *New Humanist*, Summer.

Metropolitan Police (2000). *Policing Diversity: The Metropolitan Police Service Handbook on London's Religions, Cultures and Communities*. London: Metropolitan Police.

Metropolitan Police Authority (2004) *Report of the MPA Scrutiny on MPS Stop and Search Practice*. London: Metropolitan Police Authority.

Metropolitan Police Authority (2004) *Gun Crime Scrutiny: Final Report*. London: Metropolitan Police Authority.

Miller, J., Bland, N. and Quinton, P. (2000) *The Impact of Stop and Searches on Crime and the Community*. London: Home Office Police Research Paper 127.

Nagshbandi, M. (2006) *Problems and Practical Solutions to Tackle Extremism*, Shrivenham Papers No 1, Cranfield Defence College.

Ouseley, H. Sir (2001) *Community Pride Not Prejudice: Making Diversity Work in Bradford*. Bradford: Bradford Vision.

Phillips, T. (2005) *After 7/7: Sleepwalking to Segregation*, Speech to Manchester Council for Community Relations, 22 September.

Ritchie, D. (2001) *One Oldham, One Future*. Report of Independent Review.

Rowe, M. (ed.) (2004) *Policing, Race and Racism*. Cullompton: Willan.

Scarman, Lord (1981) *The Scarman Report: The Brixton Disorders 10–12 April 1981*. London: HMSO Cmnd 8427.

Waddington, P., Stenson, K. and Don, D. (2004) 'In Proportion: Race and Police Stop and Search'. *British Journal of Criminology* 44 (6): 889–914.

Young, T., Fitzgerald, M., Hallsworth, S. and Joseph, I. (2007) *Groups, Gangs and Weapons*. London: Youth Justice Board.

CHAPTER 6

Health and Health Care

JAMES Y. NAZROO

Introduction

Differences in health across ethnic groups, in terms of both morbidity (the presence of illness and disease) and mortality, have been repeatedly documented in the UK (for example, Erens et al. 2001; Harding and Maxwell 1997; Marmot et al. 1984; Nazroo 2001; Sproston and Mindell 2006), as they have in the US (Department of Health and Human Services 1985; Davey Smith et al. 1998; Sorlie et al. 1992, 1995; Williams 2001), Latin America (Pan American Health Organization 2001), South Africa (Sidiropoulos et al. 1997), Australia (McLennan and Madden 1999) and elsewhere (Polednak 1989). They seem to be a consistent feature of the social distribution of health in developed countries.

In this chapter I will first describe the ethnic patterning of health – primarily using data drawn from the UK experience – and then go on to discuss possible explanations for this patterning and the role of health services in ameliorating the impact of health inequalities. Throughout I will show that ethnic inequalities in health in developed countries cannot be understood without building on an adequate understanding of ethnic/race relations and the contexts within which these operate. The core argument is that health cannot be understood outside of social context – its generation and distribution across the population is not a purely biological phenomenon – and that differences in health across ethnic groups cannot be understood without considering how they relate to the patterning of social and economic inequalities by ethnicity.

The patterning of ethnic differentials in health

Health is, of course, a multidimensional and complex concept (Blaxter 1990). Nevertheless, in statistics it is often reduced to death and/or specific disease categories (such as coronary heart disease, hypertension, or diabetes). Given this,

Table 6.1 Standardised mortality ratio by country of birth for those aged 20–64 years, England and Wales, 1991–1993

	All causes		CHD		Stroke		Respiratory disease		Lung cancer	
	Men	Women	Men	Women	Men	Women	Men	Women	Men	Women
Caribbean	89*	104	60*	100	169*	178*	80*	75	59*	32*
Indian sub-continent	107*	99	150*	175*	163*	132*	90	94	48*	34*
India	106*	–	140*	–	140*	–	93	–	43*	–
Pakistan	102	–	163*	–	148*	–	82	–	45*	–
Bangladesh	137*	–	184*	–	324*	–	104	–	92	–
East Africa	123*	127*	160*	130	113	110	154*	195*	35*	110
West/South Africa	126*	142*	83	69	315*	215*	138	101	71	69
Ireland	135*	115*	121*	129*	130*	118*	162*	134*	157*	143*

Note: *$p < 0.05$.
Source: Office for National Statistics.

it is perhaps not surprising that many of those concerned with the study of ethnicity and health are frustrated by the fact that in the UK mortality data are not available by ethnic group. However, country of birth is recorded on death certificates and mortality rates have been published by country of birth using data around the 1971, 1981, 1991 and, to a more limited extent, the 2001 Censuses. The analyses around the 1991 Census are summarised in Table 6.1, which shows variation in mortality rates by country of birth and gender (using the 'standardised mortality rate' statistic, which adjusts for differences in age profiles of different groups and where the value '100' is the average population rate, and rates higher than this indicate higher death rates). The table reproduces some repeatedly documented findings:

- Men born in the Caribbean have low mortality rates overall, and particularly low mortality rates for coronary heart disease, but high rates of mortality from stroke. Women born in the Caribbean have similarly high rates of mortality from stroke.
- These high mortality rates from stroke and low mortality rates from coronary heart disease are also found among those born in West/South Africa, who also have a high overall mortality rate.

- Men and women born in the Indian sub-continent and East Africa (presumed to be South Asian migrants) have high rates of death from coronary heart disease, with the highest rates found among those born in Bangladesh.
- Those born in the Indian sub-continent also have high mortality rates from stroke.
- Those born in Ireland have high mortality rates from all of the diseases covered in the table.
- On the whole, the non-white migrant groups have lower mortality rates from respiratory disease and lung cancer.
- Not shown in the table are the very high death rates found among non-white migrants from conditions relating to diabetes.

Although these findings are statistically robust, applying them to ethnic categories carries significant problems. First, and most obvious, it ignores the situation of ethnic minority people born in the UK, whose experiences might be quite different. Second, given forced migration patterns and the artificial construction of national borders after the 'fall' of the British Empire, country-of-birth groupings do not necessarily reflect ethnic groups (for example, the heterogeneity of those born in South Asia or India, the large South Asian population who migrated to Britain from the Caribbean). Third, British colonial history means that a significant number of white people were born in ex-colonies and migrated back to Britain after the Second World War. And, fourth, some of those recorded as living in the UK at the time of the Census will return to their country of birth over the period covered by the mortality data. The combination of the third and fourth problems means that white migrants to the UK will be included in data reporting immigrant mortality rates and ethnic minority migrants who return to their country of birth will be missing from the numerator in the estimate of rates of deaths.

Although the UK does not have mortality data by ethnicity, there has been a growth in data on ethnic differences in morbidity over the last decade. These, perhaps not surprisingly, contain some contradictions with the immigrant mortality data (Nazroo 2001), but are basically similar. Figure 6.1, drawn from the 1999 Health Survey for England (Erens et al. 2001), shows differences in self-reported general health across ethnic groups. It charts the odds ratio and 95 per cent confidence intervals (CI), in comparison with a white English group (who consequently are indicated by the value of '1'), for a broad measure of health-reporting your health as fair, bad or very bad rather than good or very good. So a value greater than '1' indicates a greater risk of fair, bad or very bad health than white English people (and a value less than '1' indicates a smaller risk), and if the line indicating 95 per cent CI does not cross the value of '1', the difference can be considered statistically significant. Immediately obvious is

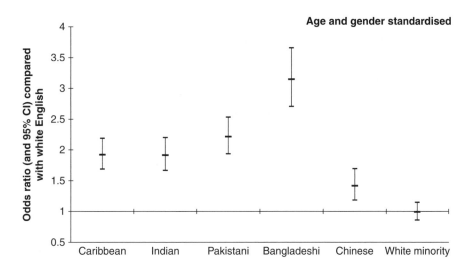

Figure 6.1 Ethnic differences in reported fair or bad general health in England.
Source: Health Survey for England 1999, see Erens et al. 2001.

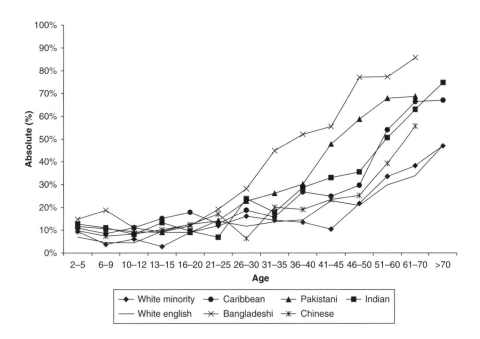

Figure 6.2 Fair/bad health by ethnic group and age.
Source: Health Survey for England 1999, see Erens et al. 2001.

the heterogeneity in experience across ethnic groups. Most notable is the wide variation for the three South Asian groups – Indian, Pakistani and Bangladeshi.

The data in Figure 6.1 are age-standardised to deal with differences in age profiles, and consequent risk of poor health, across ethnic groups. Figure 6.2 shows how ethnic differences in self-reported fair or bad health vary by age group. As expected, for each ethnic group there is an increase in the proportion reporting fair or bad health with age. Interestingly, the figure suggests that the ethnic differences at the youngest ages disappear in late childhood and early adulthood, and then re-emerge in the mid-20s, becoming very large by the mid-30s and continuing to grow with age. For Bangladeshi people, the group with the poorest health, from the mid-40s onwards rates are around 50 per cent higher in absolute terms than those for white English people. How far these differences across age are a consequence of differences between cohorts, perhaps as a consequence of migration, varying generational experiences or the accumulation of disadvantage with age is uncertain (see Nazroo 2004 for further discussion of this), but something to which I will return later in this chapter.

In the US there is a similar diversity of outcomes across race/ethnic groups. Mortality data, with race/ethnicity typically assigned by the person completing the death certificate, show that non-Hispanic Black people and Native Americans have high rates of mortality in comparison with non-Hispanic whites (though these reduce at older ages), while Hispanic people and Asian/Pacific Islanders have low rates of mortality in comparison with non-Hispanic whites (Nazroo and Williams 2005).

But how do we make sense of the data showing differences in health across ethnic groups? The temptation is to read meaning directly into the categories the statistical data provide. Just as we might say that Pakistani men have high rates of unemployment, or Caribbean families are more likely to be headed by a lone parent, so we might say that Bangladeshi people have poor health. The step from this simple assertion to seeking explanation in the nature of what it is to be Bangladeshi (in this example), that is a resort to explanation based on an understanding of a reified and stereotyped category, is easy to make. So, just as we might seek explanations for higher rates of lone parenthood in Caribbean cultures, we can seek explanations for high rates of illness or disease in the cultures and genes of the ethnic categories with these higher rates. And this becomes more obvious to do when we see a diversity of outcomes across ethnic groups or across disease categories. So, if Pakistani people have high rates of heart disease, but Caribbean people do not, how can this be explained on the basis of shared ethnic disadvantage? And if the low rates of respiratory illness and lung cancer among Pakistani people can be explained as a consequence of low rates of smoking, cannot 'their' high rates of cardiovascular disease be similarly explained as a consequence of cultural or genetic traits?

In fact, the high rates of coronary heart disease found in South Asian populations provide a good example of how this reductionist explanatory approach
operates. A British Medical Journal editorial (Gupta et al. 1995) used research
findings to attribute this to a combination of genetic and cultural factors that
are apparently associated with being 'South Asian'. Concerning genetic factors,
the suggestion was that 'South Asians' have a shared evolutionary history that
involved adaptation 'to survive under conditions of periodic famine and low
energy intake'. Here it is postulated that the evolutionary development of a
'thrifty' gene in South Asian populations, to deal with inconsistent food sup-
plies, has led to a greater likelihood for people in these ethnic groups to develop
non-insulin-dependent diabetes in the form of 'insulin resistance syndrome',
which apparently underlies 'South Asian's' greater risk of coronary heart disease
(McKeigue et al. 1988). Of course this perspective requires crude 'race' thinking, allowing 'South Asians' to be viewed as a genetically distinct group with
a unique evolutionary history. In terms of cultural factors, the use of ghee in
cooking, a lack of physical exercise and a reluctance to use health services were
all mentioned in the editorial – even though ghee is not used by all of the ethnic
groups that comprise 'South Asians' – and evidence suggests that 'South Asians'
do understand the importance of exercise (Beishon and Nazroo 1997) and do use
medical services (Nazroo 1997; Rudat 1994). And this example is by no means
unique – see, for example, discussions of being 'Black' and risk of hypertension (Wild and McKeigue 1997) and of being a young 'South Asian' woman and
suicide (Soni Raleigh and Balarajan 1992). Rather, if we are to understand the
significance of ethnic differences in health, we have to consider how they relate
to wider social and economic inequalities.

Connections with social and economic inequalities

It is worth noting that the ethnic patterning of health shown in Figure 6.1 mir-
rors the broad patterning of socioeconomic inequality across ethnic groups.
However, although there are substantial data describing health differences
across ethnic groups, the role that socioeconomic inequalities may play in
determining these, rather than cultural or genetic differences, remain contested despite the long history of work in this area. In 1845 Engels attributed
the poor health and high mortality rates of Irish people living in England to
their poor social circumstances (Engels 1987) and in 1916 Trask concluded that
higher death rates among Blacks compared with whites in the US reflected less
favourable social circumstances, rather than any 'inherent' differences (Trask
1916). Indeed, in the UK there has been a long tradition of investigating the
inequalities in health that are associated with factors such as class and area

(Gordon et al. 1999). This work has produced strong evidence demonstrating that these are a consequence of socioeconomic inequalities (Marmot and Wilkinson 2005). But, in the main, this work has not been drawn upon by those investigating ethnic inequalities in health in contemporary times, perhaps as a consequence of Marmot and colleagues' now classic study of immigrant mortality rates (Marmot et al. 1984). Published shortly after the Black report had firmly placed socioeconomic inequalities in health on the research agenda (Townsend and Davidson 1982), this study used the combination of British census and death certificate data to explore the relationship between country of birth and mortality rates. A central finding was that there was no relationship between occupational class and mortality for immigrant groups, even though there was a clear relationship for those born in the UK. These findings led to the conclusion that differences in socioeconomic position could not explain the higher mortality rates found in some migrant groups in the UK.

Since then, it took until 1997 for socioeconomic position to reappear in published national data exploring the relationship between ethnicity and health in the UK (Harding and Maxwell 1997; Nazroo 1997). The work on morbidity suggested that socioeconomic factors made a major contribution to ethnic differences in health (Nazroo 1997), but again conclusions drawn from analysis of immigrant mortality data did not appear to support a socioeconomic explanation for the different rates of mortality across immigrant and non-immigrant groups (Harding and Maxwell 1997). So, some continue to claim that socioeconomic inequalities make a minimal, or no, contribution to ethnic inequalities in health (Wild and McKeigue 1997), and others suggest that even if they do contribute, the cultural and genetic elements of ethnicity must also play a role (Smaje 1996).

Given the empirical and theoretical sophistication of work on ethnicity, it is worrying that in the health field crude explanations based on cultural stereotypes and claims of genetic difference persist (Gupta et al. 1995; Soni Raleigh and Balarajan 1992; Stewart et al. 1999), despite a lack of concrete evidence, more than 100 years of research exposing the limitations of the assumptions underlying such explanations (Bhopal 1997). Part of the problem is, perhaps, that in both the US and the UK data limitations have greatly hampered investigations of ethnic inequalities in health and how they might be structured by social and economic disadvantages, particularly as obvious data limitations are often ignored by investigators. Perhaps foremost of these limitations is the inadequate measurement of ethnicity in many studies, reflecting a lack of theoretical depth in the handling of the concept of ethnicity. So, the heterogeneity of ethnic groups is ignored (for example, the use of a 'South Asian' category described earlier), observer-assigned ethnicity is used instead of self-reported ethnicity, and surrogates such as country of birth are used instead of ethnic identity. The need to consider context, history, generation/period, and so on is difficult to meet and easily ignored when using crudely quantified categories, resulting in the consideration of ethnicity in fixed and reified terms. Also important is the lack of good, or any, data on economic position in health studies, let alone data that can deal with other elements of social disadvantage faced by ethnic minority groups, such as inequalities related to geography and experiences of racial discrimination and harassment.

Although data limitations have hampered research on ethnic inequalities in health, it is still worth reviewing what the evidence has to say about the importance of social and economic inequalities.

Evidence on the socioeconomic patterning of health within and across ethnic groups

It is now reasonably clear that a socioeconomic patterning of health is present within ethnic groups in developed countries. Analysis of the US MRFIT data showed that all-cause mortality rates over its 16-year follow-up period had a very clear relationship to median income in the area of residence of respondents for both Black and white men (individual socioeconomic data were not included in the study, so income data from the US Census were used to determine median family income of white and Black households in the area of residence of the individual). Mortality rates increased with decreasing income, resulting in a twofold difference in mortality rates between those in the top ($27,500 or higher) and those in the bottom (less than $10,000) annual income bands for both Black and white men (Davey Smith et al. 1998). Figure 6.3 shows data from England giving rates of reporting fair or bad general health by household income (equivalised to account for variations in household size and banded into tertiles) for a range of ethnic groups (Nazroo 2003). As for the US data, there is a clear relationship between reported general health and income for each ethnic group.

Important here is that both sets of data point to heterogeneity within broad ethnic groupings. It is misleading to consider, for example, Black Americans to be uniformly disadvantaged in terms of their health; those in better socioeconomic positions have better health. There is nothing inevitable, or inherent, in the link between being Black American, Bangladeshi, and so on and a greater risk of mortality and morbidity. This immediately points to the need to move beyond explanations that appeal to essentialised and fixed ethnic or race effects.

If socioeconomic position is related to health within groups, it seems probable that inequalities in socioeconomic position across ethnic groups might be related to ethnic inequalities in health. Figure 6.4 explores the impact of socioeconomic factors on ethnic differences in reporting fair or bad general

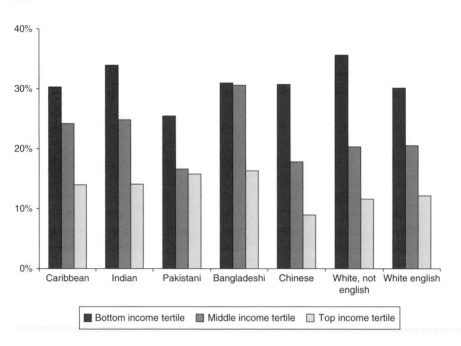

Figure 6.3 Reported fair or bad health by ethnic group and income tertile in England.

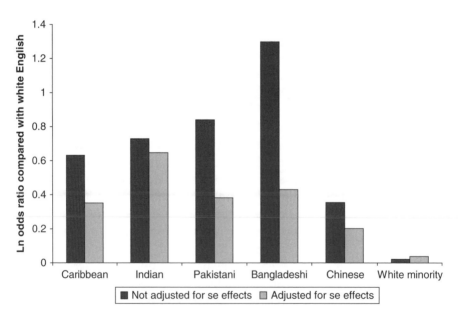

Figure 6.4 Reduction in (ln) odds ratio of reporting fair or bad health compared with white English after adjusting for socioeconomic effects.

health across the same range of ethnic groups in England (Nazroo 2003). Once adjustments had been simultaneously made for a variety of socioeconomic indicators (income, housing tenure, economic activity), there is a clear and large reduction in odds ratio for most ethnic minority groups (the natural logarithm of the odds ratio in comparison with white English people is used, to give an accurate visual impression of the size of change in odds, so a value greater than 0 (the value for the white English group) indicates a greater risk) – exceptions are the white minority group (which has an odds close to 1) and the Indian group (for whom the reduction in odds ratio is small).

Similarly, analysis of the US MRFIT data showed that standardising for mean household income in area of residence greatly reduced the relative risk for all-cause mortality of Black compared with white men – it dropped from 1.47 to 1.19, so about two thirds of the elevated mortality risk among Black men was statistically explained by this income measure (Davey Smith et al. 1998). Conversely, adjusting the Black–white mortality differential for a number of medical risk factors (diastolic blood pressure, serum cholesterol, cigarette smoking, existing diabetes, and prior hospitalisation for coronary heart disease) only decreased the relative risk from 1.47 to 1.40. This demonstrates that socioeconomic position – as indexed by income of area of residence – is a considerably more important determinant of Black–white differentials in mortality among men in the US than the biological markers of risk and behavioural factors, such as cigarette smoking or diet (to the extent to which the diet influences serum cholesterol and blood pressure), that are typically targeted in health promotion activities.

Additional evidence to support the interpretation that socioeconomic inequalities are important contributors to ethnic inequalities in health is provided by Figure 6.5. This explores the contribution of socioeconomic effects to ethnic inequalities in health for three broad ethnic minority groups and six different health outcomes, using data from the Fourth National Survey of Ethnic Minorities (Nazroo 2001). Figure 6.5 shows the natural logarithm of the relative risk statistic to compare how risk for ethnic minority compared with white respondents to have ill health changes once socioeconomic position is partially adjusted for using an indicator of standard of living. In the figure a risk equivalent to that for whites is represented by the X-axis (that is, the value 0), and a figure above this represents a greater risk, while a figure below this a smaller risk. In all cases the risk for each ethnic minority group compared with whites is reduced once the socioeconomic control has been applied.

Overall, then, the impression is that across ethnic groups, across countries, and across outcomes, socioeconomic factors contribute to ethnic inequalities in health. However, these data also raise the possibility that socioeconomic inequalities are not adequate for a full explanation of ethnic inequalities in

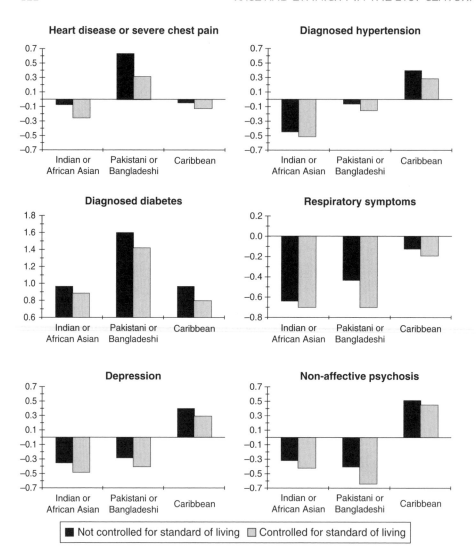

Figure 6.5 Reduction in (ln) relative risk of ill health compared with whites after controlling for standard of living (UK Fourth National Survey of Ethnic Minorities).

health. For most groups and for most outcomes, differences remain once the adjustment for the socioeconomic indicator has been made. Here, it is important to recognise that the process of standardising for socioeconomic position when making comparisons across groups, particularly ethnic groups, is not straightforward. As Kaufman and colleagues (1997, 1998) point out, the process of standardisation assumes that all necessary factors are accounted for by the measures available. Evidence from the Fourth National Survey of

Ethnic Minorities illustrates the fallacy in this. In that survey analysis of ethnic differences in income within class groups showed that within each class group ethnic minority people had a smaller income than white people (Nazroo 2001). Indeed, for the poorest group – Pakistani and Bangladeshi people – differences were twofold and equivalent in size to the difference between the richest and the poorest class groups in the white population. Similar findings have been reported in the US. For example, Oliver and Shapiro (1995) report that within occupational groups white people have higher incomes than Black people, among those below the poverty line Black people are more likely to remain in this situation than white people, and within income strata Black people have considerably lower wealth levels than white people and are less likely to be home owners.

The implication of this is clear: using either single or crude indicators of socioeconomic position is of little use for 'controlling out' the impact of socioeconomic position. Within any given level of a particular socioeconomic measure the circumstances of ethnic minority people in the UK and the US are less favourable than those of white people. Nevertheless, research typically presents data that are 'standardised' for socioeconomic position, leaving both the author and the reader to mistakenly assume that all that is left is an 'ethnic/race' effect, be that cultural or genetic. Rather, taking on board the limitations of empirical models, such as those presented in Figures 6.4 and 6.5, strongly suggests that differences in socioeconomic position make a key contribution to ethnic inequalities in health. It is also worth emphasising that the analyses shown here simply reflect current socioeconomic position; data on the life-course and data on other forms of social disadvantage were not included and are almost universally not available in existing studies of ethnic inequalities in health. Next I will examine the evidence on one important element of social disadvantage experienced by ethnic minority groups – the links between health and experiences of racism and discrimination.

Impact of experiences of racial harassment and discrimination on health

The empirical investigation of the relationship between experiences of racial harassment and discrimination and health is even more complex than the investigation of the influence of socioeconomic inequalities (Karlsen and Nazroo 2006). Most important is the difficulty with good measurement of exposure to racism and discrimination, given that these are a central, but often subtly expressed, feature of the lives of ethnic minority people in developed countries. Nevertheless, experiences of racial harassment and discrimination appear to be related to health in the few, but growing number of, studies that have been conducted. US studies have shown a relationship between self-reported experiences of racial harassment and a range of health outcomes, including hypertension, psychological distress, poorer self-rated health, and days spent unwell in bed, and have also found that differences in rates of hypertension between Black and white respondents were substantially reduced by taking into account reported experiences of, and responses to, racial harassment (Krieger 2000; Krieger and Sidney 1996; Williams et al. 2003). In the UK, analyses of the Fourth National Survey of Ethnic Minorities also suggested a relationship between experiences of racial harassment, perceptions of racial discrimination, and a range of health outcomes across ethnic groups (Karlsen and Nazroo 2002). This analysis showed that reporting experiences of racial harassment and perceiving employers to discriminate against ethnic minority people were related to likelihood of reporting fair or poor health independently of each other, and that this relationship was also independent of socioeconomic effects as indexed by occupational class. It could be argued that this represents three dimensions of social and economic inequality operating simultaneously: economic disadvantage (as measured by occupational class); a sense of being a member of a devalued, low status, group (British employers discriminate); and the personal insult and stress of being a victim of racial harassment. Further analysis of these data also showed that reporting being fearful of racism was related to poor health (Karlsen and Nazroo 2004), and more recent data have shown the relationship between experiences of racism and discrimination and mental health outcomes for a wider range of ethnic groups in the UK (Karlsen et al. 2005). Finally, recent analysis of data from New Zealand has shown the impact on health of reported experiences of racism and discrimination in a number of domains of life for both migrant and indigenous minority groups (Harris et al. 2006a, 2006b).

Age, the life-course and migration: the significance of context

There is growing evidence that socioeconomic conditions across the life-course can influence current health (Kuh and Ben-Shlomo 1997). This could occur in two ways. First, an early 'exposure', perhaps pre-natal or in early childhood, might set adverse biological process in train. For example, low birthweight, which is strongly influenced by adverse material circumstances acting over the lifetime of the mother, is associated with high rates of diabetes, coronary heart disease, respiratory disease, and hypertension in adult life (Barker 1991). Similarly, short stature, influenced by nutrition in early life, is related to an increased risk of respiratory and cardiovascular mortality. Second, the impact of socioeconomic disadvantage on health might accumulate across the life-course, a process that has been referred to as 'weathering' with respect to the health of Black women in the US (Geronimus 1992).

The data shown in Figure 6.2 suggests that ethnic inequalities in health in the UK increase with age, with relatively small differences at younger ages and differences beginning to emerge from the mid-30s onwards. Variations in ethnic inequalities in health across the life-course are also apparent in US data, but they take the opposite form with an apparent narrowing of differences at old ages and much discussion of possible 'cross-over' effects for Black–white differences and how far these might be a survival (of the fittest) effect, or an artefact in the data (Kestenbaum 1992; Nam 1995). The interpretation of the contrasting UK and US patterning of ethnic inequalities in health with age is not straightforward, but such data do point to the need for sophisticated approaches to the explanation of ethnic inequality that takes account of life-course issues. In particular, we need to place ethnic inequalities in health within a wide social context. For example, the increasing ethnic inequalities in health with age could reflect a number of coexisting explanations, including accumulation of risks over the life-course and the long-term consequences of exposure to hazards in early life. In the UK context, the cross-sectional pattern of increasing differences in risk over age could also reflect differences between first- and second-generation migrants, as older people are more likely to be migrants and younger people are more likely to be born in the UK. This final point is a reminder of the need to be aware of a number of potential effects related to migration:

- Selection into a migrant group will be related to both health and human capital, potentially leading to a healthy migrant effect (Marmot et al. 1984).
- The childhood experiences of migrants will be very different from those of the second generation, so insofar as these lead to long-term adverse health outcomes, or onto pathways that lead to an accumulation of social and health disadvantage, differences in health across generations might be expected.
- The experience of migration itself will occur alongside social and economic upheavals, which might have a direct impact on health.
- Return migration might have a significant impact on the apparent relationship between age and ethnic inequalities in health, with selection into a return migrant-group being related to both health and economic capital.
- The contemporary social and economic experiences of a migrant and non-migrant generation might be quite different, with the non-migrant generation more likely to do well economically and to have less traditional ethnic identities (Nazroo and Karlsen 2003).
- And such generational differences may well also be driven by the varying influences of events particular to specific periods (for example, the civil rights movement), and the consequent reconfiguring of the nature of ethnic relations, and ethnic inequalities, over time.

Access to and quality of health care

Although the discussion to date has concentrated on the causes of differences in health, it is also worth considering the role of health services in ameliorating, or aggravating, ethnic inequalities in health. In the US data suggest that inequalities in health are, if anything, aggravated by the health care system. So, a large body of research in the US has repeatedly documented ethnic/racial inequalities in access to and quality of health care, inequalities that are consistent across a range of outcomes and types of providers. An Institute of Medicine (IOM) study, requested by Congress, identified ethnic/racial differences in health care insurance status as a key determinant of these inequalities (Smedley et al. 2003). However, the primary focus of the IOM study was on factors not related factors and the authors noted that while inequalities diminish significantly when insurance status and socioeconomic factors are controlled, some typically remain. Suggested explanations for the remaining inequalities included characteristics of institutions (language barriers, time pressures on physicians, geographic availability of health care institutions, the potentially greater adverse impact of managed care – that is, adherence to strictly defined protocols for treatment – on ethnic/racial minorities); behaviours of practitioners of health care (bias, or prejudice, against ethnic/racial minorities, uncertainty when interacting with racial/ethnic minority patients, stereotypes about the behaviour or health of racial/ethnic minorities); and behaviours of patients (refusal of, or non-compliance with, treatment, delay in seeking care) (Smedley et al. 2003).

The IOM report also noted that studies of ethnic/racial inequalities in health care that controlled for insurance status had only done so at a crude level, without accounting for the ethnic/racial differences in the extent of coverage provided (Smedley et al. 2003), a point similar to that made above in relation to attempts to estimate the extent to which ethnic inequalities in health are driven by socioeconomic inequalities. So, ethnic/racial minority people are likely to have less comprehensive coverage than white Americans and, consequently, to have a more limited choice of providers, health care settings, and types of services. One way of testing the possibility that differences in health care insurance coverage explain inequalities in access to and quality of health care is to examine the extent of ethnic/racial inequalities in health care systems with more universal access, such as health care provided by the US military and Veterans Affairs systems. Studies of these lend support to the possibility that universal, or equal, access to health care eliminates the inequalities found in other systems, although the findings are less consistent for the Veterans Affairs system (Smedley et al. 2003).

In the UK there is, of course, (almost) free universal access to its publicly funded National Health Service (NHS), so one might expect ethnic inequalities in access to health care and quality of health care to be minimal, or at least smaller than those in the US. However, it is also worth recalling the widespread evidence of institutional racism in UK public services (for example, see Home Office 1999). Insofar as there is evidence from the UK, it lends support to the possibility that inequalities in access to health care do not exist, but there are inequalities in the quality of care received, supportive of an institutional racism hypothesis. So, UK studies have shown that ethnic minority people on the whole make greater use of primary health care services than white people (with Chinese people being the exception) (Carr-Hill et al. 1996; Erens et al. 2001; Nazroo 1997; Rudat 1994), even when adjustments are made for self-reported morbidity (Nazroo 1997). However, this does not appear to be reflected in greater use of secondary care services (Nazroo 1997), and there are suggestions that the quality of services received by ethnic minorities are poorer. For example, in primary care ethnic minorities are more likely to be dissatisfied with various aspects of the care received (Airey et al. 1999; Raleigh et al. 2004; Rudat 1994), to wait longer for an appointment (Airey et al. 1999), and to face language barriers during the consultation (Nazroo 1997; Rudat 1994). Also, they are less likely to leave the surgery with a follow-up appointment (Gilliam et al. 1989) and to receive follow-up services such as a district nurse (Badger et al. 1989). Other evidence suggests that in the UK South Asian people with coronary heart disease wait longer for referral to specialist care than whites (Shaukat et al. 1993), are less likely to receive revascularisation procedures (Feder et al. 2002; Mindell et al. 2005), and one study has suggested that among those who have suffered an acute heart attack Indian patients are less likely to be treated with thrombolysis (the so-called 'clot busting' drugs) or to be referred for exercise stress tests (Lear et al. 1994a, 1994b).

The research in the UK is limited in comparison with that in the US, with only a few studies to date covering a limited range of diseases and often local rather than nationally representative populations. However, the evidence does support the possibility of institutional racism, indicating that regardless of intention health services cannot operate outside of the context of broader processes of racialisation. This is something that is addressed in the following discussion of mental health and the rate of treatment for psychotic illnesses among Black Caribbean people.

Mental health – the case of Black Caribbean people in the UK and psychotic illness

Psychotic illnesses, which include schizophrenia, are relatively infrequent (they are thought to affect around one person in 250 in the UK (Meltzer et al. 1995)), but often result in severe disability. Typically, they involve a fundamental disruption of thought processes, where the individual suffers from a combination of distressing delusions and hallucinations.

One of the most striking findings in the literature on ethnic inequalities in health – perhaps *the* most striking finding – is that Caribbean people are three to five times more likely to be admitted to a psychiatric hospital with a diagnosis of first episode of psychosis than white people (Cochrane and Bal 1989; Harrison et al. 1988; McGovern and Cope 1987; Van Os et al. 1996). This difference is larger than that for any other condition or ethnic group except diabetes, where differences between white and most ethnic minority groups are of a similar order of magnitude (Erens et al. 2001; Nazroo 2001; Sproston and Mindell 2006). However, the increased rates are even higher for young Caribbean men (Cochrane and Bal 1989), and especially British-born young men – 18 times higher in one widely cited study (Harrison et al. 1988, see also McGovern and Cope 1987).

As you might imagine, these findings have been interpreted in a number of ways by commentators. On the one hand, they are interpreted as reflecting real differences in the incidence of psychotic illnesses – the methods used in studies are considered robust and, importantly (though not often explicitly stated in papers), it is assumed that psychotic illness is sufficiently severe for all cases to appear in treatment data; that is, there is no clinical iceberg (untreated, undiagnosed conditions that are not reflected in the statistics). Such an interpretation inevitably leads to a questioning of the causes of these high rates of illness. Not surprisingly, the full range of explanations associated with ethnic categories has been examined, including the possibility that the high rates are a consequence of genetic factors that correlate with ethnic background. However, differences in the risk of psychotic illness across African Caribbean people in different contexts raise doubts about such reductionist explanations. For example, low rates of psychotic illness among the populations of Jamaica and Trinidad (Bhugra et al. 1996; Hickling 1991; Hickling and Rodgers-Johnson 1995) and the large differences in risk between those who migrated to the UK and those who were born in the UK (noted above) suggest that there is not a straightforward ethnic difference in genetic risk. So, commentators have instead expressed concern that the social circumstances of African Caribbean people in the UK might result in such consequences (Harrison et al. 1988; King et al. 1994). Not surprisingly, given the evidence presented earlier in this chapter, there is a growing body of evidence linking socioeconomic inequalities and racism and discrimination to adverse mental health outcomes, including psychosis (Karlsen et al. 2005; Nazroo 2001; Sproston and Nazroo 2002).

However, an alternative interpretation is that these high treatment rates do not reflect a real higher rate of illness, but are a consequence of the adverse

interactions between ethnic minority people and social structures as represented, in this case, by the social institution of psychiatry (Fernando 2003;
Sashidharan 1993; Sashidharan and Francis 1993). Indeed, on reviewing data
on ethnic differences in the occupancy of psychiatric wards, Jasper claimed
that 'Mental health services are institutionally racist and overwhelmingly discriminatory. They are more about criminalising our community than caring
for it' (cited in Singh and Burns 2006). It is argued that psychiatry is not
only institutional racist, but part of a broader oppressive system that configures
race relations. Evidence for this is diverse, but most central is that which has
suggested that there are differences in the routes of admission into treatment
for psychosis, with African Caribbean people over-represented among patients
compulsorily detained, more likely to have been in contact with the police or
forensic services prior to admission, and more likely to have been referred to
these services by a stranger rather than by a relative or neighbour, despite them
being both less likely than white people to display evidence of self-harm and
no more likely to be aggressive to others prior to admission (Davies et al. 1996;
Harrison et al. 1989; McKenzie et al. 1995; Rogers 1992). In addition, studies
of the prevalence of illness in community samples, rather than rates of treatment, suggest that the prevalence of psychosis is not particularly high among
African Caribbean people – at most twice as high as those in the general population (Nazroo 2001; King et al. 2005; Sproston and Nazroo 2002). And when
differences were considered across gender, age and migrant/non-migrant groups
in these community studies, it was found that the prevalence of psychotic illness
among men, young men, and men born in the UK was no greater than that for
white men (Nazroo 2001).

Taken together, the evidence suggests that there are a variety of potential
problems with straightforward interpretations of existing data (for more comprehensive reviews, see Iley and Nazroo 2001; Sashidharan 1993; Sashidharan
and Francis 1993) and, consequently, that the higher rates of psychosis reported
among African Caribbean people need to be examined critically. Given this, it is
perhaps surprising that some have provided a robust defence of both the data
and the position of psychiatric services on the basis that there is no empirical evidence of the operation of institutional racism in psychiatric practice
(Singh and Burns 2006). Unfortunately, this comment neglected to note that
the lack of evidence is because there have been only limited investigations of
institutional racism in psychiatric services, and where studies have been carried out, they have in fact indicated the existence of institutional racism (King's
Fund 1998; Sainsbury's Centre for Mental Health 1998; Webbe 1998). It seems
likely that the high rates of treatment for psychotic illness found among young
Black men are, in fact, a reflection of racialised identities, racial disadvantage and racist practices. It is worth drawing parallels with data on rates of

imprisonment, which are, of course, much higher for young Black men than any other group, and self-reported levels of criminal activity, which are not (Sharp and Budd 2005).

Concluding comments – placing ethnic inequalities in health in context

Ethnic differences in health in the developed world have been clearly documented, across countries, across groups, and over time. These are summarised briefly at the beginning of this chapter, a summary which showed that on the whole ethnic minority groups have poorer health than the ethnic majority. However, there are variations in the nature of this across ethnic groups and across specific types of disease. The detail of this variation, and a focus on specific diseases, can lead to a focus on essentialised characteristics of ethnic groups when seeking explanation. An example is the focus on genetic differences and culturally rooted health behaviours when attempting to explain the higher rates of heart disease among South Asian populations. Such an approach, however, neglects the social and relational character of ethnicity and ethnic identities. And, importantly, it detaches health experiences from the social context within which ethnicity achieves it significance. Instead, accumulating evidence suggests that variations in health across ethnic groups in developed countries can best be understood as inequalities in health – that is, they are rooted in the wider social inequalities faced by ethnic minority groups. So, evidence was presented to show the socioeconomic patterning of health within ethnic groups, that socioeconomic inequalities across ethnic groups statistically explain a large proportion of ethnic differences in health and, indeed, explain a larger proportion of the difference than the risk factors that are conventionally focused on (smoking, diet, and so on), and that this is the case across groups and national contexts and for both measures of general health and specific diseases. Evidence was also presented to show that other elements of social disadvantage faced by ethnic minority groups, such as experiences of discrimination and racism, are also strongly related to health. Inevitably, there are exceptions – the social world can never be so easily explained – with, for example, lower rates of respiratory symptoms among ethnic minority groups in the UK explained by differences in the prevalence of smoking (Nazroo 2001). But this is the general pattern.

Showing such statistical correlations only takes us part of the way to explanations, however. The implication is that to understand ethnic inequalities in health, we need to understand ethnic inequality *per se*, and to understand this we need to consider how ethnicity/race becomes central to the configuration of social relations. That is, how social relations become racialised and how racialised identities are resisted. The need is to understand the contexts which shape such experiences. The implication of this is, of course, that there are not inevitable links between ethnic/racial categories and health experiences, because the social meaning of these categories varies over time and place. Two examples will help illustrate this point.

The first concerns the health of Black migrants from the Caribbean. The relatively poor health of Black Caribbean people in England is a consistent finding in the health inequalities literature and is mirrored by the circumstances of Black Americans. Indeed, there are many similarities between the health, social, economic and demographic profiles of these two groups. However, there is now strong evidence showing that Caribbean people in the US have considerably better health than both Black Americans and Black Caribbean people in the UK, and that this difference is underpinned by much better socioeconomic circumstances (Nazroo et al. 2007). The evidence suggests that their better socioeconomic and health situation is in part related to differences in human capital between Caribbean people in the two locations – so, for example, those in the US appear to have better educational qualifications – and possibly to differences in migration context (Nazroo et al. 2007). Migrating to the UK in the 1950s and 1960s is a very different experience to migrating to the US in the post-civil rights era (1970s onwards). However, it is also worth pointing out that the extent of the experience of racial abuse and discrimination does not appear to be different between Black Americans and Caribbean people in the US, indicating the complexity of racialised social relations and the significance of a Black identity to social interactions.

The second example is the case of high death rates from suicide among young women born in South Asia but living in the UK. Although on the whole South Asian people are reported to have low relative rates of mental illness (Cochrane and Bal 1989), analyses of immigrant mortality statistics show that mortality rates from suicide are higher for young women born in South Asia, and this is particularly the case for very young women (aged 15–24), where the rate is two to three times the national average (Soni Raleigh et al. 1990; Soni Raleigh and Balarajan 1992). In contrast to the findings for young South Asian women, these studies also showed that men and older women (aged 35 or more) born in South Asia had lower rates of suicide. Attempts to explain this finding have, not surprisingly, focused on the social position of young South Asian women. Here stereotyped notions of South Asian communities have been mobilised, with family structures portrayed as highly patriarchal, demanding of young people, constraining, and conflictual, leading to the oppression of young women and the consequent high suicide rates (Soni Raleigh and Balarajan 1992). It is worth noting that this literature was largely generated in the early 1990s. In contemporary times it seems strange to be talking of 'South Asian' women in this way; rather the stereotype offered is one that is now typically, and routinely, applied to Muslim communities and Muslim women. It is, then, perhaps surprising to find that these high death rates do not apply to women born in the predominantly Muslim countries of Pakistan and Bangladesh. A more recent paper showed that rates for these women are, in fact, very low, with high rates exclusively present for those born in India and East Africa (Soni Raleigh 1996). This example illustrates both how the significance of a particular ethnic identity can change dramatically over a short period of time, with a shift from a discussion of 'South Asians' to one of 'Muslims', and also how this significance permeates social relations sufficiently to shape scientific discourse.

Overall, then, it should be clear that ethnic health inequalities are a product of racialised social relations. The nature and causes of these health inequalities can only be understood within the context in which they are generated and resisted, so how social relations are shaped in context, and the consequent social, economic and health inequalities.

Suggested further readings

Fernando, S. (2003) *Cultural Diversity, Mental Health and Psychiatry: The Struggle Against Racism*. East Sussex: Brunner-Routledge.

Kaufman, J. S., Cooper, R. S. and McGee, D. L. (1997) 'Socioeconomic Status and Health in Blacks and Whites: The Problem of Residual Confounding and the Resiliency of Race'. *Epidemiology* 8 (6): 621–8.

Nazroo, J. Y. (2001) *Ethnicity, Class and Health*. London: Policy Studies Institute.

Nazroo, J. Y. (1998) 'Genetic, Cultural or Socio-Economic Vulnerability? Explaining Ethnic Inequalities in Health'. *Sociology of Health and Illness* 20 (5): 710–30.

Singh, S. P. and Burns, T. (2006) 'Race and Mental Health: There Is More to Race Than Racism'. *British Medical Journal* 333: 648–51, and the responses to this article (available on the BMJ website).

Smaje, C. (1996) 'The Ethnic Patterning of Health: New Directions for Theory and Research'. *Sociology of Health and Illness* 18 (2): 139–71.

References

Airey, C., Bruster, S., Erens, B., Lilley, S., Pickering, K. and Pitson, L. (1999) *National Surveys of NHS Patients: General Practice 1998*. London: NHS Executive.

Badger, F., Atkin, K. and Griffiths, R. (1989) 'Why Don't General Practitioners Refer Their Disabled Asian Patients to District Nurses'. *Health Trends* 21: 31–2.

Barker, D. (1991) 'The Foetal and Infant Origins of Inequalities in Health in Britain'. *Journal of Public Health Medicine* 13: 64–8.

Beishon, S. and Nazroo, J. Y. (1997) *Coronary Heart Disease: Contrasting the Health Beliefs and Behaviours of South Asian Communities in the UK*. London: Health Education Authority.

Bhopal, R. (1997) 'Is Research into Ethnicity and Health Racist, Unsound, or Important Science?' *British Medical Journal* 314: 1751–6.

Bhugra, D., Hilwig, M., Hossein, B., Marceau, H., Neehall, J., Leff, J., et al. (1996) 'First-Contact Incidence Rates of Schizophrenia in Trinidad and One-Year Follow-up'. *British Journal of Psychiatry* 169: 587–92.

Blaxter, M. (1990) *Health and Lifestyles*. London: Tavistock/Routledge.

Carr-Hill, R. A., Rice, N. and Roland, M. (1996) 'Socioeconomic Determinants of Rates of Consultation in General Practice Based on Fourth National Morbidity Survey of General Practices'. *British Medical Journal* 312: 1008–13.

Cochrane, R. and Bal, S. S. (1989) 'Mental Hospital Admission Rates of Immigrants to England: A Comparison of 1971 and 1981'. *Social Psychiatry and Psychiatric Epidemiology* 24: 2–11.

Davey Smith, G., Neaton, J. D., Wentworth, D., Stamler, R. and Stamler, J. (1998) 'Mortality Differences Between Black and White Men in the USA: Contribution of Income and Other Risk Factors among Men Screened for the MRFIT'. *The Lancet* 351: 934–9.

Davies, S., Thornicroft, G., Leese, M., Higgingbotham, A. and Phelan, M. (1996) 'Ethnic Differences in Risk of Compulsory Psychiatric Admission among Representative Cases of Psychosis in London'. *British Medical Journal* 312: 533–7.

Department of Health and Human Services (1985) *Report of the Secretary on Black and Minority Health*. Washington, DC: U.S. Department of Health.

Engels, F. (1987) *The Condition of the Working Class in England*. Harmondsworth: Penguin.

Erens, B., Primatesta, P. and Prior, G. (2001) *Health Survey for England 1999: The Health of Minority Ethnic Groups*. London: The Stationary Office.

Feder, G., Crook, A. M., Magee, P., Banerjee, S., Timmis, A. D. and Hemingway, H. (2002) 'Ethnic Differences in Invasive Management of Coronary Disease: Prospective Cohort Study of Patients Undergoing Angiography'. *British Medical Journal* 324: 511–16.

Fernando, S. (2003) *Cultural Diversity, Mental Health and Psychiatry: The Struggle Against Racism*. East Sussex: Brunner-Routledge.

Geronimus, A. T. (1992) 'The Weathering Hypothesis and the Health of African-American Women and Infants: Evidence and Speculations'. *Ethnicity and Disease* 2: 207–21.

Gilliam, S. J., Jarman, B., White, P. and Law, R. (1989) 'Ethnic Differences in Consultation Rates in Urban General Practice'. *British Medical Journal* 299: 953–7.

Gordon, D., Shaw, M., Dorling, D. and Davey Smith, G. (eds) (1999) *Inequalities in Health: The Evidence Presented to the Independent Inquiry into Inequalities in Health, Chaired by Sir Donald Acheson*. Bristol: The Policy Press.

Gupta, S., de Belder, A. and O'Hughes, L. (1995) 'Avoiding Premature Coronary Deaths in Asians in Britain: Spend Now on Prevention or Pay Later for Treatment'. *British Medical Journal* 311: 1035–6.

Harding, S. and Maxwell, R. (1997) 'Differences in the Mortality of Migrants' in Drever, F. and Whitehead, M. (eds). *Health Inequalities: Decennial Supplement Series DS no. 15*. London: The Stationery Office.

Harris, R., Tobias, M., Jeffreys, M., Waldegrave, K., Karlsen, S. and Nazroo, J. (2006a) 'Māori Health and Inequalities in New Zealand: The Impact of Racism and Deprivation'. *The Lancet* 367: 2005–9.

Harris, R., Tobias, M., Jeffreys, M., Waldegrave, K., Karlsen, S. and Nazroo, J. (2006b) 'Racism and Health: The Relationship between Experience of Racial Discrimination and Health in New Zealand'. *Social Science and Medicine* 63 (6):1428–41.

Harrison, G., Holton, A., Neilson, D., Owens, D., Boot, D. and Cooper, J. (1989) 'Severe Mental Disorder in Afro-Caribbean Patients: Some Social, Demographic and Service Factors'. *Psychological Medicine* 19: 683–96.

Harrison, G., Owens, D., Holton, A., Neilson, D. and Boot, D. (1988) 'A Prospective Study of Severe Mental Disorder in Afro-Caribbean Patients'. *Psychological Medicine* 18: 643–57.

Hickling, F. W. (1991) 'Psychiatric Hospital Admission Rates in Jamaica'. *British Journal of Psychiatry* 159: 817–21.

Hickling, F. W. and Rodgers-Johnson, P. (1995) 'The Incidence of First Contact Schizophrenia in Jamaica'. *British Journal of Psychiatry* 167: 193–6.

Home Office (1999) *The Stephen Lawrence Inquiry Report of an Inquiry by Sir William Macpherson of Cluny*. London: The Stationery Office.

Iley, K. and Nazroo J. (2001) 'Ethnic Inequalities in Mental Health: A Critical Examination of the Evidence' in L. Culley and S. Dyson (eds) *Sociology, Ethnicity and Nursing Practice*. Basingstoke: Palgrave.

Karlsen, S. and Nazroo, J. Y. (2002) 'The Relationship between Racial Discrimination, Social Class and Health among Ethnic Minority Groups'. *American Journal of Public Health* 92: 624–31.

Karlsen, S. and Nazroo, J. Y. (2004) 'Fear of Racism and Health'. *Journal of Epidemiology and Community Health* 58: 1017–18.

Karlsen, S. and Nazroo, J. (2006) 'Measuring and Analyzing "Race", Racism and Racial Discrimination' in Oakes, J. and Kaufman, J. (eds) *Methods in Social Epidemiology*. Francisco: Jossey-Bass.

Karlsen, S., Nazroo, J. Y., McKenzie, K., Bhui, K. and Weich, S. (2005) 'Racism, Psychosis and Common Mental Disorder among Ethnic Minority Groups in England'. *Psychological Medicine* 35 (12): 1795–803.

Kaufman, J. S., Cooper, R. S. and McGee, D. L. (1997) 'Socioeconomic Status and Health in Blacks and Whites: The Problem of Residual Confounding and the Resiliency of Race'. *Epidemiology* 8 (6): 621–8.

Kaufman, J. S., Long, A. E., Liao, Y., Cooper, R. S. and McGee, D. L. (1998) 'The Relation between Income and Mortality in U.S. Blacks and Whites'. *Epidemiology* 9 (2): 147–55.

Kestenbaum, B. (1992) 'A Description of the Extreme Age Population Based on Improved Medicare Enrollment Data'. *Demography* 29: 565–80.

King, M., Coker, E., Leavey, G., Hoare, A. and Johnson-Sabine, E. (1994) 'Incidence of Psychotic Illness in London: Comparison of Ethnic Groups'. *British Medical Journal* 309: 1115–19.

King, M., Nazroo, J., Weich, S., McKenzie, K., Bhui, K., Karlsen, S., et al. (2005) 'Psychotic Symptoms in the General Population of England: A Comparison of Ethnic Groups (The EMPIRIC Study)'. *Social Psychiatry and Psychiatric Epidemiology* 40 (5): 375–81.

King's Fund (1998) *London's Mental Health: The Report to the King's Fund London Commission*. London: King's Fund Publishing.

Krieger, N. (2000) 'Discrimination and Health' in Berkman, L., Kawachi, I. (eds) *Social Epidemiology*. Oxford: Oxford University Press.

Krieger, N. and Sidney, S. (1996) 'Racial Discrimination and Blood Pressure: The CARDIA Study of Young Black and White Adults'. *American Journal of Public Health* 86 (10): 1370–8.

Kuh, D. and Ben-Shlomo, Y. (1997) *A Life Course Approach to Chronic Disease Epidemiology*. Oxford: Oxford University Press.

Lear, J. T., Lawrence, I. G., Pohl, J. E. and Burden, A. C. (1994a) 'Myocardial Infarction and Thrombolysis: A Comparison of the Indian and European Populations in a Coronary Care Unit'. *Journal of the Royal College of Physicians* 28: 143–7.

Lear, J. T., Lawrence, I. G., Burden, A. C. and Pohl, J. E. (1994b) 'A Comparison of Stress Test Referral Rates and Outcome between Asians and Europeans'. *Journal of the Royal Society of Medicine* 87: 661–2.

Marmot, M. and Wilkinson, R. G. (eds) (2005) *Social Determinants of Health*, (2nd Edition) Oxford: Oxford University Press.

Marmot, M. G., Adelstein, A. M., Bulusu, L. and OPCS (1984) *Immigrant Mortality in England and Wales 1970–78: Causes of Death by Country of Birth*. London: HMSO.

McGovern, D. and Cope, R. (1987) 'First Psychiatric Admission Rates of First and Second Generation Afro-Caribbeans'. *Social Psychiatry* 22: 139–49.

McKeigue, P., Marmot, M., Syndercombe Court, Y., Cottier, D., Rahman, S. and Riermersma, R. (1988) 'Diabetes, Hyperinsulinaemia, and Coronary Risk Factors in Bangladeshis in East London'. *British Heart Journal* 60: 390–6.

McKenzie, K., van Os, J., Fahy, T., Jones, P., Harvey, I., Toone, B., et al. (1995) 'Psychosis with Good Prognosis in Afro-Caribbean People Now Living in the United Kingdom'. *British Medical Journal* 311: 1325–8.

McLennan, W. and Madden, R. (1999) *The Health and Welfare of Australia's Aboriginal and Torres Strait Islander Peoples*. Commonwealth of Australia: Australian Bureau of Statistics.

Meltzer, H., Gill, B., Petticrew, M. and Hinds, K. (1995) *The Prevalence of Psychiatric Morbidity Among Adults Living in Private Households*. London: HMSO.

Mindell, J., Klodawski, E. and Fitzpatrick, J. (2005) *Using Routine Data to Measure Ethnic Differentials in Access to Revascularization in London*. London: London Health Observatory.

Nam, C. B. (1995) 'Another Look at Mortality Crossovers'. *Social Biology* 42: 133–42.

Nazroo, J. (2003) 'The Structuring of Ethnic Inequalities in Health: Economic Position, Racial Discrimination and Racism'. *American Journal of Public Health* 93 (2): 277–84.

Nazroo, J. Y. (1997) *The Health of Britain's Ethnic Minorities: Findings from a National Survey*. London: Policy Studies Institute.

Nazroo, J. Y. (2001) *Ethnicity, Class and Health*. London: Policy Studies Institute.

Nazroo, J. Y. (2004) 'Ethnic Disparities in Aging Health: What Can We Learn from the United Kingdom?' in Anderson, N., Bulatao, R. and Cohen, B. (eds) *Critical Perspectives on Racial and Ethnic Differentials in Health in Late Life*. Washington, DC: National Academies Press.

Nazroo, J. Y., Jackson, J., Karlsen, S. and Torres, M. (2007) 'The Black Diaspora and Health Inequalities in the US and England: Does Where You Go and How You Get There Make a Difference?' *Sociology of Health and Illness* 26 (6): 811–30.

Nazroo, J. Y. and Karlsen, S. (2003) 'Patterns of Identity among Ethnic Minority People: Diversity and Commonality'. *Ethnic and Racial Studies* 26 (5): 902–30.

Nazroo, J. Y. and Williams, D. R. (2005) 'The Social Determination of Ethnic/Racial Inequalities in Health' in Marmot, M. and Wilkinson, R. G. (eds) *Social Determinants of Health*, (2nd Edition) Oxford: Oxford University Press.

Oliver, M. L. and Shapiro, T. M. (1995) *Black Wealth/White Wealth: A New Perspective on Racial Inequality*. New York: Routledge.

Pan American Health Organization (2001) *Equity in Health: From an Ethnic Perspective*. Washington, DC: Pan American Health Organization.

Polednak, A. P. (1989) *Racial and Ethnic Differences in Disease*. New York: Oxford University Press.

Raleigh, V. S., Scobie, S., Cook, A., Jones, S., Irons, R. and Halt, K. (2004) *Unpacking the Patients' Perspective: Variations in NHS Patient Experience in England*. London: Commission for Health Improvement.

Rogers, R. (1992) 'Living and Dying in the USA: Sociodemographic Determinants of Death among Blacks and Whites'. *Demography* 29 (2): 287–303.

Rudat, K. (1994) *Black and Minority Ethnic Groups in England: Health and Lifestyles*. London: Health Education Authority.

Sainsburys Centre for Mental Health (1998) *Keys to Engagement: Review of Care For People With Severe Mental Illness Who Are Hard to Engage With Services*. London: Sainsbury's Centre for Mental Health.

Sashidharan, S. and Francis, E. (1993) 'Epidemiology, Ethnicity and Schizophrenia' in Ahmad, W. I. U. (ed.) *'Race' and Health in Contemporary Britain*. Buckingham: Open University Press.

Sashidharan, S. P. (1993) 'Afro-Caribbeans and Schizophrenia: The Ethnic Vulnerability Hypothesis Re-examined'. *International Review of Psychiatry* 5: 129–44.

Sharp, C. and Budd, T. (2005) *Minority Ethnic Groups and Crime: Findings from the Offending, Crime and Justice Survey 2003*, Home Office Online Report 33/05.

Shaukat, N., de Bono, D. P. and Cruickshank, J. K. (1993) 'Clinical Features, Risk Factors and Referral Delay in British Patients of Indian and European Origin with Angina', *British Medical Journal* 307: 717–18.

Sidiropoulos, E., Jeffery, A., Mackay, S., Forgey, H., Chipps, C. and Corrigan, T. (1997) *South Africa Survey 1996/97*. Johannesburg: South African Institute of Race Relations.

Singh, S. P. and Burns, T. (2006) 'Race and Mental Health: There Is More to Race Than Racism'. *British Medical Journal* 333: 648–51.

Smaje, C. (1996) 'The Ethnic Patterning of Health: New Directions for Theory and Research'. *Sociology of Health and Illness* 18 (2): 139–71.

Smedley, B. D., Stith, A. Y. and Nelson, A. R. (eds) (2003) *Unequal Treatment: Confronting Racial and Ethnic Disparities in Health Care*. Washington, DC: Institute of Medicine of the National Academies.

Soni Raleigh, V. (1996) 'Suicide Patterns and Trends in People of Indian Subcontinent and Caribbean Origin in England and Wales'. *Ethnicity and Health* 1: 55–63.

Soni Raleigh, V. and Balarajan, R. (1992) 'Suicide and Self-burning Among Indians and West Indians in England and Wales'. *British Journal of Psychiatry* 161: 365–8.

Soni Raleigh, V., Bulusu, L. and Balarajan, R. (1990) 'Suicides among Immigrants from the Indian Subcontinent'. *British Journal of Psychiatry* 156: 46–50.

Sorlie, P., Rogot, E., Anderson, R., Johnson, N. J. and Backlund, E. (1992) 'Black–white mortality differences by family income'. *Lancet* 340: 346–50.

Sorlie, P. D., Backlund, E. and Keller, J. (1995) 'U.S. Mortality by Economic, Demographic and Social Characteristics: The National Longitudinal Mortality Study'. *American Journal of Public Health* 85: 949–56.

Sproston, K. and Mindell, J. (2006) *Health Survey for England 2004: The Health of Minority Ethnic Groups*. London: The Information Centre.

Sproston, K. and Nazroo, J. (eds) (2002) *Ethnic Minority Psychiatric Illness Rates in the Community (EMPIRIC)*. London: The Stationery Office.

Stewart, J. A., Dundas, R., Howard, R. A., Rudd, A. G. and Woolfe, C. D. A. (1999) 'Ethnic Differences in Incidence of Stroke: Prospective Study with Stroke Register'. *British Medical Journal* 318: 967–71.

Townsend, P. and Davidson, N. (1982) *Inequalities in Health (the Black Report)*. Middlesex: Penguin.

Trask, J. W. (1916) 'The Significance of the Mortality Rates of the Coloured Population of the United States'. *American Journal of Public Health* 6: 254–60.

Van Os, J., Castle, D. J., Takei, N., Der, G. and Murray, R. M. (1996) 'Psychotic Illness in Ethnic Minorities: Clarification from the 1991 Census'. *Psychological Medicine* 26: 203–8.

Webbe, A. (1998) 'Ethnicity and Mental Health'. *Psychiatric Care* 5: 12–6.

Wild, S. and McKeigue, P. (1997) 'Cross Sectional Analysis of Mortality by Country of Birth in England and Wales'. *British Medical Journal* 314: 705–10.

Williams, D. R. (2001) 'Racial Variations in Adult Health Status: Patterns, Paradoxes and Prospects' in Smelser, N. J., Wilson, W. J. and Mitchell, F. (eds) *America Becoming: Racial Trends and Their Consequences*. Washington, DC: National Academy Press.

Williams, D. R., Neighbors, H. W. and Jackson, J. S. (2003) 'Racial/Ethnic Discrimination and Health: Findings From Community Studies'. *American Journal of Public Health* 93: 200–8.

CHAPTER 7

Education

DAVID GILLBORN AND NICOLA ROLLOCK

Introduction

A characteristic of most urban areas is their ethnic and racial diversity.[1] In this chapter we examine how race, and in particular *racism*, operates in and through contemporary education policy and practice. Building on an analysis of both quantitative and qualitative research, we show how race inequity has been influenced by the drive to improve 'standards' as defined in official policy. The principal sections of the chapter consider differences in attainment between minority ethnic groups; the issue of exclusion (expulsion) from school; and the in-school processes that shape minority students' experiences and achievements. In order to contextualise these debates, however, it is useful to begin with a brief introduction to the demographic landscape.

Populations and projections

A significant and growing number of British residents (around 4.6 million) have community backgrounds outside the UK: equivalent to around 8 per cent of the total population in the most recent national census (ONS 2001). This figure represents a growth of around 48 per cent between 1991 and 2001. Most minority ethnic communities have much younger population profiles than white communities; consequently, it is anticipated that minority ethnic communities will continue to grow substantially, both in relative and in absolute terms, over the next 20 years.[2] This will have a particular consequence for education, where the school population will continue to include a greater proportion of minority ethnic people than is true of the adult population. These changes are already well advanced. In 2006 around 17 per cent of secondary school students (aged between 11 and 16) and 21 per cent of primary students (age 5–10) were classified as being of minority ethnic heritage (DfES 2006a: 3). In the cities of London,

Birmingham and Leicester it is projected that by the end of this decade no group will account for 50 per cent or more of the population: that is, there will be no overall ethnic majority.

These demographic changes are not restricted to urban centres alone. There are few parts of the education world that are not directly affected by the multi-ethnic nature of society. Official statistics already suggest that only a minority of primary schools (around 25 per cent), and very few secondary schools (5 per cent), can accurately claim to be 'all white' (DfEE 1999: 2). Nevertheless, it remains the case that most minority ethnic students are educated in urban schools (DfES 2005a: 8–9).

Against this background of increasing diversity, the English education system currently faces a series of challenges.[3] On one hand, because of legislative changes arising from the Stephen Lawrence Inquiry (Macpherson 1999),[4] the system now has a legal duty to proactively pursue race equity; on the other hand, the system continues to produce outcomes that are deeply scarred by systematic race inequities (in, for example, rates of permanent exclusion and academic success).

Quantitative research findings

Attainment and under-achievement

The relative attainments of children in different ethnic groups has long dominated discussion of ethnic diversity in English education. The field has been plagued by widespread misunderstanding and over-simplification that have sometimes added to the problems. The notion of 'under-achievement', for example, is widely quoted but rarely subjected to proper scrutiny. In most academic and policy treatments, the term refers to a situation where the attainments of one group are significantly less than those of the majority ethnic group. This is usually judged by comparing group averages or the proportion reaching some agreed cut-off point, such as a minimum of five higher grade GCSE passes.[5] These are important measures but they do not tell us anything about *all* members of that group: although members of a particular group might be less likely to attain five higher grades overall, some *individuals* in that group will undoubtedly meet and exceed such measures. Too much attention to group-level measures can lead to over-simplification and even stereotyping. Many writers have argued that the notion of 'under-achievement' itself has become yet another stereotype – as if each individual member of an under-achieving group were destined for failure.[6] Gus John argues that if minority ethnic students continue to be presented as one-dimensional and separate groups, policy *'will succeed in projecting "ethnic minority" students as an undifferentiated mass, pathologically defined, as if the lack of attainment with which the group as a whole has come to be identified is somehow congenitally determined'* (John 2001: 3, original emphasis). These warnings are important because the pattern of attainment by minority ethnic students is considerably more complex than is usually recognised.

First, it is important to note that *every* ethnic group is capable of the highest achievement. For each of the principal ethnic groups in England (white, Black African, Black Caribbean, Black Other, Indian, Pakistani, Bangladeshi) statistical data from Local Authorities (LAs) show that there is at least one part of the country where that group has the greatest proportion of young people attaining five or more higher grade GCSE passes (Gillborn and Mirza 2000: 8–11). This important finding demolishes any notion of innate differences between groups and is a reminder of the need to guard against stereotyping on the basis of broad descriptive statistics.

A second point to remember is that the definitions and assumptions that shape official statistics also influence the terms of debate and determine policy priorities. Gypsy/Traveller children are frequently absent from considerations of minority ethnic groups. For example, they are not included in one of the British government's most detailed sources of data, the Youth Cohort Study (YCS) (DfEE 2003a; DfES 2005b). This is especially worrying because the consensus is that these children are the group *most* at risk of educational failure (see Bhattacharyya et al. 2003; Bhopal et al. 2001; DfES 2006b; OFSTED 1999; Plowden 1967; Swann 1985). A survey by the schools inspectorate (the Office for Standards in Education: OFSTED) found that Gypsy/Traveller children were massively over-represented on the register of children designated as having 'special educational needs' and

> although some make a reasonably promising start in primary school, by the time they reach secondary school their levels of attainment are almost always a matter for concern. Many, especially boys, opt out of education by Year 9 [aged 13–14] and very few go on to achieve success at GCSE or beyond.
>
> (OFSTED 1999: 11)

The 2001 Census included a 'mixed' category in the question on ethnic origin for the first time and this has subsequently been adopted in the categories used in the annual schools census. This is an especially heterogeneous group and there is some controversy about the assumptions behind the 'mixed' label (Phoenix and Owen 2002). Nevertheless, as more data emerge, it is likely that this category will begin to feature in relevant debates to a much greater extent (Tikly et al. 2004).

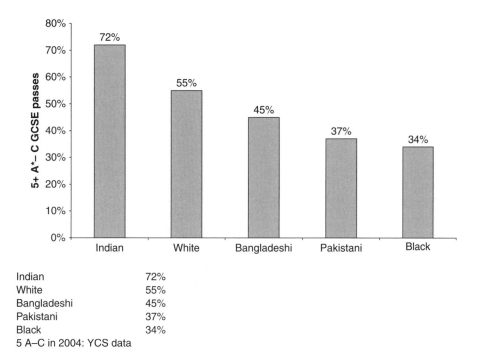

Indian	72%
White	55%
Bangladeshi	45%
Pakistani	37%
Black	34%

5 A–C in 2004: YCS data

Figure 7.1 Attainment and ethnic origin (England & Wales 2004).
Source: Table A of DfES (2005b), Youth Cohort Study: the activities and experiences of
16 year olds, SFR 04/2005 Revised. London.

Nationally, discussions of 'under-achievement' usually focus on three principal minority ethnic groups: Black (African Caribbean),[7] Bangladeshi and
Pakistani children. Although rates differ from year to year and from region to
region, children from these groups tend to achieve less well, on average, than
their white peers of the same sex and social class background. This pattern is
well established at the national level and has been found in numerous surveys.
In 2004, 55 per cent of white 16-year-olds attained five or more higher grade
(A*–C) passes in their GCSEs. In contrast, this level was attained by 34 per cent
of Black students, 37 per cent of Pakistanis and 45 per cent of Bangladeshis (see
Figure 7.1).

When considering attainment data it is important to remember that
key information is often absent from official statistics. The information in
Figure 7.1, for example, includes neither gender nor social class. And yet it is
well established that both these factors are strongly associated with differences
in average attainment: on average, girls' attainment is higher than boys in each
of the principal minority ethnic groups (Bhattacharyya et al. 2003: 12; Gillborn

and Mirza 2000: 22–5) and boys and girls from non-manual backgrounds score considerably higher on average than peers from manual households (Gillborn and Mirza 2000: 18–21). These factors are vital because they each interact. A re-analysis of official data, for example, showed that although girls categorised as African Caribbean and Bangladeshi/Pakistani were attaining higher scores on average than boys in their ethnic groups, their attainment was not only less than their white and Indian female counterparts, but also less than white and Indian *boys*. In other words, the gender gap *within* minority ethnic groups is not enough to close the wider inequities that exist *between* different ethnic groups (Gillborn and Mirza 2000: 25–6; also Rollock 2007a). Similarly, although Black students from non-manual households (including middle-class children) are likely to perform better than their Black counterparts in manual households, their attainment is less than all other non-manual groups (Gillborn and Mirza 2000: 20). It is necessary, therefore, to keep in mind the significance of class, ethnic origin *and* gender: each factor is important, but none is completely dominant.[8] However, the common assertion that gender and/or class factors 'explain' ethnic inequities is demonstrably false.

Education reform and changing patterns of attainment

The government's use of attainment scores as an indicator of 'standards' has led to a significant increase in formal assessment throughout the English education system. One consequence has been the generation of additional data that offer the possibility of further enquiry into patterns of attainment as students move through the system. Unfortunately, relatively few current statistics are available with any meaningful analyses by ethnic origin. In contrast, some LAs have been gathering ethnically based data for more than a decade and now offer the opportunity to examine the entire range of attainments at different stages (from age 5 to 16). These data suggest that patterns of minority ethnic inequity might actually worsen as students go through school (see Gillborn and Mirza 2000; Richardson and Wood 1999). However, the picture has been complicated by a change in the nature of assessments in early years' education, which draws attention to the fact that assessment itself is far from the neutral technology that is often assumed.

Attainment on entry to school

In the late 1990s the push for increased public information on educational 'standards' reached primary schools, with the requirement that all five-year-olds be subject to 'baseline assessment' when they entered schooling. A wide variety of different approaches were adopted and there was no requirement that the data be analysed by ethnic origin. However, several LAs with substantial minority populations chose to publish ethnic analyses, and the findings often confounded expectations. In particular, Black (African Caribbean) students often emerged as entering school better prepared than their peers. Unfortunately, their relative attainment was seen to fall dramatically as they moved through the system (see Gillborn and Mirza 2000; Richardson and Wood 1999).

These data suggest that schools add considerably less value for their Black students. In one large metropolitan LA in 2000, for example, Black students entered primary school attaining an average of 20 points *above* the local average in their baseline assessments but their older Black peers were leaving school (aged 16) attaining 21 points *below* the LA average in their GCSEs (see Figure 7.2). This finding became well known but, without any wider debate or

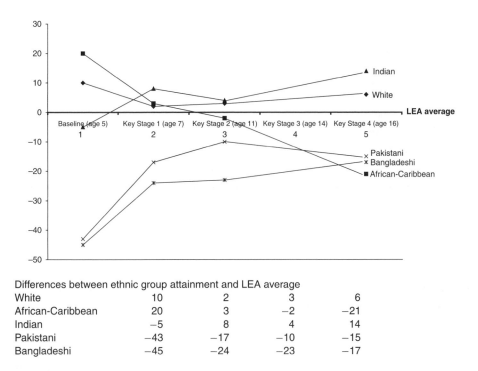

Differences between ethnic group attainment and LEA average

White	10	2	3	6
African-Caribbean	20	3	−2	−21
Indian	−5	8	4	14
Pakistani	−43	−17	−10	−15
Bangladeshi	−45	−24	−23	−17

Figure 7.2 Ethnic group inequalities: age 5–16 (one metropolitan authority, 2000).

comment, the pattern was *reversed* when, in 2002, the government introduced a new form of assessment that was compulsory in all state schools.

The 'Foundation Stage Profile' requires that all five-year-olds are assessed by their classroom teacher on a range of 13 different 'scales' (QCA 2003). Although this sounds highly technical, in fact the judgements are entirely at the practitioners' discretion. The first published results of the new system showed a marked change in the fortunes of different minority groups. In contrast to the previous 'baseline' measures, which included a wider array of different approaches, the Foundation Stage Profile has consistently placed white students ahead of *all* other groups (including their Indian and Chinese peers, who tend to perform well at 16). Black students have fared especially badly from the changes: they are now ranked lower than the national average in all different aspects of the assessment profile nationally (see Gillborn 2006). These patterns were first reported in 2005 (DfES 2005d) and the ethnic inequities have worsened in subsequent data (DfES 2006a). This dramatic change in the attainments of minority ethnic students, however, has gone unremarked by policy makers. Some of the reasons for these changes are discussed in detail in the section on qualitative research later in the chapter.

GCSE Attainment

Overall rates of success in the GCSE have risen significantly since the examination was introduced in 1988. Successive governments (both Conservative and Labour) have used the proportion of students attaining *five* or more higher grade passes as the dominant measure of educational success. Consequently, a great deal of effort has gone into attaining this measure (at both school and LA levels) and a year-on-year improvement has become the norm for more than a decade. This raises an important question: have minority ethnic groups shared in the improving rates of GCSE success? The best available data suggests that there is considerable cause for concern.

In late 2000, OFSTED published a review of evidence on 'race', class and gender in relation to educational attainment (Gillborn and Mirza 2000). Commissioned as part of OFSTED's response to *The Stephen Lawrence Inquiry* (Macpherson 1999), the report drew considerable publicity with its claim that substantial inequities of attainment between minority ethnic groups were not only persisting but, in some cases, actually *growing*:

> Indian pupils have made the greatest gains in the last decade: enough to overtake their white peers as a group.

Bangladeshi pupils have improved significantly but the gap between themselves and white youngsters is much the same.

African-Caribbean and Pakistani pupils have drawn least benefit from the rising levels of attainment: the gap between them and their white peers is bigger now than a decade ago.

(Gillborn and Mirza 2000: 14)

In apparent contrast to these findings, just a few months later the government announced new data and celebrated that 'black and Indian students and students from working class backgrounds have seen their GCSE results rising nearly three times as much as the national average since 1997' (DfEE 2001a: 1). Predictably, the news of Black students improving at such a rate drew great attention and was given much prominence in the government's subsequent plans for education reforms (see DfEE 2001b: 14). As Table 7.1 demonstrates, however, the government's pleasure was short-lived. Not only did the apparent gains look more modest over a longer time period, but subsequent data showed a further *decline* for Black students.

Youth Cohort Study: changes in attainment between 1988 and 2004

Table 7.1 charts the changing patterns of GCSE attainment from the late 1980s through to 2004. The data are drawn from the Youth Cohort Study (YCS). A disadvantage with the YCS is that it reports on a *sample* of 16-year-olds rather than the whole cohort. Although the sample is large (more than 14,000 in 2004) it is considerably smaller than the numbers involved in the Pupil Level Annual Schools Census (PLASC), which, in 2002, began to gather systematic data on the ethnicity of *every* child in the state system. However, at the time of writing the PLASC data were only available for a period of four years. In contrast, the YCS offers a unique picture of how different ethnic groups have fared over 15 years. The YCS data offer the only available information on how a nationally representative sample have fared since the start of the important reforms that began with the Education Reform Act 1988.

The data are generated by a questionnaire sent to a sample of 16- to 19-year-olds. Table 7.1 records the proportion of students in each of the main ethnic minority groups who achieved five or more higher grade GCSE passes (or their equivalent) in the most recent surveys. Alongside the relevant percentage is a calculation of the 'gap' between that group's attainment and the level of their white peers in the same survey. Hence, in 1989, 30 per cent of white young people gained five or more higher grade passes, compared with 18 per cent of Black students: this equates to a 'gap', an inequity, of 12 percentage points.

Table 7.1 Ethnic origin and GCSE attainment

Percentage gaining five higher grade GCSE passes and percentage point difference with the 'white' group

	1989		1991		1992		1994		1996		1998*		2000		2002		2004	
	%	gap	%	gap	%	gap	%	gap	%	gap	%	gap	%	gap	%	gap	%	gap
White	**30**		**35**		**37**		**43**		**45**		**47**		**50**		**52**		**55**	
Black	18	−12	19	−16	23	−14	21	−22	23	−22	29	−18	39	−11	36	−16	34	−21
Indian	na		na		38	+1	45	+2	48	+3	54	+7	60	+10	60	+8	72	+17
Pakistani	na		na		26	−11	24	−19	23	−22	29	−18	29	−21	40	−12	37	−18
Bangladeshi	na		na		14	−23	20	−23	25	−20	33	−14	29	−21	41	−11	45	−10

Notes: na = not available: separate calculations were not made for Indian, Pakistani and Bangladeshi students until the 1992 cohort.
Year = the year of the cohort being questioned: the GCSE examinations were taken in the previous calendar year.
Please note that these are the official statistics and *include* students attending independent schools.
* includes equivalent GNVQ qualifications from 1998.
Source: Adapted from DfES (2005b) Table A.

White students are the *only* group identified in the YCS that has enjoyed an improvement in every one of the surveys since 1989. The performance of the other groups has been less certain, with periods where their attainment in one study remained static or actually fell below that of the previous survey. These changes could relate to actual fluctuations nationally, but they might also be a product of relatively small changes within the sample groups. Consequently, it is advisable to treat year-on-year changes with caution and focus more on the longer-term trends.

Black students

The performance of Black students has shown a marked improvement over recent years. Over the entire period in Table 7.1 (1989–2004) the proportion of Black students attaining at least five higher grades almost doubled (from 18 per cent to 34 per cent). This improvement (of 16 percentage points), however, did not keep pace with white students (whose attainment improved by 25 percentage points over the same period). Despite improvements during the 1990s, therefore, it remains the case that the so-called 'Black/white gap' is significantly larger (at 21 percentage points) than it was more than a decade ago (12 percentage points in 1989). This comparison, however, does not tell the whole story.

The data in Table 7.1 show that the Black/white gap grew considerably during the early- to mid-1990s. This was a period of intense emphasis on raising exam performance and improving positions in the newly introduced school performance tables (first published for secondary schools in 1992). In contrast, surveys in 1998 and 2000 showed a narrowing of the Black/white gap. However, it should be noted that since 1998 the data includes the results in other forms of assessment that are judged as equivalent to GCSEs, including General National Vocational Qualifications (GNVQs). Evidence shows that Black students are disproportionately entered for these lower-status examinations (Gillborn and Youdell 2000). Further, despite the significant gains that received so much publicity in the 2000 data, figures for 2002 and 2004 showed a *fall* in the proportion of Black students attaining five or more higher grade passes, meaning that once again the inequity of attainment has begun to rise. Notwithstanding our earlier warning about fluctuations in the YCS figures, it is clear that parity of attainment remains a long way away: the Black/white inequity in the most recent data is almost as great as that at any time since the late 1980s.

Pakistani students

The pattern of attainment by Pakistani students is even more complex. Since 1992, the achievements of Pakistani young people have varied considerably:

falling in two consecutive cohorts before showing some important gains more recently. Overall, between 1992 and 2004, the proportion of Pakistani students attaining five or more higher grade passes improved by 11 percentage points (from 26 per cent to 37 per cent). This is a significant increase but it should be noted that that the gap between Pakistani students and their white peers, while fluctuating considerably, was actually smallest in 1992 when data were first gathered separately for this group.

Bangladeshi students

From a very low starting point in 1992, the Bangladeshi group showed quite dramatic improvements until the 2000 survey, when their attainment fell below the level of the previous cohort. However, the upward trend resumed in subsequent surveys and, overall, Bangladeshi students are now three times more likely to attain five higher grades than they were in the early 1990s. Nevertheless, Bangladeshi students remain less likely to achieve these higher grades than their white counterparts.

Indian students

The picture for Indian students is markedly different from the other minority ethnic groups examined above. From a position of virtual equity in 1992, when the YCS first disaggregated the composite 'South Asian' category, Indian students have improved *more* than their white peers. Although the proportion attaining five or more higher grades remained static between 2000 and 2002, overall Indian students have improved from 38 per cent in 1992 to 72 per cent, an increase of 34 percentage points: almost double the white improvement (of 18 percentage points) over the same period.

Data on ethnic origin and achievement for approximately the last 15 years, therefore, shows that none of the existing inequities are fixed. Each of the attainment inequities have varied over time, with the early and mid-1990s being a period of especially pronounced inequity. All groups have enjoyed some improvement over the period but significant problems persist. The Black/white gap is almost as great as ever and both Bangladeshi and Pakistani students have experienced periods of growing inequity.

Exclusions from school

The most serious sanction a school can take against a student is to permanently expel them ('permanent exclusion' in the official lexicon). The local state has a duty to ensure that such students receive a basic education elsewhere, usually through placement in some form of special unit or limited private tuition. Official statistics suggest that exclusion is strongly associated with negative outcomes in education and in wider life chances:

> Young people excluded from school are much less likely to achieve 5 GCSEs at grade A*–C than other groups – just one in five young people compared to more than half overall. More than four times as many young people excluded from school fail to gain any qualifications at 16 compared with those not excluded. Being out of school is a major risk factor for juvenile offending. Research has found an almost direct correlation between youth crime rates in an area and the 'out of school' population. Young people excluded from school are more than twice as likely to report having committed a crime as young people in mainstream school.
>
> (Equalities Review 2006: 41).

In view of these experiences the persistent and significant over-exclusion of Black students is a major area of controversy and concern. They have tended to be over-represented in permanent exclusions whenever relevant data have been broken down by ethnicity. In the mid-1980s, for example, 'Afro-Caribbean' students accounted for 14 per cent of London school children but made up more than 30 per cent of all exclusions in the capital (*Times Educational Supplement*, 9 September 1988). This problem became even more pressing during the 1990s when the overall number of exclusions increased dramatically: the figure for 1995/96 was 12,476, four times the number recorded at the start of the decade (Gillborn 1998: 11). In the mid-1990s new data, based on OFSTED inspections, suggested that nationally Black Caribbean children were excluded from secondary schools at almost *six times* the rate for white students (Gillborn and Gipps 1996: 53). It was calculated that this meant around 1,000 additional and potentially unjust Black expulsions every year (Gillborn 1998: 13).

In 1998, the first report of the newly created Social Exclusion Unit focused on exclusions and truancy from school. The unit's recommendations were taken up by the government and committed Labour to drastically reduce the number of permanent exclusions by a third from 12,700 in 1996/97 to 8,400 by 2002 (SEU 1998). The government abandoned this target, in 2001, arguing that the reduction had all but been achieved (at 8,600 in 1999/2000) and that no new targets were necessary (DfES 2001). Perhaps predictably, the following two years saw a rise in the number of students being permanently excluded (DfES 2003a: Table 1).

However, the official statistics on permanent exclusions are only part of the story. Indeed, there are indications that 'unofficial exclusions', which evade official recording, are becoming increasingly common (Osler et al. 2001). Further, the growth in alternative provision, including the use of referrals to 'Pupil Support Units', will have helped reduce the official numbers but do not guarantee students' access to the mainstream curriculum. Additionally, Black parents' groups have raised concerns about 'internal exclusion', where students may be repeatedly removed from class: again, a form of exclusion from equal access to schooling but not a form of exclusion that shows up in official data (see John 2006: 225–38). With these warnings in mind, the official statistics on ethnicity and exclusion are summarised in Table 7.2.

Table 7.2 shows the recorded levels of permanent exclusion since the overall peak in 1996/97. The columns show the number of students in each ethnic group formally recorded as having been permanently excluded. The percentage column shows that number of students as a percentage of their ethnic group in school; hence, the figure of 0.06 Bangladeshis in 2004/05 represents 6 students in every 10,000, and 0.39 for Black Caribbean students represents 39 in every 10,000.

The first thing to note is the complexity of the statistics. The number of white students recorded as permanently excluded declined each year between 1996/97 and the overall low of 1999/2000, but then rose in each of the next two years. In contrast, the number of Black Caribbean students excluded barely changed in the first year of the overall decline, but (having begun to fall more rapidly) then continued to decline even in 2000/01 when overall numbers began to rise once again. Indian students had the least chance of being excluded (as a percentage of their numbers in the school population) throughout the entire period in question, but the number (and proportion) of Indians excluded actually rose in 1997/98 just as overall rates began to fall. The exclusion rate for Bangladeshi students has been volatile throughout the period, including a rise in 1999/2000 (the third successive year of overall reductions), a fall in 2000/01 (when the total rate started to rise) and a steep increase in 2001/02.

In view of the limitations of the official statistics, and the volatility of figures for minority ethnic groups, it is necessary to be cautious about interpreting these data. It appears that students in each of the principal ethnic groups shared to some degree in the general reduction that occurred in the late 1990s (between 1996/97 and 1999/2000 inclusive). However, taking a longer-term view (over the whole period detailed in Table 7.2), we get a more varied picture. Comparing the numbers excluded at the start and end of this nine-year period, and disregarding the 'Black Other' composite group,[9] the greatest proportionate reduction was experienced by Black Caribbean students (down almost 50 per cent on the 1996/97 high). Students recorded as Pakistani (44 per cent), white (29 per cent) and Indian (23 per cent) experienced greater proportionate decreases than their Bangladeshi (16 per cent) and Black African (5 per cent) counterparts over the same period.

Table 7.2 Ethnic origin and permanent exclusions from school (England 1996/97 to 2004/05)

Ethnic Origin	1996/97 N	%	1997/98 N	%	1998/99 N	%	1999/00 N	%	2000/01 N	%	2001/02 N	%	2002/03 N	%	2003/04 N	%	2004/05 N	%
White	10,555	0.18	10,303	0.18	8,801	0.15	6,890	0.12	7,574	0.13	7,820	0.13	6,800	0.12	7,860	0.14	7,470	0.13
Bl. Caribbean	770	0.78	765	0.77	589	0.60	455	0.46	385	0.38	410	0.41	360	0.37	400	0.41	380	0.39
Bl. African	200	0.31	203	0.30	157	0.21	145	0.17	156	0.17	160	0.15	130	0.12	200	0.16	190	0.14
Bl. Other	334	0.71	287	0.58	268	0.50	218	0.37	236	0.39	220	0.35	90	0.32	120	0.42	100	0.36
Indian	91	0.06	116	0.07	71	0.04	54	0.03	47	0.03	60	0.03	50	0.03	40	0.02	70	0.04
Pakistani	286	0.18	218	0.13	165	0.10	129	0.07	113	0.06	170	0.09	130	0.08	130	0.07	160	0.08
Bangladeshi	60	0.10	60	0.10	42	0.07	53	0.08	44	0.07	80	0.11	40	0.06	70	0.09	50	0.06
W/Bl. Caribbean	na	na	na	na	na	na	na	na	na	na	na	na	180	0.29	240	0.37	280	0.41
W/Bl. African	na	na	na	na	na	na	na	na	na	na	na	na	40	0.26	40	0.23	50	0.24
W/Asian	na	na	na	na	na	na	na	na	na	na	na	na	40	0.11	40	0.12	30	0.09
TOTAL	12,668		12,298		10,424		8,314		9,122		9,519		9,270		9,860		9,380	

(includes some groups not shown separately above)

Notes: N = number of pupils permanently excluded.
% = number of pupils excluded in that ethnic group expressed as a percentage of that ethnic group in compulsory schooling.
na = data not available for that period.
Sources: For 1996/97–2000/01 DfES (2002); thereafter DfES (2003b), Table 2; DfES (2004), Table 4; DfES (2005c), Table 7; DfES (2006c), Table 7.

When we focus on the likelihood of exclusion within each ethnic group some more consistent patterns begin to emerge. Students of 'South Asian' ethnic heritage, for example, have almost always been *less* likely to be excluded (as a percentage of their ethnic group) than their white and Black counterparts.[10] In contrast, Black students (those categorised as Black Caribbean, Black African or Black Other) have almost always been *more* likely to be excluded than their white counterparts: a pattern that is true every year and for each of the Black groups (with the lone exception of Black African students in 2002/03, when their rate of exclusion was the same as their white peers).

The 'mixed' ethnic category has featured in official statistics on exclusions only relatively recently (since 2002/03). Students in the 'Mixed: White & Asian' group experienced the lowest exclusion rate, marked by a 25 per cent decrease between 2003/04 and 2004/05 compared to a 25 per cent *increase* for 'Mixed: White & Black African' students for the same period. Data for 'Mixed: White & Black Caribbean' students reveals a particularly high rate of exclusion, similar to Black Caribbean students, with a 55 per cent increase since data on this group was first collected.

Additional official data on short 'fixed-term' exclusions (when students are temporarily barred from a school) has only recently been collected but shows similar patterns as the permanent exclusions; that is, students in the 'Mixed: White & Black Caribbean', Black Caribbean and other Black groups tend to experience fixed-term exclusions around twice the rate of their white peers and the national average (DfES 2005c, 2006c).

Factors contributing to the disproportionate exclusion of Black students

The over-representation of Black students in the numbers excluded from school is a topic that generates considerable debate and controversy. Despite academic research (Blair 2001; Wright et al. 2000) and community-based initiatives (John 2006) that highlight the inequitable treatment of Black students in schools, the popular media continue to repeat crude stereotypes that reinforce powerful deficit images of Black communities in general and Black young men in particular (see Rollock 2006).

There is growing evidence that the over-representation of African Caribbean students is the result of harsher treatment by schools rather than simple differences in behaviour by students. Twice in recent years OFSTED has published special inspections concerning discipline and exclusions from school. In both cases they have found evidence that Black students are treated somewhat more harshly than their peers of other ethnic origins. In the mid-1990s inspectors found that the profile of 'Caribbean' excludees was significantly different to that of other excludees: with the former judged of higher prior attainment and having less pronounced histories of disruption (OFSTED 1996: 11). More recently, OFSTED reported that 'many black pupils who find themselves subject to disciplinary procedures perceive themselves to have been unfairly treated': inspectors noted that 'the lengths of fixed-period exclusions varied considerably in some schools between black and white pupils for what were described as the same or similar incidents' (OFSTED 2001: 23). These comments are all the more powerful when read within a context where OFSTED itself has been heavily criticised for failing to take a sufficiently active role in debates on race equity (Osler and Morrison 2000). Indeed, a research report funded and published by the DfES has noted that 'Ofsted school inspections rarely comment on disproportionality in exclusions' (Parsons et al. 2004: 1). The report noted that even where evidence of over-representation was contained within the reports themselves, it usually went unremarked:

> None of the seven Ofsted inspection reports published on secondary schools [in the sample] commented on disproportionality of minority ethnic exclusions, which was evident in the tables published in six of them.
>
> (Parsons et al. 2004: 50)

In late 2006 the issue of race and exclusions made front-page headlines when the *Independent on Sunday* newspaper published extensive extracts from what it claimed was a DfES 'priority review' into the issue. According to the published extracts, the DfES had concluded that the weight of evidence was clearly against the common stereotypes:

> While a compelling case can be made for the existence of institutional racism in schools, there is a comparatively weak basis for arguing that street culture has a more persuasive influence on black young people than it has on other young people.
>
> (Unpublished DfES report quoted in the *Independent on Sunday*, 10 December 2006: 8–9)

Nevertheless, the government minister responsible (Lord Adonis) was reported to have decided against making the report's conclusions public. The *Independent on Sunday* stated that 'In the event, Lord Adonis ducked the issue, arguing that since the report does not baldly conclude that Britain's entire school system is "institutionally racist", the term – and issue – could be quietly shelved' (Griggs 2006: 8). The DfES briefed journalists that 'ministers had concluded that it would be inaccurate and counterproductive to brand the school system racist' (BBC News 2006). The *Daily Telegraph's* reaction to the story was to describe the review as 'a collection of antiquated Leftist platitudes' and, in a sentence that demonstrates the nature of the problem precisely, the newspaper dismissed the criticism of media stereotyping as

> ...an insult to teachers for whom the cult of violence adopted by many fatherless black youths represents a daily threat to their physical safety.
>
> (*Daily Telegraph*, 11 December 2006: 23)

As if to seal the argument the General Secretary of the country's largest head teachers' organisation was later quoted as follows:

> behaviour that disrupts the education of others must always be acted upon. Where there is an external culture of violence, anarchy and lack of respect for authority, that clash of cultures poses a huge problem for our schools.
>
> (Mick Brookes, *National Association of Head Teachers*, quoted in Stewart 2006)

These assumptions ('cult of violence', 'fatherless black youths', 'a daily threat', 'culture of violence', 'anarchy', 'lack of respect') shape the everyday school experiences of Black boys and young men, and go some way to explaining the patterns of inequity highlighted above (see Rollock 2007b).

This episode is important for several reasons. First, it highlights the significance of exclusions as a touchstone for issues concerning race and education. The over-exclusion of Black students frequently emerges as one of the most important issues for Black teachers, parents and students (see Greater London Authority 2003; Richardson 2005). Second, it highlights the highly charged political climate that surrounds any discussion of 'institutional racism'. This is a complex area where the limitations of quantitative data become especially apparent. In order to understand these issues, and the school-level processes involved, it is necessary to make use of qualitative research.

Qualitative research findings

School processes and racism

> It's not blatantly there. I mean, you can't, you wouldn't be able to just walk in the school and say 'Oh the school's racist.' You have to take time before you knew that. (Marcella, a 14-year-old African Caribbean student)[11]

Detailed research on life in multi-ethnic schools has revealed much about the significance of 'race' and ethnic identity for students and teachers. In many cases the influence of ethnicity is quite subtle: in others, the ethnicised nature of interactions is more obvious. Among the latter are cases where students feel themselves the victim of racial harassment. Unfortunately, despite its often overt form, racial harassment between students is frequently not recognised by teachers, whose inaction can result in spiralling conflict.

Racist incidents and institutional racism

In an important study of the school experiences of South Asian students Ghazala Bhatti documents aggression from fellow students and notes how teachers' reactions can play an active role in shaping further resentments and conflicts. The following episode, for example, describes a classroom dispute between John (a white boy) and Shakeel (an Asian classmate):

> The atmosphere was getting charged. Miss Paine was busy writing the date on the blackboard. Lot of general noise in class which sounds incoherent on tape. Shakeel looking very provoked, shoved the book aside and pushed the chair back. Lull in noise level.

> *John*:   Look at him! Paki Pakora [Latter said in a near whisper but audible to Shakeel, Asad and me]
> *Shakeel*: I'll smash your face in, you clown [said very loudly]
> *AP*:   [turning around] Right that's enough. Shakeel leave the class this minute.
> *Shakeel*: But Miss . . .
> *AP*:   Out! Go and stand outside . . . God these boys!

> I wrote in my field notes that Shakeel made a lot of noise collecting things and putting them in his bag. There was a look of great satisfaction on John's face. There was pin-drop silence in the class.
>
> (Bhatti 1999: 192)

Bhatti accompanies this description with her own reflections on the incident and explains that the following day three white and three Asian boys were involved in a fight away from the school: both John and Shakeel took part. Bhatti notes that other students had been making noise and remarks on her surprise that 'Miss Paine did not keep the quarrelling parties behind to try and ascertain the circumstances which had led to the incident'; neither did she 'leave the classroom to explore what had happened'. Had the teacher sought an explanation from Shakeel, she could have been in a position to defuse the conflict and to challenge John's racism. In this case, however, only one party was disciplined and the dispute was intensified. Additionally, Bhatti notes, the incident would not have had racist connotations if both boys had been of the same ethnic origin. But in this example, ethnicity is clearly a key factor. Shakeel is reacting to racist name-calling and the teacher's decision solely to punish the Asian student 'was racist in its outcome if not in intention' (1999: 192).

This kind of conflict is compounded by some teachers' reluctance to address racism. If racist name-calling (or worse still, racist physical violence) goes unpunished by teachers then witnesses will draw their own conclusions. White students may think that teachers condone such perspectives and minority ethnic students will rightly question the school's commitment to equity and justice. This situation may sound exaggerated to some (see, for example, Foster et al. 1996), but qualitative studies of schools suggest that racial harassment is a regular (for some a daily) occurrence.

The Stephen Lawrence Inquiry

Following *the Stephen Lawrence Inquiry*, the Home Office issued a new code of practice on reporting racist incidents. The document recommended the following definition:

> A racist incident is any incident which is perceived to be racist by the victim or any other person .... The purpose of this definition is not to pre-judge whether a perpetrator's motive was racist or not: that may have to be proved ... rather (it is) to ensure that investigations take account of the possibility of a racist dimension to the incident and that statistics of such incidents are collected on a uniform basis.
>
> (*Home Office Code of Practice on Reporting and Recording Racist Incidents*, quoted in London Borough of Lambeth nd: 16)

This approach emphasises the importance of people's perceptions; it insists that racism be recorded wherever a participant experiences it and adds to the impetus for a serious investigation and subsequent action. Too often, racist incidents (especially racist name-calling) have been denied significance mainly – but not exclusively – by white people who have failed to understand the meaning of such assaults. Over 20 years ago an official enquiry, the Swann Report (1985), complained of this problem and it is still in evidence: the following quotations, for example, are taken from two studies of teachers' views *after* the publication of the Stephen Lawrence Report:

> I haven't seen any instance of what I would call a serious racist incident. I've heard silly name-calling. I suppose it's got to be taken seriously, but within reason: kids do call each other names, to start panicking and saying 'it's

terrible, it's being racist' is just not the case. (White primary school teacher) their first line of defence is that, 'Oh, the teacher's racist' ... it's an easy cop-out. (White secondary school teacher).

(Kemp and Gillborn 2000)

Also this thing that you know 'oh that teacher's racist' or 'that teacher doesn't like Black boys'. That is nonsense! I wouldn't say that you know, yes people could give me six case studies of it and they are genuine but you know, it's the minority, it's not the majority ... what happens is that some of the Black boys are too easily distracted from learning and they come into school and learning does not feature on their agenda (Black secondary head teacher).

(Rollock 2006:147)

These quotations are significant for several reasons. First, they suggest that even post-Lawrence, some teachers remain unwilling to take seriously accusations of racism or incidents where racism is clearly in play. The primary teacher who views racist name-calling as 'silly' rather than 'serious' not only runs counter to current official advice but also shows a lack of awareness of the realities of racism by ignoring the historical and contemporary denigratory treatment and inferences made to various minority ethnic groups.

The secondary teachers' comments are also significant. They evidence a common fear among some teachers that minority ethnic students will use the notion of racism as a weapon to make spurious accusations and deflect criticism: as the quote from the secondary head teacher demonstrates, this is not a perspective solely held by white teachers. This is an important concern and one that anti-racist institutions must work through seriously (see Bhavnani 2001; Bonnett 2000, Gillborn 1995). To automatically deny the possibility that the student has a genuine grievance, however, is not only disrespectful, but also refuses any possibility of engagement and, effectively, rejects the case for anti-racism. It is a position that is untenable in contemporary education. In many ways this kind of rejection trades on an assumption (common among many white people) that 'racism' is crude and obvious, seen in violent attacks or the language of neo-Nazi political parties. However, the thrust of many contemporary critiques (and increasingly a view enshrined in formal equity legislation in Britain) is that racism can actually be much more subtle and even unintended. This is the position underlying the Stephen Lawrence Inquiry Report's definition of 'institutional racism':

The collective failure of an organisation to provide an appropriate and professional service to people because of their colour, culture, or ethnic origin. It can be seen or detected in processes, attitudes and behaviour which amount to discrimination through unwitting prejudice, ignorance, thoughtlessness and racist stereotyping which disadvantage minority ethnic people.

(Macpherson 1999: 28)

This definition is highly relevant to education because research has increasingly revealed numerous ways in which teachers' assumptions (for example, about behaviour, 'ability' and motivation) can operate to the disadvantage of particular minority ethnic groups. Research, in both the US and the UK (and for at least two decades), has shown consistently that when teachers are asked to judge the relative ability, motivation and behaviour of their students, it is likely that Black students, and Black *boys* in particular, will be systematically disadvantaged. For example, recent research examining the experiences of academically successful Black students found that staff in an inner-city school were unable to think about or identify Black boys as successful; instead, they automatically situated them as disinterested in school and likely to fail:

> when they [Black boys] haven't got all that gear on, you know, they're not an individual within a school. When you look at them they are students ... but when you got your hat on and this on, you're individual and it's individual behaviour and sometimes it can be a bit threatening ... you know, like ... what's depicted on the TV about the American sort of influence and stuff. Once they haven't got their Nike on, you know, their anything else, on *they become more receptive students* (Black member of support staff, secondary school).

(Rollock 2006: 111, emphasis added)

This quotation is significant for a number of reasons. First, it reveals the way in which perceptions about certain forms of dress, associated with Black boys, are seen as unquestioningly at odds with a willingness to engage in schooling. Second, it shows one way in which Black boys become positioned as agents of intimidation and fear simply because of their choice of clothing (Rollock 2005). Finally, it challenges the view common among some practitioners that Black staff will automatically be able to engage with and understand the experiences of Black pupils, simply on account of their shared ethnicity (Maylor et al. 2006: 44; Rollock 2006: 127).

Black students are also typically *under*-represented in high-status teaching groups (Hallam 2002; Oakes 1990; Sukhnandan and Lee 1998). In some cases, teachers' differential expectations mean that Black students are placed in lower groups than white counterparts with inferior test scores (Wright 1986). Additionally, Black students are *over*-represented in low-status groups, which artificially lowers their attainment because grouping students according to teachers' expectations creates institutional barriers to success. Lower-ranked groups frequently receive a more limited curriculum, which has a cumulative effect as students move through school (Plewis 1996). A further area of disadvantage relates to differences within the dominant examination itself, the GCSE.

GCSE examinations: denied access and hidden limits on attainment

Most GCSE examinations are now 'tiered', meaning that teachers have to enter students into one of two separate hierarchically ordered question papers for which only a limited range of grades are available. Students can only attain the highest pass grades (A*, A and B) if they are entered in the top tier; but Black students tend to be under-represented in this level (Gillborn and Youdell 2000; Qualifications and Curriculum Authority 2000). The present system of tiering in mathematics includes an additional tier, with the effect that students entered in the lowest tier can only attain a grade D at best, despite the fact that D and below are commonly seen as *failures* in the job market and in competition for places in further and higher education. Research in two London secondary schools found that two thirds of Black students were placed in the lowest of three tiers for mathematics (Gillborn and Youdell 2000). Consequently, in one of the most important core subjects, two in every three Black students had been denied the opportunity of attaining a higher pass grade before they had even seen the question paper. From the summer of 2008 onwards mathematics examinations will adopt the two-tier model: nevertheless, there is evidence to suggest that Black students will continue to be under-represented in the top tier, removing any possibility of attaining the best results – often essential for continued study at advanced level.

To date the largest sample of tiering decisions to be examined by ethnicity was generated as part of a study of *Aiming High*, a government initiative meant to raise the attainments of Black Caribbean students in 30 secondary schools (Tikly et al. 2006). Despite receiving additional resources and other support to help them focus on Black achievement, the schools repeated the pattern of placing disproportionate numbers of Black students in the lowest examination tiers:

> Black Caribbean pupils, were on average less likely to be in the top-set. For example, just 10.5% of Black Caribbean boys and 14.5% of Black Caribbean girls were in the top set compared to 30% of Indian boys and girls, 31% of White girls and 25% of White boys (Tikly et al. 2006: 26).
>
> ... on average 3% of pupils were not entered for GCSE mathematics in 2004 and 2005 and 22% were entered for the Foundation paper. Black Caribbean boys and White/Black Caribbean mixed heritage boys were more likely than

average to be entered for the Foundation paper (37%) and Black Caribbean boys were more likely than average to be not entered (7%) (Tikly et al. 2006: 26–7).

On average over 2004 and 2005, 69% of Black Caribbean boys were entered for the Foundation paper in GCSE English and 5% were not entered for the examination. This compares to an average for all *Aiming High* school pupils of 48% entered for the Foundation paper and 2% not entered for the examination.

(Tikly et al. 2006: 27)

For South Asian students, there is evidence that language needs are frequently misinterpreted, leading to stereotyping and the denial of learning opportunities. There is often a failure to distinguish between *language* needs and *learning* difficulties. This can lead to students with English as an Additional Language (EAL) being defined as having special educational needs (SEN) and then being passed over for subsequent opportunities because of issues related to teacher expectations, curriculum coverage and examination attainment (Cline and Shamsi 2000; Gillborn and Youdell 2000; Hallam and Toutounji 1996; Troyna and Siraj-Blatchford 1993).

Conclusion

The best available evidence – both quantitative and qualitative – shows that race inequities continue to scar the English educational system. Worse still, education policy appears to be actively implicated in the processes that sustain, and in some cases extend, race inequity. Some of the processes can appear subtle; for example, concerning teachers' differential expectations and the cumulative effects of internal selection within schools. But their effects can be gross, including the fact that Black children are disproportionately removed from the mainstream system altogether (via exclusion) and refused the chance even to enter examinations that could offer the highest possible grades.

Following the *Stephen Lawrence Inquiry*, there has been a good deal of policy debate about race and racism but the politicians' rhetoric has not been matched by action. Although the Department for Education lauds occasional special initiatives, the main thrust of education policy continues to promote a colour-blind 'standards' agenda (Gillborn 2005). Despite assurances that all students will benefit from these changes, as we have shown, the lessons of the past suggest that deep-rooted race inequities will not only persist, but will become worse.

Notes

1. There is no such thing as 'race' in the strict biological sense of significantly different sub-species of *homo sapiens*. The groups that are commonly known as 'races' are viewed differently at different time points and between different contemporary societies. However, the idea of race remains a powerful social construct that requires constant interrogation. It is in this sense, sometimes called 'social race', that the term is used in this chapter.

2. Around 16 per cent of white people are aged 65 or over, compared with approximately 3 per cent of Africans, Bangladeshis and Pakistanis. Conversely, it is estimated that 20 per cent of whites are less than 16 years old, compared with 43 per cent of Bangladeshis, 35 per cent of Pakistanis and 32 per cent of Africans (Parekh et al. 2000: 375). It is officially estimated that people of minority ethnic heritage will account for around half the growth in the working-age population between 1999 and 2009 (Cabinet Office 2003: 4).

3. A limited form of devolution within the UK means that although a single British Parliament resides in Westminster, certain powers (including those to determine the curriculum and education regulations) are now held separately in England, Wales, Scotland and Northern Ireland. In this chapter we focus specifically on the situation in England. There are several reasons for this. First, the largest proportion of Britain's minority ethnic population reside in England. There are significant demographic and historical differences between the minority ethnic populations of different parts of the UK and, in a chapter of this length, it makes sense to deal with one country in detail, rather than merely skim across several. Second, and most important, the majority of relevant research has been conducted in English schools. This means that we know a good deal more about how race and racism operate in the English system.

4. Stephen Lawrence, an 18 year old Black college student, was stabbed to death by a group of white youths on a London street in April 1993. Following a prolonged campaign for justice, led by his parents Doreen and Neville Lawrence, in 1997 an official inquiry was launched into the murder and the failed police investigation. The inquiry reported in 1999 (Macpherson 1999).

5. The General Certificate of Secondary Education (GCSE) is the most common examination at the end of compulsory schooling in England. The following grades can be awarded: A*, A, B, C, D, E, F, G, U. With the exception of U (ungraded), all other grades are considered to be 'passes' but grades A*–C are described as 'higher pass grades'. The latter are usually given preference in competition for entry to professional training and higher education.

6. For this reason we prefer to talk of inequities in attainment rather than 'under-achievement'. This has the advantage of accurately describing the situation while avoiding the common misconceptions linked to 'under-achievement' (see Bhattacharyya et al. 2003; Gillborn & Mirza 2000; Wright 1987).

7. In this chapter we use the word 'Black' to refer to those children with family heritages in Africa and/or the Caribbean. There is no universally agreed protocol on the use of such terms but this approach does at least have the advantage of reflecting the preferred self-identification of many of the people so labelled.

8. The government has recently begun to release data broken down by ethnic origin and receipt of Free School Meals (FSM). It should be remembered, however, that FSM is only a crude proxy for social class. Receipt of FSM is an indicator of family poverty but there

are very many working-class children who do not receive FSM. This is important when considering such data because the great variety of experience within different groups could be masked by such a blanket category as 'non-FSM'. It is certainly *not* the case that non-FSM equates to 'middle class' in a sense that would be widely understood.

9. 'Black Other' is a composite group that can be prone to dramatic fluctuations in size from one year to the next.
10. The only exception to this pattern was in 1996/97, when the percentage of Pakistanis excluded was the same (0.18) as the white rate.
11. Quoted in Gillborn & Youdell (2000: 186).

Suggested further readings

Bhavnani, R., Mirza, H. S. and Meetoo, V. (2005) *Tackling the Roots of Racism: Lessons for Success*. Bristol: Policy Press.

Gillborn, D. and Youdell, D. (2000) *Rationing Education: Policy, Practice, Reform and Equity*. Buckingham: Open University Press.

John, G. (2006) *Taking a Stand: Gus John Speaks on Education, Race, Social Action & Civil Unrest 1980–2005*. Manchester: The Gus John Partnership.

Ladson-Billings, G. and Gillborn, D. (eds) (2004) *The RoutledgeFalmer Reader in Multicultural Education*. New York & London: RoutledgeFalmer.

Hooks, B. (1991) *Yearning: Race, Gender and Cultural Politics*. London: Turnabout.

Osler, A. (1997) *Exclusion from School and Racial Equality*. London: Commission for Racial Equality.

Rollock, N. (2007) 'Failure by Any Other Name? Educational policy and the continuing struggle for Black academic success'. *Runnymede Perspectives*. London: Runnymede Trust.

References

BBC News (2006) *Expulsions 'fuelled by prejudice'*. http://news.bbc.co.uk/1/hi/education/6168285.stm (last accessed 10 January 2007).

Bhattacharyya, G., Ison, L. and Blair, M. (2003) *Minority Ethnic Attainment and Participation in Education and Training: The Evidence*. London: Department for Education & Skills.

Bhatti, G. (1999) *Asian Children at Home and at School: An Ethnographic Study*. London: Routledge.

Bhavnani, R. (2001) *Rethinking Interventions in Racism*. Stoke-on-Trent: Trentham.

Bhopal, K., Gundara, J., Jones, C. and Owen, C. (2001) *Working Towards Inclusive Education: Aspects of Good Practice for Gypsy Traveller Children*. DfEE Research Paper 238, London: DfEE.

Blair, M. (2001) *Why Pick on Me? School Exclusion and Black Youth*. Stoke-on-Trent: Trentham.

Bonnett, A. (2000) *Anti-Racism*. London: Routledge.

Cabinet Office (2003) *Ethnic Minorities and the Labour Market: Final Report*. London: The Strategy Unit.

Cline, T. and Shamsi, S. (2000) *Language Needs or Special Needs? The Assessment of Learning Difficulties in Literacy Among Children Learning English as an Additional Language: A Literature Review*. London: DfEE.

Department for Education & Employment (DfEE) (1999) *Ethnic Minority Pupils and Pupils for Whom English is an Additional Language 1996/97*. Statistical Bulletin 3/99. London: DfEE.

Department for Education & Employment (DfEE) (2001a) *Black and Indian Students See Big Improvement in GCSE Results*. Press notice 2001/0033. London: DfEE.

Department for Education & Employment (DfEE) (2001b) *Schools Building on Success: Raising Standards, Promoting Diversity, Achieving Results*, Cm 5050. London: The Stationery Office.

Department for Education & Skills (DfES) (2001) *New Measures Will Tackle Violent Pupils and Parents and Help Promote Good Behaviour: Estelle Morris*, Press notice 2001/0300. London: DfES.

Department for Education & Skills (DfES) (2003a) *Permanent Exclusions from Schools and Exclusion Appeals, England 2001/2002 (provisional)*. SFR 16/2003. London: DfES.

Department for Education & Skills (DfES) (2005a) *London Schools: Rising to the Challenge*. London: Department for Education & Skills.

Department for Education & Skills (DfES) (2005b) *Youth Cohort Study: The Activities and Experiences of 16 Year Olds: England and Wales 2004*. SFR 04/2005 Revised. London: Department for Education & Skills.

Department for Education & Skills (DfES) (2005c) *Permanent and Fixed Period Exclusions from Schools and Exclusion Appeals in England, 2003/04*. London: DfES.

Department for Education & Skills (DfES) (2005d) *Ethnicity and Education: The Evidence on Minority Ethnic Pupils*. Research Topic paper: RTP 01–05. London: Department for Education & Skills.

Department for Education & Skills (DfES) (2006a) *Ethnicity and Education: The Evidence on Minority Ethnic Pupils Aged 5–16*. Research Topic paper: 2006 edition: ref 0208-2006DOM-EN. London: Department for Education & Skills.

Department for Education & Skills (DfES) (2006b) *National Curriculum Assessment, GCSE and Equivalent Attainment and Post-16 Attainment by Pupil Characteristics in England 2005/06*. (Provisional). SFR 46/2006. London: Department for Education & Skills.

Department for Education & Skills (DfES) (2006c) *Permanent and Fixed Period Exclusions from Schools and Exclusion Appeals in England, 2004/05*. London: DfES.

Equalities Review (2006) *The Equalities Review: Interim Report for Consultation*. London, Equalities Review. Available at www.theequalitiesreview.org.uk (last accessed 10 January 2007).

Foster, P., Gomm, R. and Hammersley, M. (1996) *Constructing Educational Inequality: An Assessment of Research on School Processes*. London: Falmer Press.

Gillborn, D. (1995) *Racism and Antiracism in Real Schools: Theory, Policy, Practice*. Buckingham: Open University Press.

Gillborn, D. (1998) 'Exclusions from School: An Overview of the Issues' in Donovan, N. (ed.) *Second Chances: Exclusion from School and Equality of Opportunity*. London: New Policy Institute.

Gillborn, D. (2005) 'Education Policy as an Act of White Supremacy'. *Journal of Education Policy* 20 (4): 485–505.

Gillborn, D. (2006) 'Rethinking White Supremacy: Who Counts in "WhiteWorld"'. *Ethnicities* 6 (3): 318–40.

Gillborn, D. and Gipps, C. (1996) *Recent Research on the Achievements of Ethnic Minority Pupils*. Report for the Office for Standards in Education London: HMSO.

Gillborn, D. and Mirza, H. S. (2000) *Educational Inequality: Mapping Race, Class and Gender – A Synthesis of Research Evidence*. Report #HMI 232. London: Office for Standards in Education.

Gillborn, D. and Youdell, D. (2000) *Rationing Education: Policy, Practice, Reform and Equity*. Buckingham: Open University Press.

Greater London Authority (2003) Delegate Survey, *Towards a Vision of Excellence: London Schools and the Black Child 2002 Conference Report*. London: GLA, pp. 48–51.

Griggs, I. (2006) 'Institutionally Racist'. *Independent on Sunday*, 10 December, pp. 8–11.

Hallam, S. (2002) *Ability Grouping in Schools*. Perspectives on Education Policy, number 13. London: Institute of Education, University of London.

Hallam, S. and Toutounji, I. (1996) *What Do We Know About the Grouping of Pupils by Ability? A Research Review*. London: Institute of Education, University of London.

John, G. (2001) *Implementing 'Schools – Building on Success': Proposals for the Consideration of Estelle Morris, Secretary of State for Education and Skills*. Rawtenstall: JTN Consultancy.

John, G. (2006) *Taking a Stand: Gus John Speaks on Education, Race, Social Action & Civil Unrest 1980–2005*. Manchester: The Gus John Partnership.

Kemp, S. and Gillborn, D. (2000) *Achievement in Southwark: A Qualitative Study*. Presentation at the Southwark Teachers' Centre, London Borough of Southwark, 1 December.

London Borough of Lambeth (no date) *Challenging Racism & Promoting Race Equality: Guidance for Schools*. London, London Borough of Lambeth.

Macpherson, W. (1999) *The Stephen Lawrence Inquiry*. CM 4262-I. London: The Stationery Office.

Maylor, U., Ross, A., Rollock, N. and Williams, K. (2006) *Black Teachers in London*. London: Greater London Authority.

Oakes, J. (1990) *Multiplying Inequalities: The Effects of Race, Social Class, and Tracking on Opportunities to Learn Mathematics and Science*. Santa Monica, CA: The Rand Corporation.

Office for National Statistics (ONS) (2001) *2001 Census*. London: ONS www.ons.gov.uk/census2001

Office for Standards in Education (OFSTED) (1996) *Exclusions from Secondary Schools 1995/6*. London: OFSTED.

Office for Standards in Education (OFSTED) (1999) *Raising the Attainment of Minority Ethnic Pupils*. London: OFSTED.

Office for Standards in Education (OFSTED) (2001) *Improving Attendance and Behaviour in Secondary Schools*. London: OFSTED.

Osler, A. and Morrison, A. (2000) *Inspecting Schools for Race Equality: OFSTED's Strengths and Weaknesses*. Stoke-on-Trent: Trentham.

Osler, A., Watling, R., Busher, H., Cole, T. and White, A. (2001) *Reasons for Exclusion from School*. DfEE Research Brief no 244. London: DfEE.

Parekh, B. (2000) *The Future of Multi-Ethnic Britain*. London: Profile Books.

Parsons, C., Godfrey, R., Annan, G., Cornwall, J., Dussart, M., Hepburn, S., et al. (2004) *Minority Ethnic Exclusions and the Race Relations (Amendment) Act 2000*. Research Report 616. London: Department for Education & Skills.

Phoenix, A. and Owen, C. (2002) 'From Miscegenation to Hybridity: Mixed Relationships and Mixed-Parentage in Profile' in Bernstein, B. and Brannen, J. (eds) *Children, Research & Policy*. London: Taylor & Francis.

Plewis, I. (1996) 'Inequalities and the National Curriculum' in Bernstein, B. and Brannen, J. (eds) *Children, Research and Policy*. London: Taylor & Francis.

Plowden Report (1967) *Children and Their Primary Schools*. London: HMSO.

Qualifications & Curriculum Authority (2000) *Pupil Grouping and Its Relationship with Gender, Ethnicity and Social Class: A Summary of the Research Literature*. Report by QCA Research, May, London: QCA.

Qualifications & Curriculum Authority (2003) *Foundation Stage Profile: Handbook*. London: QCA.

Richardson, B. (ed.) (2005) *Tell It Like It Is: How Our Schools Fail Black Children*. London: Bookmarks.

Richardson, R. and Wood, A. (1999) *Inclusive Schools, Inclusive Society: Race and Identity on the Agenda*. Report produced for Race on the Agenda in partnership with Association of London Government and Save the Children. Stoke-on-Trent: Trentham.

Rollock, N. (2005) 'Dressed to Fail? Black Male Students and Academic Success'. *Runnymede Bulletin*, June (342): 17–18.

Rollock, N. (2006) *Legitimate players? An Ethnographic Study of Academically Successful Lack Pupils in a London Secondary School*. Unpublished PhD Thesis: Institute of Education, University of London.

Rollock, N. (2007a) Black Pupils Still Pay an Ethnic Penalty – Even If They're Rich. *The Guardian*, 4th July. Available at www.guardian.co.uk/commentisfree/2007/jul/04/comment.education (last accessed 12 September 2008).

Rollock, N. (2007b) Failure by Any Other Name? Educational Policy and the Continuing Struggle for Black Academic Success. *Runnymede Perspectives*. London: Runneymede Trust.

Social Exclusion Unit (1998) *Truancy and School Exclusion Report by the Social Exclusion Unit*, Cm 3957. London: SEU.

Stewart, W. (2006) Racism Charge Rejected by NAHT, *Times Educational Supplement*, 15 December, at http://www.tes.co.uk/search/story/?story_id=2320758 (last accessed 21 January 2007).

Sukhnandan, L. and Lee, B. (1998) *Streaming, Setting and Grouping by Ability*. Slough: National Foundation for Educational Research.

Swann, Lord (1985) *Education for All: Final Report of the Committee of Inquiry into the Education of Children from Ethnic Minority Groups*. Cmnd 9453, London: HMSO.

Tikly, L., Caballero, C., Haynes, J. and Hill, J. (2004) *Understanding the Educational Needs of Mixed Heritage Pupils*. Research Report 549. London: Department for Education & Skills.

Tikly, L., Haynes, J., Caballero, C., Hill, J. and Gillborn, D. (2006) *Evaluation of Aiming High: African Caribbean Achievement Project*. Research Report RR801. London: DfES.

Troyna, B. and Siraj-Blatchford, I. (1993) 'Providing Support or Denying Access? The Experiences of Students Designated as "ESL" and "SN" in a Multi-Ethnic Secondary School'. *Educational Review* 45 (1): 3–11.

Wright, C. (1986) 'School Processes – An Ethnographic Study' in Eggleston, J., Dunn, D. and Anjali, M. (eds) *Education for Some: The Educational & Vocational Experiences of 15–18 year old Members of Minority Ethnic Groups*. Stoke-on-Trent: Trentham.

Wright, C. (1987) 'Black Students – White Teachers' in Troyna, B. (ed.) *Racial Inequality in Education*. London: Tavistock.

Wright, C., Weekes, D. and McGlaughlin, A. (2000) *'Race', Class and Gender in Exclusion from School*. London: Falmer.

CHAPTER 8

Media Representations of Diversity: The Power of the Mediated Image

MYRIA GEORGIOU

Introduction

'Asylum seekers eat our donkeys' was the front-page story of the *Daily Star* on 21 August 2003, a story to follow a previous 'revelation' (04 July 2003) by *The Sun* that asylum seekers eat the Queen's swans. Headlines like these have made huge impression and attracted a lot of audiences' attention in the early years of the twenty-first century. These stories appeared while heated debates have been taking place in public political platforms about asylum and migration. Headlines like these, which occasionally still appear in the press, have been the exception in the coverage of ethnicity, migration and asylum; however, the intense interest in such stories and others about 'bogus asylum seekers' and crime and terrorism in the quarters of diasporic and refugee communities has not. According to an ICAR report (2005), asylum is highly newsworthy in the British press, especially for the highest circulation publications. Migration and multiculturalism have also attracted huge media interest, especially in post-9/11 and post-7/7 times. Rarely a day goes by without a story appearing in the national press or in broadcast media about migration policy, multicultural politics, religious diversity or crimes and terrorist threats involving members of migrant and ethnic minority groups. As the most widely consumed media spend a significant amount of space on stories about race, ethnicity, migration and their politics, it becomes apparent that the way media address diversity can be of great significance in the ways the public and politicians think about these issues.

Representing difference in the media in a fair, realistic and coherent manner has never been an easy task and it has raised concerns among academics and activists since the 1970s (cf. Hall, 1977b; Hartmann and Husband, 1974). Representation has two distinct dimensions, both equally important in assessing the role of the media in covering race, ethnicity and diversity. On the one hand, representation relates to employment and the role of ethno-cultural minorities and migrants in media production. On the other hand, representation relates to the media images and narratives, as seen in the pages of the press and on television screens and as heard on airwaves. Both kinds of representation – in production and in content – have consequences for the ways audiences construct perceptions about migration, race and ethnicity. In studying representation, it can be argued that the side of the audience is the most revealing of all. In media consumption we can actually observe how appealing and influential headlines about donkeys and swans or how others promoting understanding and dialogue can be.

This chapter discusses both kinds of representation, focusing primarily on national broadcast media and the popular press – the two most widely consumed kinds of media and arguably the most influential. The discussion also takes into account transnational and diasporic media, which often reveal different editorial values, journalistic practice and ideology about representation of ethno-cultural particularity. This chapter also aims to engage with all three sides of the media process – production, content and consumption – in order to offer a more comprehensive approach to the important question of representation. The focus is on Britain, though transnational dimensions of media and diversity provide the context for discussion. The main part of the chapter consists of four distinct sections. The first section introduces some important theoretical debates on representation. The second focuses on the representation of ethno-cultural minorities in the production of mainstream media. The third section looks at representations of minorities on television screens and the press. The fourth section pays closer attention to migrant and diasporic media, as these are domains of media culture offering alternative representations of difference and cultural particularity vis-à-vis the mainstream. All sections touch upon the relation between media representations of difference and media consumption.

Media representation: research approaches

Data from across Europe shows that for a large majority of citizens, knowledge about different cultural groups is primarily mediated.[1] Information that relates to ethnic and religious groups, locations and experiences beyond one's own and politics and policies of representation are learned through the media; they are filtered and interpreted in discussions around the television set and in public and private domains; alternative viewpoints are searched online and in local and community radio and fished through interpersonal and political networks' propositions. Everyday culture increasingly becomes media culture

(Silverstone, 1994). The position that different groups take in mediation processes – as producers, as consumers, as neither or both – has multiple implications for participation in communication and, to a significant extent, to the wider social and political processes. The struggles around representation take place at times when media are growing in numbers and in influence. From television to the Internet and the mobile phone, media technologies saturate everyday life and surpass space and time restrictions in exchange of information (Rantanen, 2004). Media are diversifying as communication markets grow and become more global (Chalaby, 2005). At the same time, cultures become more transnational and struggles for power, control and distribution of media are less and less bounded within one national geographical territory (Thussu, 2006). Taking that migration, diversity and intercultural dialogue are inherently attached to processes of transnational mobility, media representations are also inevitably transnational. Thus, and while the most widely consumed media are still the national – with terrestrial television channels such as BBC, ITV and Channel 4 still dominating consumption – different media originating from within the nation and other nations or some emerging in transnational spaces challenge singular representations of difference.

Racism and discrimination in the representation of difference in the media has been addressed in relevant literature since the 1970s. Stuart Hall's work (1977a, 1977b, 1981) has been very influential in the debate. Stuart Hall's early work, drawing from Marxist and structuralist thought, emphasised the role of the media in reproducing inequalities in the society. In his very influential work, Hall explains that the media misrepresent social injustice and attribute problems such as crime to the behaviour of specific (ethnic) groups, rather than dealing with it as an outcome of an economically dividing system. For example, in the mid-1970s, media constantly portrayed young black males as street muggers, creating a black menacing stereotype against people who were actually facing racial discrimination by employers and the police (Hall, 1977a). Stuart Hall has repeatedly emphasised one of the key elements of the problem with fair representation: minorities tend to appear in the media primarily as part of 'the immigration problem' and/or as the usual suspects in crime stories; the complex and diverse experience of minorities is not reflected in the media, he argues (1977a, 1981). Hall's work remains a key point of reference for at least two reasons: (i) he has established the central role of media as a 'filtering' system for social and political communication and participation; (ii) he developed an articulate analysis of the ways ethnic and racial identities are interconnected with social processes of exclusion, discrimination, racism and ascriptions (partly in the media) of specific identity models.

Another important early study is that of Hartmann and Husband (1974). In one of the first studies to look at both media production and media consumption, Hartmann and Husband (1974) analysed the relation between media and racism. In both its method and analysis, the study became influential and groundbreaking. In relation to media production, the authors explored the significance of professional responsibility and practice of journalism in the way media portray race. They argue that partly stereotyped and discriminating images derive from journalists' professional values, such as newsworthiness. Turning to journalism values as a problem but also as a possible solution, the authors invite professionals in the media to address questions of fairness, dismiss sensationalism and adopt a positive stand towards race relations. Hartmann and Husband also express important concerns with relevance to the media and to policy-makers. Their arguably prophetic account of media's role in (not) addressing the consequences of racism relates to phenomena currently observed, especially in urban life:

> It seems probable that if the news media do not attempt to make known to white Britain the personal cost of prejudice to the Black British, then black alienation may in the long run breed violence and conflict that is not readily 'manageable'. The news media are spoken of as 'setting the agenda' for the population's concerns. If they fail to include the possible consequences of racism and discrimination on the agenda then they may ultimately destroy the status quo they seek to protect.
>
> (1974: 212)

Hartmann and Husband's study (1974) has also been influential in positioning the discussion at the crossroads of direct experience and mediated ideologies. They argue that the level of actual contact between minorities and white media consumers is important in the way the white majority perceives difference. In particular, they show how responses to specific events in people's lives primarily relate to direct experience, while beliefs largely derive from the media. Media definition of belief systems has two dimensions: 'on one hand people have been kept aware of the hostility and discrimination suffered by coloured immigrants. . . . On the other hand, and simultaneously, people have derived from the media a perception of the coloured population as a threat and a problem' (Hartmann and Husband, 1974: 208).

Many studies within sociology and cultural studies that followed developed further research into inherent institutional racism in the media, stereotyping that emerges because of journalists' own preconceptions and a culture of sensationalism undermining more comprehensive approaches to news that involve minorities. Gordon and Rosenberg (1989), for example, analyse the uncritical connections they see made by a section of the media between crime, anti-social behaviour and minority cultures. As they write, such social problems are often taken out of a social and policy context, resulting in the production of racist representations (especially as regards black people). The importance of such racist representations in the press is enormous, they continue, as media play a key role as opinion-formers among both politicians and citizens.

Empirical studies in the last three decades have advanced research concerned with citizenship, equality/inequality and racism (cf. Downing and Husband, 2005), have also moved away from analysis of media as part of the problem with racism. Most recent research has tended to emphasise the complexity of the media, both as organisations and as players in social, cultural and political affairs; current research tends to look at media not only as systems of control, but also as cultural players contested in the society (Fiske, 1987; Hall, 1997b; Hartley, 1992; Kellner, 1995). The focus of the debate has somehow shifted through empirical studies, which have found out that media don't take a homogenous position towards the representation of diversity. Law et al. (1997) argue that most media present a balanced, and even positive, approach to migration and race issues; only a small minority of the media stereotypes minorities and, even then, this happens only in exceptional cases.

Importantly, all studies – both those critical to the media and those arguing that media are doing a good job in representing difference – confirm one important point: media are interested in stories about migration, asylum and diversity. The interpretation of the reasons for this intense interest varies from being a reflection of an inherently racist culture in the media, to reflecting commercial interests and the tendency of a number of media towards sensationalism.

Media producers

Research on media production and the significance of representation of minority media professionals behind the camera and in the newsroom has been addressed only recently (cf. Campion, 2005; Cottle, 1997; http://www.olmcm.org/). Such research has argued for the significance of fair professional representation of minorities for two reasons: firstly, professionals of ethno-cultural backgrounds have not been given equal opportunities to work in the media; and secondly, participation of all cultural groups in production can have a positive effect in fairer representation on the screen and in the press. Online/More Colour in the Media (http://www.olmcm.org/), the European network of media practitioners, academics and NGOs, has initiated numerous cross-European campaigns, bringing together the two elements of representation and arguing for the central role of employment in better understanding diversity in media coverage. Also, many media organisations realised the effects of limited employment of minority journalists, especially after the events of 7/7.

Major media organisations have recently been concerned with the low levels of Muslim representation among their staff and the effect this fact has on their coverage of the events (e.g. access to specific communities for reporting has been restricted[2]).

Campion's study (2005) of media production and representation of difference has been revealing about the attitudes within the media as regards coverage and representation of minorities. This is probably the most comprehensive account of media production and diversity so far. Campion interviewed more than 100 programme-makers working in different genres across the broadcasting industry to try to understand the barriers to cultural diversity in media output. Her conclusion is that the existing policy, which is based on quotas and targets – that is, a quantitative approach – is ineffective. This approach, she argues, provides a misleading picture of progress and does not address the qualitative elements of exclusion and divides in media production. Additionally, minority media professionals find themselves competing for filling 'the one job' that is supposed to go to minority staff (ibid.). Very often, minority producers said that they find themselves treated not as professionals but as token representatives of groups that media need to 'represent'.

Campion's interviewees expressed several times their disengagement from existing policies. They often noted that the media industry is concerned about meeting numerical targets, but there is very little long-term and in-depth understanding of the complexities of social diversity across Britain and within ethno-cultural minorities. Additionally, an important conclusion that comes out of Campion's project is that the statistical representation given to the public is often misleading, as it often includes non-production staff. The division between the white media producers and the minority staff (e.g. from accountants to cleaners) shows more about the existing and insisting divide in the media than the official singular presentation of numbers.

Representation in media production

Ethnic minorities are under-represented in the British mainstream media, with percentages of minority journalists and executives being minimal on the higher levels of production and management. The Parekh Report on multicultural Britain (2000) revealed a grim picture, with Blacks and Asians being even less represented in the senior decision-making level in the BBC, Channel 4 and ITV in 2000 compared to 1990. The limited representation of minorities in the media is a concern expressed by minority community leaders, national professional bodies such as the National Union of Journalists (NUJ) and lobby organisations for equal representation in the media (e.g. Presswise). Though the

British communication policy has been changing in order to address the new challenges of digitalisation (e.g. diversity of output; abundance of frequencies; entry of new international channels into mainstream platforms), it has for long avoided direct interference in decision-making by media corporations regarding employment. The media sector is dominated by the ideology and the practice of self-regulation and most organisations have their own codes of practice that relate to issues of representation of minorities in the production and the content of the media. Some broadcasting media – especially the BBC, but also Channel 4 – demonstrate high levels of sensitivity when it comes to the representation of minorities; however, employment has remained an area where progress is slow. In the 1990s – which was a time of intense debates around multiculturalism in Britain – Channel 4 had officially established and promoted multicultural programming. These tendencies are now either on the retreat or have taken new forms. Channel 4 has actually abolished its special section for multicultural programming, arguing that the development of special programmes – *minority programmes* – promote more segregation and stereotyping than inclusion and participation. BBC, on the other hand, still sets goals for the fair representation of minorities both on the screen and on the production side. However, the BBC, like most broadcasting organisations, still has not met its own goals for increasing the representation of minorities, especially on editorial and management levels.

As far as print media are concerned, there is still a lot of work to be done in order to establish a fair presence of minorities in production and reporting of news and current affairs. Ironically, the relative invisibility of news people in the press – unlike broadcasting, where image predominates – has not helped the cause of representation of difference in the newsroom. The condition is even grimmer on editorial and managerial levels. Additionally, the fierce competition between newspapers has not allowed any initiative for collaborative efforts within the industry to hold on. Each organisation applies its own rules and only a few of the major media have codes of conduct that promote the employment of ethnic minorities. Though there are now a few journalists of ethno-cultural minority background in the press industry, the numbers are still minimal. Especially when it comes to print media, information about the representation of minorities in production is little and usually only internally available.

Focus on electronic media

In the last few years, and even more intensively, since the establishment of Ofcom,[3] both the British government and the media have promoted self-regulation and initiatives from within the industry vis-à-vis legislation restrictions. It is fair to say that centralised legislation for monitoring the media industry is on the decline while affirmative action is hardly part of the agenda. At the same time, there is a centralised government strategy for supporting action taken by the industry itself. According to relevant legislation (Communications Act), Ofcom has a general duty to have regard to '... the different interests of persons in the different parts of the United Kingdom, of the different ethnic communities within the United Kingdom...' as they consider relevant in the circumstances. More specifically, the Act requires Ofcom's review of Public Service Broadcasting (PSB) to take account of the extent to which PSB services '... include what appears to Ofcom to be a sufficient quantity of programmes that reflect the lives and concerns of different communities and cultural interests and traditions within the UK, and locally in different parts of the UK'. There is a particular requirement for Channel 4 to provide '... a broad range of high quality and diverse programming which ... appeals to the tastes and interests of a culturally diverse society' under the Public Service Remit (Ofcom website, accessed 31 January 2007).

A significant initiative taken by the television industry in 2000, reflecting the best of self-regulation practice, is the establishment of the Cultural Diversity Network (CDN). Presently, all mainstream terrestrial and digital broadcasting organisations (BBC, Sky, Channel 4, five, GMTV, ITN, ITV, PACT and SMG Television) are part of the initiative which aims to promote fairer representation of minorities on the screen and on the production side of the media. One of the tangible tasks taken up by the CDN is the establishment of a database with media producers and members of the creative industry with different ethno-cultural backgrounds (http://www.channel4.com/diversity). Minority media practitioners are invited to submit their data so that the mainstream industry can gain direct access to them (and they can thus gain the, otherwise and often, difficult access to mainstream broadcasting). It still remains to be seen if the CDN will indeed make a significant contribution to the fairer representation of minorities in the mainstream media. So far progress is reported but the network is only beginning to make an impression.

In 2004, the time CDN published the last available report for its activities, certain progress was noted. By 2004, most broadcasting organisations – public and commercial – had established a system of encouraging entry of minorities in the media and a formal portrayal monitoring system of media representations and programmes distribution. The 2004 report notes that drama production has been diversified with a growing representation of minorities. This latest CDN report provides a detailed and largely quantitative analysis of the work done across the media industry. The diversity achievements of the CDN, according to its 2004 report (from the BBC website, accessed 30 January 2007) include a number of initiatives that fall under three categories:

(i) Setting up targets for employment of minorities (e.g. BBC aimed at a 12.5 per cent of all staff and 7 per cent of senior management to be achieved by the end of 2007; ITV aimed for 7 per cent across the whole organisation; Channel 4 aimed at 13 per cent among all staff and 6 per cent among senior staff; SKY has not set specific targets).
(ii) Launching programmes and media with minorities being main characters and main intended audiences (e.g. BBC's first Asian soap *Silver Street* and Asian Network; ITV's *My Life as a Popat*; Channel 4 introduced various debates and documentaries on diversity, as well as entertainment programmes such as *Bollywood Star* and *God is Black*.
(iii) Offering training to minority professionals for increasing their employability in mainstream media (e.g. ITV Yorkshire's training of minority journalists; Channel 4's networking events for minority producers and commissioning editors; ITN's technical training and placements)

The CDN tends to report the present condition and future targets in numbers. However, these figures require critical caution in evaluating their significance. Campion (2006) argues that presented figures give the impression that British ethnic minorities are *over-represented* on television. However, figures about minority reporters and actors are misleading as they often include imported American programmes, which tend to have a higher number of ethnic minority actors.

Broadcasters' targets for on-screen representation of difference have undoubtedly led to a marked increase in the visibility of black and Asian faces on screen. However, as representation of diversity is about reflection of different social and cultural experiences and not just about the colour of actors' skin (Campion, 2005), audiences' dissatisfaction with on-screen representations remains high.

A 2002 report titled *Multicultural Broadcasting: Concepts and Reality*, commissioned by BBC (www.bbc.co.uk/race) confirms Campion's argument. The research shows that there are still significant numbers of people that mistrust the media when it comes to fair representation of minorities in media production and on the screen.[4] Interviewees were asked if it is harder for ethnic minorities professionals to get jobs in the media. Among them, 57 per cent of Asian interviewees and 54 per cent of Black interviewees said that this is the case, while even among white respondents a significant 32 per cent agreed that it is easier for white professionals than minority professionals to become employed in the media.

Media content: stereotyping or reflection of society?

Media content and the representation of race and ethnicity on front pages and on the screen have attracted a lot of attention among media scholars and among activists and audiences consuming such images and narratives. Headlines that point the finger to asylum seekers and minorities as responsible for social problems, crime stories that (re-)produce stereotypes about specific ethnic groups' anti-social behaviour and editorials that predict doomsday scenarios about the end of the national culture under migration pressures are extreme, yet regular occurrences in the popular press. Khiabany and Williamson (2007) refer to an editorial by *The Sun*'s political editor Trevor Kavanagh titled 'Beware the rise of Muslim hardliners' (published 20 February 2006) as an example where the columnist invites his audience to resist threats by a minority culture to 'our way of life'. In a similar tone, an editorial in the non-tabloid *Daily Telegraph*, argued, 'Britain is basically English speaking, Christian and white, and if one starts to think it might become basically Urdu speaking and Muslim and brown one gets frightened' (Greenslade, 2005: 6). Next to these opinion articles, infamous front-page headlines and 'investigative reporting' stories include the already mentioned 'revelations' about donkey- and swan-eating refugees. *The Sun*'s 'Swan Bake: Asylum seekers steal the Queen's birds for barbecues', followed by the paper's revelation 'Now they eat our fish!' and the similar-in-tone *Daily Star*'s 'Asylum Seekers eat our donkeys', as well as the 'political' *Daily Express* front-page story 'Plot to kill Blair: Asylum seekers with high-tech equipment and maps caught half a mile from PM's home' (Greenslade, 2005: 28) are some of the most characteristic examples. Yet, as research reveals, the way media represent race, ethnicity and migration can be complex and not always fitting a 'black and white' (i.e. racist versus fair and democratic) model of representation.

Press

During the last two decades, research on press coverage of ethnicity and race has been extensive. Most research shows that media do not necessarily, singularly or intentionally reproduce stereotypical or discriminating representations of migrant, diasporic and refugee communities, though in some cases – especially in the case of newcomers – coverage is more likely to become hostile (Greenslade, 2005). Law et al. (1997), in their empirical study of press coverage of race and ethnicity, observed that three quarters of the news coverage of diversity issues adopted a broadly anti-racist perspective. At the same time, and increasingly so, it seems that the anti-racist stand of most media does not correspond to coverage on migration and refugee stories; anti-racism dominates stories about established ethnic minorities, but coverage of recent arrivals reveals a visible anti-migrant stand (ibid.).

One of the most recent projects, *Reporting Asylum* (2005) conducted by The Information Centre about Asylum and Refugees in the UK (ICAR), confirmed that most media offer accurate accounts of asylum, especially after the introduction of guidelines by the Press Complaints Commission (PCC). Only one per cent of press articles studied used inaccurate terminology and only rarely media might have breached PCC guidelines. What this report shows, however, is that journalists are preoccupied with a system of 'chaos' in asylum politics and policies. Another more recent research conducted by ICAR for the Mayor of London (2006) shows that local London press is much more balanced and sympathetic to asylum seekers and refugees than the national press (www.icar.org.uk, accessed 02 April 2007). This finding reflects the positive effect of direct contact between media professionals and minorities in representing race and ethnicity beyond preconceptions and stereotypes. An Institute for Public Policy Research (IPPR) study (Greenslade, 2005) confirms that the media sometimes – and historically this has often been the case – tend to be hostile towards newcomers. This study makes a specific mention of the role of columnists, whose writing tends to challenge politics and policies. In writing in a provocative manner, columnists sometimes make generalisations with effect on the way migrants and refugees are portrayed (ibid.).

Overall, the coverage of asylum through the lens of a 'chaotic' condition, which sometimes dehumanises refugees and undermines their traumatic experiences, has caused alarm among organisations engaged in refugee politics (e.g. Refugee Council) and other research and policy-advising bodies. The Refugees, Asylum and the Media (RAM) project and Presswise are two of the most active lobbies, promoting fairer representation of migrants and refugees in the media. These organisations are particularly concerned with the coverage in tabloid press, which is also the most widely read. Forward Maisokwadzo of Presswise said during a speech (2004) that

Over the last ten years, the asylum seeker has entered the tabloid stage as a new stock character with a set role in the daily performance. The fact that the refugee will find it difficult to speak for herself, not least because of the fear that it will affect her asylum claim, means that she can become a screen on to which all manner of evils can be projected, without fear of contradiction. Asylum seeker stories have become a staple of the tabloid diet, with a front page story almost once a week and inside stories almost every day. Among the tabloids, the variation between different titles is minimal: the Mail's viciousness stands out; the Mirror is sometimes more generous. But it is the uniformity of the characterisation that is striking, the lack of dissident voices or opposing viewpoints. Almost without exception, asylum stories feed into the mythology of suspicion and deterrence: they can't be trusted; we need tighter controls.

(http://www.presswise.org.uk/files/uploaded/Forward%20speech.pdf, accessed 20 March 2007)

Apart from the unease caused in the coverage of asylum stories among refugees and the refugee support community, more recently the representations of Muslims, especially in relation to terrorism, has alarmed not only activists and community leaders, but also wide sections of Muslim audiences. Khiabany and Williamson (2007), in a detailed account of the coverage of 'the veil' in *The Sun*, refer to numerous examples where connections between the Muslim female veil and terrorism are made. In a story linking airport security and veil-wearing women, *The Sun* wrote that when a *Sun* Page 3 girl went through the airport disguised and wearing a Muslim veil, she had no difficulty passing through security (9 October 2007; in Khiabany and Williamson, ibid.). A series of stories on veil and airport security were followed by the paper's campaign to enforce a measure so that all women have to uncover their faces when they go through airports. Such recent press preoccupations with Islamist terrorist threats have led campaign organisations, the, then, Commission of Racial Equality and even the Parliament to express concern about representations of Muslim communities as threatening.

Broadcasting

While coverage of issues of migration and race in the popular press tends to grasp public imagination and attract criticism, data shows that coverage of diversity in broadcasting media can also be problematic (Greenslade, 2005); not so much in this case because difference is misrepresented but mostly because it is just not represented. Unlike the intentions and the strategic declarations of the broadcasters' Cultural Diversity Network, the statistics as regards actual representation of minorities on screen still raise concerns. What is actually observed in the industry is a decline in diversity programming, as well as a lesser financial commitment of broadcasting organisations in multicultural projects. According to an Ofcom report, the total volume of multicultural programmes on all main channels, including the BBC's digital services in 2002 was 2.8 hours a week on average, a figure that has gradually reduced – by 21 per cent since 1998. (For the five main channels, 2002 output was 2.0 hours a week – a reduction of 42 per cent since 1998.) Additionally, Ofcom estimates the total spend on such programmes at £5.2 million in 2002, compared with £6.8 million (in 2002 prices) five years previously (www.ofcom.org.uk, accessed 31 January 2007).

On the BBC channels, the total volume amounted to 69 hours (1.3 hours a week) in 2002, a figure which has fluctuated a little over the years but averaged 63 hours (1.2 hours a week) over the period. However, the amount shown by BBC Two reduced from 59 hours a year in 1998 to 28 hours in 2002 (a reduction of 53 per cent) with 39 hours transferring to the BBC's digital channels. BBC Two titles included programmes targeted at Asian viewers, including *Goodness Gracious Me*, *Network East* and *Bombay Blush*. However, there are very few programmes available covering other ethnic minorities, such as the Afro-Caribbean community. Channel 4's output in 2002 totalled 1.4 hours a week, a reduction of 32 per cent, compared with the volume broadcast in 1998. Programme titles included *Trouble at the Mosque*, *Unreported World* and editions within the *Dispatches* series, such as *Halabja* (www.ofcom.org.uk). These examples again focus on the largest groups and become one more indication of the little progress achieved in addressing and including in the media smaller and newer migrant groups (e.g. Eastern European, East Asian).

The decline in actual commitment of the mainstream broadcasting organisations is even more worrying when taking into account the growing diversification of their outputs with the use of digital and satellite technologies (e.g. many new programmes and channels have been established since 2002 on digital platforms and are now available online, on digital and satellite television). The decreasing percentages in funding and output show that most of the mainstream organisations have missed the opportunity – at least so far – to take advantage of technological developments in order to address more diverse audiences and sections of the society. In this case, again, the smaller, newer and less affluent minority groups are the ones with the most limited representation on screen and behind the camera.

In addition to the main terrestrial TV channels, dozens of satellite channels target niche audiences, including diasporic and migrant media consumers. While most of them are part of transnational conglomerates, they target specific audiences. Such cases are ACTV, BEN, OBE and MTV Base, targeting primarily black audiences. Linguistic diversity in media production is also gaining ground fast. For South Asian viewers, commercial transnational media are growing in popularity. Zee, Star, Sony Entertainment TV Asia and B4U (Movies and Music) are the largest ones. Phoenix Television is very popular among East Asian audiences, while Middle Eastern channels are achieving great success, with Al Jazeera being the most well known among dozens of Arabic news and entertainment channels on satellite and digital platforms. All of these media adopt specific perspectives, sometimes have distinct ideological takes and offer unprecedented linguistic diversity. However, it is important to note the inequality within this diverse field. While in the case of some languages and cultures (e.g. South Asian, Middle Eastern), local, national and transnational production is significant, in the case of other regions and groups (e.g. African and Caribbean) production of media is very limited (www.ofcom.org.uk).

Interpreting coverage: what audiences think

While research on production and content reveal a changing and sometimes positive image about the role of the media in representing in a fair manner ethnic, cultural and religious diversity, audiences still express concern over media coverage, raising issues about mistrust in the media and exclusion from the public sphere. The question whether audiences 'see themselves' in mainstream media has not been given satisfactory answers by the industry. However, research shows that either the media still need to do a lot to gain the trust of audience in terms of fair representation of diversity, or they need to communicate in a more coherent manner their initiatives to audiences.

According to the 2002 BBC-commissioned report *Multicultural Broadcasting: Concepts and Reality* (www.bbc.co.uk/race), there is a mixed picture when it comes to audiences' perspective on media and the representation of diversity. For that research, 1,576 people aged 18 and over were interviewed. The interviews were conducted face to face and quotas were used to ensure that at least 500 interviews were conducted with people from white, black and Asian backgrounds. One of the key findings of the survey is that half of the people interviewed believe that Britain is still a racist society. However, similar number of people believe that Britain is more tolerant when it comes to race compared to ten years ago. The overall picture, as it unfolds in this report, shows that there is a sense of progress in race relations and representations of minorities in the society and in the media in particular, but there is still much to be done. As regards representations of diversity and of minorities on the screen, the findings are revealing. Less than half of black and only 42 per cent of Asian interviewees think that there is enough representation of minorities on television. Disapproval of television representations becomes even higher when it comes to drama and soaps. To the question 'Do soaps and dramas accurately reflect the lives of ethnic minorities', 37 per cent of white respondents answered 'yes' and a mere 28 per cent among black respondents and a 35 per cent among Asian respondents agreed. Importantly, the majority of respondents agreed that representation of minorities has improved in the last 10 years with 80 per cent of white interviewees believing so, and 73 per cent of black and 67 per cent of Asian respondents agreeing.

Also an interesting finding is the unevenness of a sense of self-representation among different minority groups. For some minority groups, such as the Cypriots, the Chinese and the Muslims, an intense sense of being invisible or misrepresented in the media was expressed. Other research (cf. After 11 September 2002; Georgiou, 2005, 2006) shows that this sense of unfair representation or invisibility in mainstream media is often the reason minorities turn to ethnic, diasporic and transnational media. Notably, however, this same research explains how minorities who turn to ethnic and diasporic media do *not* switch off the mainstream national and commercial media. Rather, what is increasingly observed in the case of minority audiences' media consumption is the growing diversification of their media use (mainstream and minority media; local, national and transnational), especially in the case of younger generations.

As it becomes apparent, especially among the minority interviewees, there is a large percentage of expressed dissatisfaction with the representation of race and ethnicity in the media. Though the overwhelming majority across various ethnic groups agrees that the representation of minorities in the media has improved, for many members of such groups the sense of exclusion and marginalisation remains.

Diasporic and ethnic media: a challenge to the mainstream

Ethnic and diasporic media have been making important advances in British society. Al Jazeera, one of the most well known cases among transnational media with great success among diasporic Muslim audiences, has raised concerns in the British broadcasting industry and polity. Concerns about competition on the one hand and about the effect of such successful imported media on political and cultural cohesion on the other hand have been widely expressed by media executives and politicians. Britain still retains one of the most liberal frameworks in Europe as regards restrictions and access to diasporic and ethnic media. Consumers can gain access to virtually all media as long as they are available via satellite, digital, analogue and cable technologies. This openness in the legal framework relates to two significant characteristics of media and communications' history in Britain. On the one hand, governments since the 1990s have adopted a liberal economic approach to the field of communications (i.e. advancement of free market values, unrestricted competition, etc.). Such policies, which have intensified in the last two decades, encourage less legislation, more self-regulation and more diversification in the media and communications available to consumers. On the other hand, media and communications policy – like cultural policy overall – reflects the ideology of multiculturalism that recognises ethno-cultural diversity as an important and positive element of Britain. Thus, policy and the state encourage (at least as a rhetoric, though not always as a practice) the development of media projects which reflect societal diversity.

The openness towards communication and media diversity has informed polity's attitude towards minority media. The liberal approach came with limited support of the state to such projects. For example, British minority media have benefited less from subsidies than those in most other European countries. The ones which managed to establish their presence adopt a commercial medium identity. The results of a diversified media terrain in Britain have become most visible after the advent of the Internet and the expansion of satellite services offering limitless choice to audiences. Minority media projects available in the UK – on local media, on internet, on digital radio and television, and of course as seen in the production and consumption of transnational channels on satellite – now have a significant presence. Some of the most successful ones are commercially viable and competitive and have started attracting the attention of mainstream media (e.g. especially some radio and internet media addressing the numerically significant South Asian diaspora in Britain). There are two distinct characteristics of this success worth mentioning:

(i) The successful and long-lived minority media are very few, unlike the many ambitious projects that often emerge. As this sector has not benefited from subsidising and has faced severe constraints because of the state control of radio frequencies until recently, a handful of projects originating in Britain have managed to survive in the long run. These include projects which address large audiences (and thus can gain from advertising revenue), like Sunrise Radio in West London addressing South Asian communities. Small and less affluent communities often have no access to media output in their original language or representation of their group in the production side of the media.

(ii) The existing industry framework is restrictive to local and small initiatives; the dominant market ideologies and forces have privileged transnational media which address minorities in Britain vis-à-vis home-grown initiatives. Successful media, usually based in the country of origin of migrant and diasporic groups, are easy and cheap to access on satellite. In this way, such media have grown to be a regular and everyday reference to the numerous diasporic and ethnic communities in Britain. For some groups, as the recently arrived Eastern European migrants, satellite broadcasts offer the only kind of diasporic media they have access to (with the exception of a few local newspapers).

While liberal values have posed no restrictions to transnational media for the last two decades, after 9/11 and even more so after the 7/7 London bombings, the growing popularity of ideologies of integration has had an effect on diasporic and migrant media. These media have often found themselves under attack.

Though not directly addressed as a sector, the political and security concerns about the role of certain media, and the Internet in particular, in harbouring extremism and fundamentalism, will probably have long-term effects in the way non-minority populations perceive the role of ethnic and diasporic media. At the same time, the suspicion towards alternative cultural references and the victimisation of Muslim minority populations and their religion has created an atmosphere of tension with consequences for media consumption on a national level. As the research project *After September 11: TV News and Transnational Audiences* (2002), among other studies, has shown, mistrust of mainstream media has grown since 9/11, especially among Muslim populations in the UK. The sense of being excluded and stereotyped will probably have irreversible consequences for British mainstream media. Many people interviewed for the above project confirmed that they turn to transnational media in trying to balance their consumption and to get an alternative viewpoint to mainstream British and other dominant Western media. It is worth mentioning, however, that the vast majority of people asked have not stopped using mainstream British media (ibid.).

Political and cultural polarisation after 9/11 and the war in Iraq has scarred the field of media and communications and has raised suspicion regarding representation among both mainstream and minority audiences (especially the latter). At the same time, many of the mainstream programmes addressing issues relating to minorities have started focusing on terrorism and extremism. This shift has only intensified minority audiences' mistrust of the media.

What is rarely observed is collaboration between mainstream and minority media and a sustainable effort for mutual understanding. British media have addressed minority audiences' suspicions by developing their own versions of minority media. Such cases include two very important initiatives taken by BBC and available through its digital platform: the Asian Network (24-hour broadcast with a focus on South Asian cultures) and 1Xtra (a Black urban music digital BBC radio).

Conclusions

The above discussion aimed at illustrating the condition of minority representation in the media. What is most interesting and worth addressing is the complexity of this condition that includes progress in terms of advancement of anti-racist discourse on the one hand and growing stereotyping of Muslim and refugee communities on the other. Though there are strong arguments criticising limitations in terms of policy and media industry initiatives for fair representation in production and on the screen and in the press, the picture is not completely grim. Initiatives like the Cultural Diversity Network have at least a symbolic role in recognising and keeping the issue of representation of diversity on the agenda. However, beyond the rhetoric of recognition, action is much more limited and much less effective. Media producers and journalists feel there is much more that can be done, and this goes beyond numbers and quotas (Campion, 2005). Affirmative action – popular in other European countries – is not even part of the agenda in Britain. At the same time, culturally diverse audiences are increasingly critical of mainstream media and either turn to transnational media or engage with mainstream media from a position of relative mistrust.

At times of cultural and political tension around diversity, both on national and transnational levels, representation and its politics become even more important than in the past. Fair representation on the screen and in the press and adequate representation in the production of probably the most influential cultural institutions of our times – the media – are important issues not only for the specific industry but also for democratic representation in the society as a whole. The public sphere and the contribution of citizens to public debates that take place within it are often mediated – filtered, enabled, restricted – by the media and communication technologies. If the media system is one that actually restricts access and participation of a significant section of the population in the public sphere, then the consequences for democracy can be many and grim (Downing and Husband, 2005). Especially, for culturally diverse societies like those of Western Europe and North America, fair representation of different social and cultural groups is a prerequisite for an inclusive democracy. Based on the above discussion, there are certain directions of the politics of representation we see emerging in the media worth concluding with. These directions are more parallel than mutually exclusive. Firstly, the initiatives observed from within the industry, the polity and the non-governmental sector for fairer representation of minorities are no doubt unprecedented; such pressure will continue making the media more representative of cultural difference. Secondly, the growing diversification of the media, with digitalisation and liberalisation, will 'dilute' the consequences of misrepresentation of difference, as different sections of the audience can turn to various media for consuming kinds of representation more acceptable to them. The diversification of the media terrain, with various media serving different groups, is a likely element of the multi-ethnic public sphere and not necessarily a dividing element of contemporary media cultures (Downing and Husband, 2005). Thirdly, the phenomena of mistrust and alienation, which are recorded across some sections of the audience, as a result of media misrepresentations of minorities, can further mistrust between sections of the society and strain inter-ethnic relations. The hostile attitudes of much of the British popular press towards asylum seekers, for example, have arguably played a role in public expressions of hostility towards this group. These three directions of the mediated politics of representation are shaped at present and will continue being shaped in the near future; they are outcomes of developments in the media industry, technology progress and wider politics and policies on diversity, ethnicity and race. Which of these three directions will become more dominant is still uncertain. As politics and policies for representation of difference are currently shifting within the UK and Europe, the three directions named above will be terrains of negotiation, and even of tension, for the years to come.

Notes

1. Data from the UK, Denmark and Ireland (Georgiou, 2003) shows that for the vast majority of the non-minority populations, familiarity with diasporic and migrant cultures is mediated. In Denmark, 80 per cent of Danes have no interpersonal relation with migrants, while in the UK, two thirds of those asked said that they get their information about Muslims from the media (ibid.).
2. This information has been derived from various discussions I had with BBC producers and managers after the London bombing.
3. Ofcom is the independent legislation organisation responsible for the whole of the electronic communications industry.
4. Findings relating to the representation of minorities in media programmes are discussed in the next section.

Suggested further readings

Downing, J. and Husband, C. (2005) *Representing 'Race': Racisms, Ethnicities and Media*. London, Thousand Oaks, New Delhi: Sage.
Entman, R. M. and Rojecki, A. (2000) *The Black Image in the White Mind: Media and Race in America*. Chicago: University of Chicago Press.
Georgiou, M. (2006) *Diaspora, Identity and the Media: Diasporic Transnationalism and Mediated Spatialities*. Cresskill, NJ: Hampton Press.
Greenslade, R. (2005) *Seeking Scapegoats: The Coverage of Asylum in UK Press*. London: IPPR.

References

After September 11 (2002) *TV News and Transnational Audiences. Research Report*. Available at http://www.afterseptember11.tv/
BBC (2002) *Multicultural Broadcasting: Concepts and Reality* (www.bbc.co.uk/race) (Accessed 05 February 2007).
Campion, M. J. (2005) *Look Who's Talking. Cultural Diversity, Public Service Broadcasting and the National Conversation*. Oxford: Nuffield College.

Campion, M. J. (2006) 'Diversity, or Just Colour by Numbers?' *British Journalism Review* 17 (1): 71–6.

Chalaby, J. (2005) 'Towards an Understanding of Media Transnationalism' in Chalaby, J. (ed.) *Transnational Television Worldwide: Towards a New Media Order*. London: I. B. Tauris.

Cottle, S. (1997) *Television and Ethnic Minorities: Producers' Perspectives*. Aldershot: Avebury.

Downing, J. and Husband, C. (2005) *Representing 'Race': Racisms, Ethnicities and Media*. London, Thousand Oaks, New Delhi: Sage.

Fiske, J. (1987) *Television Culture*. London: Methuen.

Georgiou, M. (2003) *Mapping Diasporic Media Across the EU: Addressing Cultural Exclusion*. Report for the European Commission. Available at http://www.lse.ac.uk/collections/EMTEL/main1.html

Georgiou, M. (2005) 'Mapping Diasporic Media Cultures: A Cultural Approach to Exclusion' in Silverstone, R. (ed.) *From Information to Communication: Media, Technology and Everyday Life in Europe*. London: Ashgate.

Georgiou, M. (2006) *Diaspora, Identity and the Media: Diasporic Transnationalism and Mediated Spatialities*. Cresskill, NJ: Hampton Press.

Gordon, P. and Rosenberg, D. (1989) *Daily Racism: The Press and Black People in Britain*. London: Runnymede Trust.

Greenslade, R. (2005) *Seeking Scapegoats: The Coverage of Asylum in UK Press*. London: IPPR.

Hall, S. (1977a) 'Culture, the Media and the Ideological Effects' in Curran, J., Gurevitch, M. and Woollacott, J. (eds) *Mass Communication and Society*. London: Arnold.

Hall, S. (ed.) (1977b) *Representation: Cultural Representations and Signifying Practices*. London, Thousand Oaks, New Delhi: Sage.

Hall, S. (1981) 'The Whites of their Eyes: Racial Ideologies and the Media' in Bridges, G. and Brunt, R. (eds) *Silver Linings: Some Strategies for the Eighties*. London: Lawrence and Wishart.

Hartley, J. (1992) *Tele-ology: Studies in Television*. London: Routledge.

Hartmann, P. and Husband, C. (1974) *Racism and the Mass Media*. London: Davis-Poynter.

Kellner, D. (1995) *Media Culture*. London and New York: Routledge.

Khiabany, G. and Williamson, M. (2007) 'Veiled Bodies, Naked Racism: Culture, Politics and Race in the British Media'. Paper presented at the International Association for Mass Communication Research Conference, Paris, July 23–25.

Law, I., Svennevig, M. and Morrison, D. (1997) *Privilege and Silence: 'Race' in the British News during the General Election Campaign, Report for the CRE*. Leeds: Leeds University Press.

Maisokwadzo, F. (2004) 'UK Media Coverage of Asylum Seekers and Refugees'. Available at http://www.presswise.org.uk/files/uploaded/Forward%20speech.pdf (accessed 08 April 2007).

Parekh, B. (2000) *The Future of Multi-Ethnic Britain*. London: Runnymede Trust.

Rantanen, T. (2004) *The Media and Globalization*. London, Thousand Oaks, New Delhi: Sage.

Thussu, D. (2006) *International Communications*, 2nd edition. London: Arnold.

Silverstone, R. (1994) *Television and Everyday Life*. London: Routledge.

Smart, K., Grimshaw, R., McDowell, C. and Crosland, B. (2005) *Reporting Asylum: The UK Press and the Effectiveness of PCC Guidelines*. London: ICAR.

Smart, K., Grimshaw, R., Crosland, B. and McDowell, C. (2006) *Reflecting Asylum in London's Communities*. London: ICAR.

CHAPTER 9

Identity and Public Opinion

ANTHONY HEATH, CATHERINE ROTHON AND SUNDAS ALI

Introduction

The aim of this chapter is to explore how, on the one hand, ethnic minorities resident in Britain identify themselves and relate to British society. Do they think of themselves, for example, as being primarily British, as being primarily members of a minority group or as both? Do they share British values? And how, on the other hand, do members of the majority group (that is, people of white British origins) perceive and treat minorities? How widespread is racial and ethnic prejudice? Is it greater against recent migrants, refugees or 'visible' minorities? And what are the implications of the majority's attitudes for minority reactions?

These issues, and the policy responses to them, have been much debated in Britain and more widely throughout Western Europe. Following the immigration into Western Europe over the past half-century, many countries have seen the rise of the so-called 'far-right' political parties pursuing unambiguously racist and exclusionary policies. One of the most notable has been the Front National in France, which won the second highest number of votes (over 16 per cent) in the 2002 Presidential elections, reaching the second round after defeating Lionel Jospin of the Socialist Party. More recently in the 2008 elections in Austria, the two far-right parties together amassed nearly 30 per cent of the vote. In Britain the racist British National Party has never achieved the same success, but has nonetheless gained over 50 council seats, and won just over 5 per cent of the popular vote in the 2008 London Mayoral election.

The Labour government has also become concerned about issues of integrating minorities. The prime minister has repeatedly emphasized the importance of migrants learning 'British values' and we have seen the introduction of citizenship tests and citizenship ceremonies designed to promote integration. Most recently, Lord Goldsmith conducted a review of Citizenship for the Prime

Minister which laid considerable stress on a common bond of citizenship: 'I do not assume that there is a crisis about our sense of shared citizenship. Levels of pride and belonging in the UK are high. However, we are experiencing changes in our society which may have an impact on the bond that we feel we share as citizens' (Goldsmith 2008). His review proposed a range of measures intended to promote a shared sense of belonging and to encourage citizens to participate more in society.

A helpful framework for analysing these issues is provided by Berry (1992), who argues that there are two important issues that individuals and groups confront in culturally diverse societies. The first relates to the maintenance (or development) of one's own cultural identity, where greater or lesser priority can be attached to the retention of one's own cultural identity. The second relates to the nature of relationships with the wider society, and in particular whether it is considered to be of value to maintain (or develop) relationships with the other groups in society. This leads Berry to present a fourfold typology of possible options (which he terms 'acculturation options'), namely assimilation, integration, separation and marginalization (Figure 9.1).

Assimilation is where members of a minority relinquish a distinctive minority cultural identity and merge into the larger society. Berry emphasizes that this can occur through the absorption of a non-dominant group into an established dominant group (cf. Park and Burgess 1921; Gordon 1964) or alternatively by groups merging to form a new hybrid society, as with the concept of the 'melting pot' (the title of a play by Israel Zangwill in 1909). Integration implies the maintenance of some degree of cultural distinctiveness while cooperating with other groups, for example in the economy and civil society. Multiculturalism can perhaps be seen as a contemporary version of the integration strategy.

Berry defines separation as the case where there is maintenance of ethnic identity and traditions but without substantial relations with the dominant group. He sees separation as resulting when this strategy is chosen by the

		Is it considered to be of value to maintain cultural identity and characteristics?	
		Yes	No
Is it considered to be of value to maintain relationships with other groups?	Yes	Integration	Assimilation
	No	Separation/Segregation	Marginalization

Figure 9.1 Four acculturation strategies.
Source: Berry 1992.

minority, segregation when it is imposed by the dominant group. This can be linked to the concept that other writers have developed of a plural or 'pillarized' society with parallel institutional structures (for example, separate schools, separate churches, separate workplaces, separate political parties and so on) of which the classic example was the Netherlands, with separate pillars for Catholics and Protestants (Bagley 1973), and a contemporary version might be Bosnia and Herzegovina, where there are separate pillars for the Bosniak, Croat and Serb communities.

Finally, marginalization occurs where groups lose cultural and psychological contact both with their traditional culture and with the larger society. Marginalization may well occur when indigenous minorities – such as aboriginals in Canada or Australia or Roma in Europe – abandon their traditional communities and ways of life but find that they are persecuted or stigmatized by the dominant majority group. As Berry demonstrates empirically, this last option is likely to be associated with high levels of psychological distress (Berry et al. 1987).

While Berry's typology emphasizes the value orientations of the minority group, his account of which strategy will occur in practice takes account of the values, attitudes and behaviour of the majority group too. Thus assimilation or integration may be possible only if the majority group is open to contact and friendship with members of the minority. Racial prejudice and discrimination may force a minority to adopt the separation strategy. Discrimination in the housing market, for example, may well be a primary cause of geographical segregation of 'visible' minorities.

It is thus crucial to examine the interplay between the value orientations of members of both minority and majority groups. Indeed, one important possibility is that, where a group suffers rejection by the dominant majority, 'reactive ethnicity' or 'oppositional culture' may be the result (Fordham and Ogbu 1986; Ogbu 1978). While the so-called 'melting pot' may occur where majority and minority engage in mutual acculturation, the opposite may emerge where there is mutual rejection. In other words, a threatened minority may develop a distinctive culture substantially different from that of its country of origin. (Andrew Greeley (1999) has shown, for example, how the value orientations or world views of Northern Irish Catholics are substantially different from those of the Southern Irish, and he attributes this in part to a 'defensive ethnicity' on the part of Catholics in the North.)

In the British context, groups of European origin might be expected to follow the assimilation strategy, and Richard Alba has convincingly told a story of the 'twilight of European ethnicity' in the American context (Alba 1985). Some groups of Asian origin such as the Chinese, who have been economically successful while at the same time celebrating traditions such as Chinese New Year, might be expected to adopt predominantly the integration strategy. In contrast, some commentators have suggested that some groups of South Asian origin, perhaps Bangladeshis, who continue to have high rates of geographical segregation, might be following the separation strategy (Bisin et al. 2008). And one might argue that some refugee groups, who have been dispersed around the country away from their fellows and are also denied work, may be forced into marginalization.

We begin therefore by looking at the orientations of the majority group – people of white British origin. We look first at attitudes towards groups from different origins. Are the white British more accepting of voluntary migrants than of refugees? Are they more accepting of European migrants than of visible minorities who typically come from less-developed countries? And how similar are the white British in these respects to the dominant groups in other Western European countries?

Attitudes towards ethnic minorities, refugees and asylum seekers

There are three main theories about why some groups might be more stigmatized than others: the realistic threat (or ethnic competition), symbolic threat and contact theories.

The realistic threat theory essentially postulates that members of the dominant group may feel that certain resources (for example, jobs) belong to them and that when these resources are perceived to be threatened by a minority group, members of the dominant group are likely to react with hostility. Fear that one's job may be taken away by minority-group members who may be willing to work for lower wages may thus be a source of hostility and prejudice towards immigrants or minorities (Blalock 1967; Blumer 1958; Bobo 1999). This suggests that there may be particular hostility towards large-scale immigration, especially from labour migrants.

A second theory is that of symbolic threat. In essence, this is a theory of cultural distance and postulates that groups which are culturally different from the dominant majority – for example, groups of non-Christian religion, wearing non-Western dress or espousing non-Western values (such as arranged marriages) – may experience greater prejudice. These ideas were initially developed in the American context in order to explain prejudice against African Americans: 'Symbolic racism represents a form of resistance to change in the racial status quo based on moral feelings that blacks violate such traditional American values as individualism and self-reliance, the work ethic, obedience and discipline' (Kinder and Sears 1981: 416).

Racial prejudice is usually defined as 'an antipathy based on a faulty and inflexible generalization' (Allport 1954: 9); that is, a negative attitude based on a faulty stereotype about the group in question. Many scholars, including Allport himself, have suggested that contact with the group in question may be an effective way of discovering that the stereotype is actually faulty. Social contact and, in particular, friendship between equals may thus be expected to lead to diminished prejudice while lack of contact will allow stereotypes to continue unchallenged. (For reviews of the contact theory see Hamberger and Hewstone 1997; McLaren 2003.)

There may well be some degree of association between these processes of ethnic competition, symbolic racism and inter-group contact. Thus we may tend to have more contact with culturally similar groups who pose less symbolic threat. Similarly, the greater the realistic threat, the more the groups may establish 'bright' boundaries (to use Alba's evocative term (2005)) and reduce contact. It may thus be quite difficult to disentangle exactly which one of these processes is actually fundamental.

These theories all suggest that there should be least hostility and prejudice towards culturally similar groups, especially when they have entered the country in small numbers and pose little competitive threat, such as members of the Old (that is, white) Commonwealth. There might be more hostility towards culturally more distant groups that have different religious or cultural traditions (for example, Chinese Buddhists). And highest levels of prejudice may be reserved for culturally distant groups who have arrived in large numbers and live in more segregated communities (for example, some South Asian groups).

The British Social Attitudes (BSA) survey asked a highly relevant question in 1996 (although unfortunately it has not been replicated since then). Their respondents were asked as follows:

> Britain controls the numbers of people from abroad that are allowed to settle in this country. Please say, for each of the groups below, whether you think Britain should allow more settlement, less settlement, or about the same amount as now.

> Australians and New Zealanders
> Indians and Pakistanis
> People from European Union countries
> West Indians
> People from Eastern Europe
> People from Hong Kong
> Africans

To be sure, the context has changed quite considerably since 1996. We should also note that at the time the question was asked there was considerable concern about immigration from Hong Kong following the return of the colony to the People's Republic of China. In interpreting the results we must therefore bear in mind the historical context.

Table 9.1 shows rather clearly that on balance the British public tends to favour less rather than more settlement, even for the most culturally similar groups. In every single case, the percentage favouring less settlement is substantially larger than that preferring more settlement. There is, however, least opposition to immigration of Australians and New Zealanders, probably the culturally most similar group, followed at some considerable distance by West Europeans from the EU. Chinese from Hong Kong and East Europeans came next in 1996, although one suspects that hostility towards East Europeans may well have increased following the recent high rates of immigration after these countries' accession to the EU. (As we can see from Table 9.1, East Europeans were a relatively small group in 2001.) The relatively favourable attitude towards the Hong Kong Chinese is quite interesting. This may reflect the relatively small size of the group or perhaps the fact that many of them will have spoken English and in this respect at least will have been culturally similar.

The two black groups (many of whom will have been Christian and will have spoken English) come next and the least favourable attitudes are reserved for Indians and Pakistanis. It is rather unfortunate that the BSA lumped Indians and Pakistanis together but at the time the concerns over Muslims and

Table 9.1 Attitudes towards settlement in Britain of people from different origins

	% preferring less settlement	% preferring about the same/don't know	% preferring more settlement	Size of migrant group in UK in 2001
Australians and NZ	30	61	9	164,320
EU people	41	53	6	880,804
HK Chinese	46	44	10	94,611
East European	48	48	4	43,182
African	52	45	3	476,042
West Indians	52	46	2	254,740
Indian and Pakistani	56	42	2	787,183

Source: columns 1–3 – BSA 1996, self-completion supplement, N = 1989; column 4 – Born Abroad Database: An Immigration Map of Britain, BBC 2001.

their alleged cultural difference had not become nearly as prominent as it did after 9/11.

Somewhat similar results also come from a Guardian/ICM poll of 2001, reported by Saggar and Drean (2001). Most groups of white British tended to approve of white South African asylum seekers coming to live in their neighbourhood and, just as in the 1996 BSA survey, they also approved of Chinese asylum seekers. They disapproved, in contrast, of Romanian, Afghan and Iraqi asylum seekers coming to live in their neighbourhood, and there were mixed responses to Black Africans. This is broadly in line with a cultural distance explanation.

Other questions in the Guardian/ICM poll asked about the different sorts of migrants who should be allowed to enter. There was general approval for the entry of qualified people such as doctors, teachers and nurses who are in short supply in Britain but there was little support for the entry of unskilled migrants or those who could not support themselves financially. This is more in line with the realistic threat theory.

From these two sets of results we cannot unambiguously decide whether cultural dissimilarity and symbolic threat or realistic threat and competition is the key explanation. Probably there is some truth in both.

As well as comparing groups, some studies have compared different types of migrants such as labour migrants, asylum seekers and refugees. Labour migrants, for example, might be expected to pose more of a competitive threat than asylum seekers (who are not allowed to work on arrival in Britain). One might also expect more compassionate responses towards refugees and asylum seekers who have in essence been forced to migrate, whereas labour migrants are typically regarded as voluntary migrants. (In practice, however, these distinctions might not be clear-cut since many labour migrants might be 'pushed' from their countries of origin by unemployment or economic hardship.) A useful source on this was the Eurobarometer 2000, which asked about the acceptance of 'people fleeing from countries where there is serious internal conflict' (refugees) and of 'people suffering from human rights violations in their country, who are seeking political asylum'. The survey also asked about acceptance of Muslims and people from Eastern Europe 'who wish to come and work in the EU' (that is, labour migrants) as well as about citizens of other EU countries who wish to come to settle. This enables us to put the figures for refugees and asylum seekers into some kind of context. Table 9.2 shows the results for Britain (although we must be careful not to make direct comparisons with Table 9.1 because of differences in wording).

Table 9.2 shows that the British public made very little distinction between the different categories. They tended to be the most restrictive towards asylum seekers, and made little distinction between refugees and labour migrants and

Table 9.2 Acceptance of different types of migrants (row percentages)

	Should not be accepted	Should be accepted with restrictions	Should be accepted without restrictions	Don't know
People seeking political asylum	23	55	12	11
People fleeing countries with internal conflict	18	56	15	11
People from Muslim countries who wish to work	17	56	16	11
People coming from Europe who want to work	17	57	16	11
Citizens of other EU countries who wish to settle	14	50	25	12

Source: Eurobarometer 2000, UK only (EUMC 2001). N = 1370 Sample: citizens of the EU aged 15 and over residing in the UK.

were only slightly more favourable to immigrants from the EU. In this respect British public opinion was somewhat different from that in the EU15 (as it then was) as a whole, where opinion tended to be rather more favourable to refugees and asylum seekers than to labour migrants.

Crawley (2005), in her review of this evidence, has emphasized the lack of knowledge among the British public about these distinctions. She points out that the terms 'refugee' and 'asylum seeker' have very different meanings and connotations and yet are often used interchangeably. She concludes:

In a context where terms themselves have become loaded with meaning and significance, it is difficult to ask respondents about their attitudes specifically about asylum issues without evoking responses about immigration of ethnic minorities more generally. Conversely, questions about immigrants or ethnic minorities often elicit responses about asylum issues that may not be of direct relevance to the issues being explored.

(Crawley 2005: 10)

It is, however, rather puzzling that the British public appears not to differentiate clearly between these different concepts whilst the public in other Western European countries does appear to distinguish between them. One possibility is that this lack of knowledge on the part of the public reflects the loose way in which terms are used and arguments constructed in British political and media circles.

Trends in racial prejudice over time

The realistic threat, symbolic threat and contact theories also offer some suggestions about how patterns of prejudice might be expected to change over time. Contact, in particular, might be expected to increase with the passage of time, while symbolic threat might be expected to decline as the immigrant groups gradually acculturate. However, events like 9/11 might be expected to lead to a resurgence of symbolic threat. Working in the opposite direction might be realistic threat, especially in periods (such as the 1990s) when unemployment was increasing and competition in the labour market was becoming more intense.

We have one series of questions on immigration that spans 40 years. The 1964, 1966 and 1979 British Election Studies (BES) and the 2005 BSA survey all asked their (non-minority) respondents a general question on immigration: *Do you think that too many, or not too many, immigrants have been let into the country or not?* An overwhelming majority of respondents during the 1960s, the later part of the 1970s and even almost three decades later in 2005 felt that too many immigrants had been allowed into Britain, continuing at a rate of over 80 per cent with no discernible trend either up or down (Table 9.3).

This is not an ideal question as the wording invites a reflection on the current level of immigration, which has of course been changing over time. Since

Table 9.3 Attitudes towards immigration 1964–2005

Too many immigrants let into GB?

	% saying 'Too many'	% saying 'Not too many'
1964	85	15
1966	86	14
1979	86	14
2005	83	17

BES 1964, 1966 and 1979, Valid N = 680, 686 and 1793. BSA 2005, Valid N = 2013.

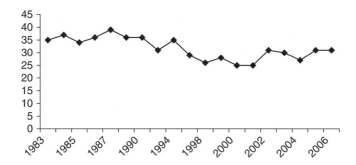

Figure 9.2 Self-reported racial prejudice: percentage who see themselves as 'very prejudiced' or 'a little prejudiced': 1983–2006.

the minority population of Great Britain has steadily increased over this period, one might argue that underlying opposition to immigration must have declined. We could think of it this way: in 1964 when the annual inflow was under 300,000 85% of the population said too many immigrants had been let into Britain. In contrast, in 2005 when the annual inflow was around 500,000 (and when the total foreign-born population was about twice that of 1964), there was no increase in opposition, so in a sense we could say that British people have become somewhat more liberal.

A second time series is also available, although over a shorter time span. The BSA surveys have asked a question on respondents' self-reported level of prejudice more or less annually over the period 1983–2006 (Figure 9.2). Respondents were asked as follows:

> *How would you describe yourself . . . as very prejudiced against people of other races, a little prejudiced, or not prejudiced at all?*

The percentage of respondents who claimed to be prejudiced in any way varies considerably, from a high of 39 per cent in 1987 to a low of 25 per cent in 2000 and 2001. Each year before 1996, the proportion of people who rated themselves as prejudiced lay between 30 and 40 per cent. From 1996 until 2001 the figures were between 25 per cent and 30 per cent, suggesting that there had been some decline in prejudice. However, from 2002 onwards the number of people who see themselves as either 'a little prejudiced' or 'very prejudiced' has been somewhat higher at around 30 per cent although never regaining the levels of the 1980s.

Various explanations for this resurgence in prejudice after 2001 have been explored (McLaren and Johnson 2004; Rothon and Heath 2003). McLaren and

Johnson conclude that 'The best explanation we could find for this change related to the overall increase in numbers of immigrants, which appears to have stimulated a rise in media coverage of immigration, and perhaps more importantly produced an increase in government statements and proclamations on the subject, many of which were quite negative in tone and content' (p. 196).

A concern that has been frequently raised about questions such as these is that they could represent little more than a superficial verbalization of socially approved norms. Some scholars have argued that it has become less tolerable over the past half-century to express openly negative attitudes towards minority ethnic groups. Hence we may not be measuring how respondents actually feel but instead may simply be measuring how people think they should report feeling, especially in the interview situation. What we may have seen is simply a decline since the 1980s in the willingness to express 'blatant' prejudice, but 'subtle' prejudice may be continuing unabated. (For the distinction between blatant and subtle prejudice see Pettigrew and Meertens 1995.) The two time series that we have reported here can be regarded as measures of blatant prejudice, and unfortunately we do not have a time series available to measure subtle prejudice. This issue therefore remains open. On balance, however, we incline to the view that blatant prejudice has declined slightly, probably reflecting increased contact, but it remains widespread and continuing decline cannot be taken for granted.

Britain in comparative perspective

How does Britain compare with the other Western European countries that have also experienced substantial immigration over the last few decades? From the Eurobarometer (and from other cross-national studies such as the European Social Survey) we can see how Britain fares in comparative perspective. The Eurobarometer quoted above makes a number of important distinctions between attitudes towards immigration policy, attitudes towards assimilation or integration policy for those who have been allowed entry, attitudes towards anti-discrimination legislation and the like. Table 9.4 shows the cross-national comparisons for the item on acceptance without restriction of 'people from Muslim countries who wish to work in the EU' together with an item measuring attitudes towards cultural assimilation: 'In order to become fully accepted members of [the] society, people belonging to these minority groups must give up their own culture.' We have presented the results such that higher percentages indicate more positive attitudes (so in column 2 we have presented the percentages for those who disagree with the statement that minorities must give up their own culture).

Table 9.4 Attitudes towards immigration and integration in the EU (Percentages)

	Acceptance of people from Muslim countries	Minorities must give up their own culture	% non-EU immigrants (1995)
Sweden	35	76	4.05
Spain	30	74	0.62
Italy	30	79	3.66
Denmark	27	69	4.02
Finland	21	65	3.12
Portugal	18	55	2.06
Ireland	16	63	2.92
UK	16	60	0.96
France	14	63	0.98
Austria	13	59	1.19
Belgium	12	54	0.64
Netherlands	11	62	3.65
Greece	10	54	6.39
Luxembourg	9	71	5.98
Germany	6	53	1.03
EU15	17	65	

Source: columns 1–2 – Eurobarometer 2000 (EUMC 2001); column 3 – Scheepers et al. 2002.

While there are some quite big discrepancies between countries in their rank-ordering on the two items, the general picture is quite clear with Sweden, Spain, Italy and Denmark being more liberal on both items than the EU 15 average, while Germany, Greece, Austria, Belgium and the Netherlands are below average. Britain is quite close to the average on both items. (For other studies which broadly confirm these patterns see Scheepers et al. 2002; Quillian 1995.)

In general, then, there is some, though far from perfect, correlation between the different dimensions, with countries that are relatively liberal on one tending to be relatively liberal on other dimensions too. A number of scholars have attempted to explain these cross-national variations, focusing in particular on theories of realistic threat and ethnic competition. Quillian (1995), for example, shows that the average degree of prejudice in a Western European country is strongly linked to the relative size of the subordinate group (defined as non-EEC immigrants) in that country, and to the prevailing economic situation of the country as a whole. Thus countries which exhibited the highest level of prejudice were those, such as Germany, France and Belgium, which had (in 1988 when the data used by Quillian were collected) the largest percentage of immigrants from outside Western Europe. Countries which displayed least anti-immigrant prejudice were ones, such as Italy, Greece, Spain and Portugal, which at that time had very little immigration. Scheepers et al. (2002) have reached rather similar conclusions.

However, by focusing on the number of non-European migrants in a country, these studies have tended to conflate the realistic threat and the symbolic threat theories. If the level of anti-immigrant prejudice is really a matter of realistic competition rather than of symbolic threat, then it should not matter whether the immigrants come from within Europe or from outside. However, the British evidence that we reviewed in Table 9.1 suggests that prejudice is likely to be particularly strong against minorities that are perceived to be the most distinct culturally. We would suggest, therefore, that it is too soon to abandon the symbolic threat theory as an explanation for cross-national variation. It is perhaps worth noting that Germany, Austria and Belgium, three of the most anti-immigrant countries, all have very large Muslim minorities.

Relatively little attention has been given to the contact theory as an explanation of cross-national differences, largely because actual rates of contact have not been measured in any of the cross-national survey programmes. There is, however, some instructive comparative work from within Britain, comparing levels of prejudice in different regions of the country. Saggar and Drean (2001) report that tolerance correlates positively with the proportion of ethnic minorities in an area with 75% of people in the North-East feeling that too much is done to help immigrants compared with just 39% of Londoners. London of course has a much higher proportion of minorities and so on the competitive threat theory might have been expected to show higher levels of intolerance. Higher levels of inter-ethnic contact in the London context provide a plausible alternative interpretation of the lower level of prejudice among Londoners.

However, as with so much of the literature in this field, results and interpretations are ambiguous or controversial. Dustmann and Preston (2001), for example, reach the opposite conclusion about the effects of contact on tolerance. They conclude from an analysis of BSA data that areas with higher proportions of minorities exhibit higher levels of intolerance, although they also point out that the much larger American literature has produced very mixed results. However, Dustmann and Preston's conclusion does depend upon the use of econometric techniques that make strong and unverifiable assumptions, and in any event measures of concentration do not necessarily tell us anything about levels of contact.

There are perhaps two key points here. First, most existing studies simply make guesses about levels of contact from the actual numbers present in each area. But of course an area occupied by two polarized communities might have low levels of contact. Second, social psychologists have demonstrated that not all forms of contact will increase tolerance. As we noted earlier, it is only those forms of contact that lead to personal knowledge of the other person that are likely to break down stereotypes. The debate is likely to continue.

Ethnic and religious identities among minority groups

We turn now to consider the identities and values of ethnic minorities in Britain. Following Berry's typology of acculturation strategies that we described earlier, we are particularly interested to explore minorities' orientations both to their own community and to the wider British society. One might expect to find an inverse relationship between the two, with groups that are more strongly oriented towards their own community being less strongly oriented to the wider society. We might also expect to find that groups that have been economically more successful (such as the Chinese or Indians) in the British labour market might be more favourably disposed towards British society, whereas more disadvantaged groups (such as the Pakistanis, Bangladeshis or Black Caribbeans) would be less favourably disposed.

There has in fact been very little research on the orientations of ethnic minorities in Britain, but the most recent (2007) Citizenship Survey (which is sponsored by the Department for Communities and Local Government and contains large ethnic minority 'booster' samples) does include some relevant questions. The survey has asked respondents two questions that tap orientations to the wider society:

How strongly do you belong to Britain?
Do you agree that different ethnic and religious groups should adapt and blend into the larger society?

The survey also asked two questions that tap orientations to one's own ethnic community:

How important is ethnic or racial background to your sense of who you are?
Do you agree that different ethnic and religious groups should maintain their customs and traditions?

Table 9.5 breaks down the responses by the main ethnic groups that the survey distinguishes.

A number of points stand out from Table 9.5. First, the ethnic minorities tend to be much more strongly oriented towards their own ethnic group than is the

Table 9.5 Orientations to Britain and to one's own ethnic group (row percentages)

	Belong strongly to Britain	Strongly agree ethnic groups should adapt	Ethnic background very important	Strongly agree ethnic groups should maintain their customs	Base
White	48	43	33	17	8492
Mixed	44	46	48	27	480
Indian	47	48	53	42	1351
Pakistani	46	40	56	52	810
Bangladeshi	51	31	61	55	291
Caribbean	40	45	70	35	804
African	39	48	66	39	808
Chinese	21	40	43	36	163

Source: Citizenship Survey 2007. The base is for columns 1 and 3. The items reported in columns 2 and 4 were asked of a half sample.

white majority. For example, over 50% of most minorities agree that ethnic or racial background is very important to 'your sense of who you are' compared with only 33% of the white respondents. But, in contrast, there is very little difference between minorities and the majority in their orientations towards the wider society. Thus around 40% of most minorities strongly agree that 'different ethnic and religious groups should adapt and blend into the larger society', a comparable figure to the 43% of whites who agree with the statement. This strongly suggests that the minorities tend to belong in the integration category of Berry's typology rather than in the assimilation or separation categories. To be sure the Bangladeshis have a rather lower percentage who strongly agree that ethnic groups should adapt but the Bangladeshi group has one of the highest levels of belonging to Britain. So the case for thinking that the Bangladeshis favour separation is not at all strong.

Secondly, we do not see any clear inverse correlation between orientations towards one's own community and to the wider society. For example, Indians are one of the minorities most strongly attached to the wider society, but they are also strongly attached to their own community. In contrast, the Chinese have the weakest levels of attachment both to their own community and to the wider society.

This immediately suggests that attachment to the ethnic community and to the wider society are not either/or concepts. Instead it is possible to be attached to both simultaneously. This is shown clearly by a question asked in the Ethnic Minority Election Survey of 1997. Respondents were asked,

Which of these statements on this card best describes how you see yourself?
 [Ethnic group] not British,
 More [ethnic group] than British,
 Equally [ethnic group] and British,
 More British than [ethnic group],
 British not [ethnic group].

Where we have put square brackets, the interviewer gave the name of the respondent's own ethnic group; for example Indian, Pakistani and so on.

This question enables us to distinguish those respondents who feel exclusively British or exclusively ethnic minority from those who have dual identities. As we can see from Table 9.6, the great majority of respondents had dual identities as both British and ethnic, with very few people having an exclusively ethnic identity. The Black Africans had the highest proportions giving an exclusively ethnic identity, but it is worth remembering that the Black Africans have been the most recent of the four groups to arrive in Britain, and other research

Table 9.6 Ethnic and British identities (column percentages)

	Indian	Pakistani	Black Caribbean	Black African
[Ethnic group] not British	6	8	6	22
More [ethnic group]	17	7	19	28
Equally	55	57	61	38
More British	19	16	6	2
British not [ethnic group]	1	10	1	2
Other answers, none, DK	1	2	6	9
Base	*228*	*122*	*142*	*101*

Source: British Election Study 1997, ethnic minority sample. For further details see Heath and Roberts 2008.

(Heath and Roberts 2008) has shown that the length of residence in Britain is (unsurprisingly) strongly related to the acquisition of a British identity.

This question was based on one that has been used for understanding the relationship between English, Welsh, Scottish and British identities and which has also demonstrated the predominance of dual identities. Interestingly, however, the Scots and Welsh showed a higher incidence of exclusively Scottish or Welsh identities than we find in Table 9.6 for ethnic minorities. (See Heath and Roberts 2008.) One way of looking at this is that Britain has long been a multinational or multi-ethnic society composed of separate English, Welsh, Scottish and Irish ethnic groups, who share (to a greater or lesser extent) an overarching British identity. In this respect, ethnic minorities' integration is no different from that of these various white ethnic groups.

The extent to which minorities subscribe to British values has also been much discussed. What actually count as British values is highly debatable, and many of the values that we like to think of as core British values are almost certainly widespread in Western Europe, and probably around the world too. Tony Blair, when prime minister, gave one fairly typical list (although it surprisingly excludes any mention of freedom of speech):

> But when it comes to our essential values – belief in democracy, the rule of law, tolerance, equal treatment for all, respect for this country and its shared heritage – then that is where we come together, it is what we hold in common; it is what gives us the right to call ourselves British. At that point no distinctive culture or religion supersedes our duty to be part of an integrated United Kingdom.
>
> (Blair 2006)

However, it should be noted that a rather similar list appears in the UN Millenium Declaration, adopted by the General Assembly, which listed the values of 'freedom', 'equality', 'solidarity', 'tolerance', 'respect for nature' and 'shared responsibility' (although not democracy). These were signed by more than 150 states, including some of the most repressive regimes in the world.

The Citizenship Survey has included some questions that more or less tap Blair's list of British values. Respondents were asked,

> *Which of these things, if any, would you say are the most important values for living in Britain. Please choose up to five.*

There then followed a list of 16 values, which included among others

> *Tolerance and politeness towards others*
> *Respect for the law*

> *Everyone should vote*
> *Equality of opportunity*
> *Justice and fair play*
> *Pride in country/patriotism*

We can roughly equate these with the British values in Blair's list although pride in Britain, which is the nearest we can get from the list in the survey to Blair's 'respect for this country', is not really the same as respect for Britain. Pride is essentially an affective or emotional concept, whereas respect has rather different connotations. We should also note that respondents are being asked to pick out the ones that they deem to be the five most important values. So it could be that a particular value is not mentioned because some other value, such as 'respect for all faiths' (which Blair did not pick out as a British value), is given higher priority.

Table 9.7 suggests that minorities very largely share these five British values, or at least are more or less as likely to mention them as important as are members of the white majority population. Indeed minorities are more likely than the white British to subscribe to the value of equality of opportunity (perhaps because they do not feel that they are actually being offered equality of opportunity by British society). None of the minority groups is significantly

Table 9.7 Adherence to British values (% mentioning the value as important)

	Duty to vote	Respect for the law	Tolerance and politeness towards others	Equality of opportunity	Patriotism	*Base*
White	13*	58	57*	35*	24*	*8504*
Mixed	13	48*	54	51*	12*	*483*
Indian	18*	58	50*	51*	11*	*1388*
Pakistani	15	61	51*	43	8*	*807*
Bangladeshi	23*	63	46*	41	5*	*286*
Caribbean	13	54*	57	51*	10*	*799*
African	15	63*	51*	51*	8*	*810*
Chinese	13	58	50	52*	7*	*165*
All	14	58	55	40	19	

Source: Citizenship Survey 2007. * indicates that the cell percentage is significantly different from the figure for 'all' in the bottom row of the table.

less likely than the majority group to mention the duty to vote (and two are significantly more likely to mention it); only Caribbeans and the mixed group are less likely to mention respect for the law; several groups are less likely to mention tolerance and politeness towards others, but in general high proportions of all groups alike mention this as important and the differences are substantively small. On the other hand, there are markedly lower levels of patriotism; even the majority group are rather unlikely to mention this as one of their top five values. (It should also be noted that patriotism is strongly related to age, and the minorities tend to have younger age profiles than the majority group.)

Furthermore, as with our previous measures, there is no sign here that any particular minority is especially alienated from British society. There is no particular minority that is consistently and significantly lower than the others in their support for British values. The differences between ethnic groups tend to be rather small, and the central story is really how similar all the minorities are to the white British majority group in their support for these values.

Overall, then, this is a rather optimistic picture. However, there are two important caveats. Firstly, we must remember that this evidence is all based on survey research, and it is quite possible that alienated individuals will be unlikely to respond to surveys. There may well therefore be some individuals (from the white group as well as from the minorities) who do not share British values or identities. The survey research therefore probably paints a somewhat over-optimistic picture. The optimistic picture almost certainly holds for the 'average' man or woman within each minority, but we cannot rule out the possibility that small subgroups of alienated individuals who perhaps support separation or indeed terrorism have simply not responded to the surveys.

Secondly, the survey evidence also suggests some worrying features among those who did respond to the survey. Thus Maxwell's analysis of the Citizenship Survey, while it confirmed that Muslims and South Asians are almost as likely as the majority group to identify themselves as British, also showed that perceived discrimination substantially reduced the likelihood of feeling strongly British. He concludes:

... arguments about alienated Muslims and South Asians are exaggerated .... While it is true that Muslims and South Asians face a variety of difficulties in Britain based on low economic resources and spatial segregation into ghettos, it is important to understand the complex ways in which Muslims and South Asians experience these environments. Specifically, discrimination is more harmful than simple socio-economic difficulties for British identification.

(Maxwell 2006: 749)

Since, as we have shown earlier, there is widespread prejudice within British society, there is a real risk for minorities that they will experience discrimination.

Conclusions

On the one hand, we have found widespread prejudice among the white majority population, especially against less-skilled migrants from culturally different societies. Britain is not perhaps any worse in this respect than some other European countries, and Britain is perhaps getting slightly less racist over time, especially among younger generations. However, Britain should not be complacent and the evidence from the Nordic countries suggests that considerable improvement is feasible.

On the other hand, despite their experiences of hostility and discrimination, minorities exhibit high levels of attachment to Britain and have adopted dual identities as members of both British society and their minority group. Most groups are clearly following the 'integration strategy' (to use Berry's terminology) of maintaining a strong and positive relationship both to their own ethnic community and to the wider British society. This may reflect the fact that minorities have been largely voluntary migrants who chose to come to Britain and who started from a position of being well disposed. There is little or no evidence that any of the main minorities on which we have data either have followed the separation strategy or have been forced into marginalization.

However, it is crucial that Britain offers minorities the equality of opportunity that, like other liberal Western societies, Britain professes. This is surely appropriate simply from an ethical point of view. While ethical arguments rarely cut much ice with governments, self-interest should also encourage more serious attempts to ensure genuine equality of opportunity. There is clear evidence that experiences of discrimination undermine attachment to British society and that they increase alienation and reduce trust. The lesson, from Northern Ireland, that entrenched discrimination in the long run leads to social disorder needs to be learned.

Unfortunately, the evidence is that equality of opportunity is not actually realized in Britain, with minorities continuing to have unemployment rates double those of comparably qualified white British peers and experiencing substantial 'ethnic penalties' (see, for example, Heath and Li 2008). Successive governments have fought shy of introducing more robust measures to promote equality of opportunity, such as the American affirmative action programme, almost certainly because of worries about the kind of white backlash against affirmative action measures that has been seen in the US. (However, we should acknowledge that the government's new Equality Bill does propose 'to extend positive action so that employers can take into account, when selecting between two equally qualified candidates, under-representation of disadvantaged groups, for example women and people from ethnic minority communities'.)

While the evidence of ethnic minority commitment to Britain that we have offered suggests that there is no large-scale crisis of British identity as yet, it is also important to recognize that some young men from minority backgrounds, especially the second generation of Caribbean heritage, are more likely to feel alienated, possibly because of their experiences of discrimination in the labour market or from the police and the courts (Heath and Roberts 2008). This might also be true of young Muslim men who feel attracted to extremism. The best recipe for avoiding alienation or hostility is almost certainly to ensure that members of all minority groups are able to compete for good education, good jobs and decent houses on equal terms with their white peers.

Suggested further readings

Crawley, H. (2005) 'Evidence on Attitudes to Asylum and Immigration: What We Know, Don't Know and Need to Know'. Working paper No 23, Centre on Migration, Policy and Society (COMPAS), Oxford.

McLaren, L. (2003) 'Anti-Immigrant Prejudice in Europe: Contact, Threat Perception and Preferences for the Exclusion of Migrants'. *Social Forces* 81: 909–36.

McLaren, L. and Johnson, M. (2004) 'Understanding the Rising Tide of Anti-Immigrant Sentiment', in Park, A., Curtis, J., Bromley, C. and Phillips, M. (eds) *British Social Attitudes. The 21st Report*. London: Sage.

Rothon, C. and Heath, A. F. (2003) 'Trends in Racial Prejudice' in Park, A., Curtice, J., Thomson, K., Bromley, C. and Phillips, M. (eds) *British Social Attitudes, the 20th Report: Continuity and Change Over Two Decades*. London: Sage, pp. 189–213.

Saggar, S. and Drean, J. (2001) *British Public Attitudes and Ethnic Minorities*. Performance and Innovation Unit, Cabinet Office, London.

References

Alba, R. (1985) 'The Twilight of Ethnicity Among Americans of European Ancestry: The Case of Italians'. *Ethnic and Racial Studies* 8: 134–58.

Alba, R. (2005) 'Bright Versus Blurred Boundaries: Second-Generation Assimilation and Exclusion in France, Germany and the United States'. *Ethnic and Racial Studies* 28: 20–49.

Allport, G. W. (1954) *The Nature of Prejudice*. New York: Addison-Wesley.

Bagley, C. (1973) *The Dutch Plural Society: A Comparative Study of Race Relations*. London: Oxford University Press.

Berry, J. W. (1992) 'Acculturation and Adaptation in a New Society'. *International Migration* 30: 69–85.

Berry, J. W., Kim, U., Minde, T. and Mok, D. (1987) 'Comparative Studies of Acculturative Stress'. *International Migration Review* 21: 491–511.

Bisin, A., Patacchini, E., Verdier, T. and Zenou, Y. (2008) 'Are Muslim Immigrants Different in Terms of Cultural Integration?' *Journal of the European Economic Association* 6: 445–56.

Blair, T. (2006) 'The Duty to Integrate: Shared British Values'. Speech on multiculturalism and integration, 8 December 2006. www.number10.gov.uk/page10563

Blalock, H. M. (1967) *Toward a Theory of Minority-group Relations*. New York: Wiley.

Blumer, H. (1958) 'Race Prejudice as a Sense of Group Position'. *Pacific Sociology Review* 1: 3–7.

Bobo, L. (1999) 'Prejudice as Group Position: Micro-Foundations of a Sociological Approach to Racism and Race Relations'. *Journal of Social Issues* 55 (3): 445–72.

Crawley, H. (2005) 'Evidence on Attitudes to Asylum and Immigration: What We Know, Don't Know and Need to Know'. Working paper No 23, Centre on Migration, Policy and Society (COMPAS), Oxford.

Dustmann, C. and Preston, I. (2001) 'Attitudes to Ethnic Minorities, Ethnic Context and Location Decisions'. *The Economic Journal* 111: 353–73.

Fordham, S. and Ogbu, J. U. (1986) 'Black Students' School Success: Coping with the Burden of "Acting White" '. *The Urban Review* 18 (3): 176–206.

Goldsmith, Lord (2008) *Citizenship: Our Common Bond*. www.justice.gov.uk/docs/citizenship-report-full.pdf

Gordon, M. M. (1964) *Assimilation in American Life: The Role of Race, Religion, and National Origins*. New York: Oxford University Press.

Greeley, A. (1999) 'The Religions of Ireland' in Heath, A. F., Breen, R. and Whelan, C. T. (eds), *Ireland, North and South: Perspectives from Social Science*, Proceedings of the British Academy 98. Oxford: Oxford University Press, pp. 141–60.

Hamberger, J. and Hewstone, M. (1997) 'Inter-Ethnic Contact as a Predictor of Blatant and Subtle Prejudice: Tests of a Model in Four West European Nations'. *British Journal of Social Psychology* 36: 173–90.

Heath, A. F. and Li, Y. (2008) 'Period, Life-Cycle and Generational Effects on Ethnic Minority Success in the British Labour Market'. *Kolner Zeitschrift fur Soziologie und Sozialpsychologie*, 48: 277–306.

Heath, A. F. and Roberts, J. (2008) *British Identity: Its Sources and Possible Implications for Civic Attitudes and Behaviour*. Research report for Lord Goldsmith's Citizenship Review. http://www.justice.gov.uk/docs/british-identity.pdf

Kinder, D. R. and Sears, D. O. (1981) 'Prejudice and Politics: Symbolic Racism Versus Racial Threats to the Good Life'. *Journal of Personality and Social Psychology* 40: 414–31.

Maxwell, R. (2006) 'Muslims, South Asians and the British Mainstream: A National Identity Crisis?' *West European Politics* 29: 736–56.

McLaren, L. (2003) 'Anti-Immigrant Prejudice in Europe: Contact, Threat Perception and Preferences for the Exclusion of Migrants'. *Social Forces* 81: 909–36.

McLaren, L. and Johnson, M. (2004) 'Understanding the Rising Tide of Anti-Immigrant Sentiment' in Park, A., Curtice, J., Bromley, C. and Phillips, M. (eds) *British Social Attitudes. The 21st Report*. London: Sage.

Ogbu, J. U. (1978) *Minority Education and Caste: The American System in Cross-cultural Perspective*. New York: Academic Press.

Park, R. E. and Burgess, E. W. (1921) *Introduction to the Science of Sociology*. Chicago: University of Chicago Press.

Pettigrew, T. F. and Meertens, R. W. (1995) 'Subtle and Blatant Prejudice in Western Europe'. *European Journal of Social Psychology* 25: 57–76.

Quillian, L. (1995) 'Prejudice as a Response to Perceived Group Threat: Population Composition and Anti-Immigrant and Racial Prejudice in Europe'. *American Sociological Review* 60: 586–612.

Rothon, C. and Heath, A. F. (2003) 'Trends in Racial Prejudice' in Park, A., Curtice, J., Thomson, K., Bromley, C. and Phillips, M. (eds) *British Social Attitudes, the 20th Report: Continuity and Change Over Two Decades*. London: Sage, pp. 189–213.

Saggar, S. and Drean, J. (2001) *British Public Attitudes and Ethnic Minorities*. Performance and Innovation Unit, Cabinet Office. London.

Scheepers, P., Gijsberts, M. and Coenders, M. (2002) 'Ethnic Exclusionism in European Countries: Public Opposition to Civil Rights for Legal Migrants as a Response to Perceived Ethnic Threat'. *European Sociological Review* 18: 17–34.

Zangwill, I. (1909) *The Melting Pot*, The Comedy Theatre, Washington, DC: Liebler & Co.

CHAPTER 10

Race and Ethnicity in Britain: Into the 21st Century

ALICE BLOCH AND JOHN SOLOMOS

This book has constructed an account of the changing patterns of ethnic and racial inequalities and relations at the beginning of the 21st century. It has focused on the analysis of the key facets of contemporary race and ethnic relations. Each chapter has provided an overview of the substantive areas that we have sought to cover in this book, as well as engaging with the most up-to-date empirical research. Taken together, they make up an overview of the changing dynamics of race and ethnic relations in the current environment, including debates about what kinds of policies we need in order to tackle forms of inequality and discrimination.

By way of conclusion we want to bring this book to a close by exploring the changing social and policy context of race and ethnic relations in contemporary British society. We shall return to some of the main themes that emerged in the preceding chapters, but they will be examined alongside the ways in which they impact on and affect changing research agendas in the areas of race and ethnicity. The chapter will then move on explore the key issues that are likely to shape questions of race and ethnicity in this early part of the 21st century. Our main concern throughout this chapter will be to suggest ways in which we can begin the process of thinking critically about the questions and issues that are likely to confront societies such as Britain over the coming period.

Migration, sociology and policy

At the beginning of the 20th century the black American scholar and activist W. E. B. Du Bois argued that it was likely to be the century of 'colour line'. As we stand at the beginning of the 21st century it is also clear that Du Bois was in many ways perceptive in his prediction. Yet it is also important to broaden our field of vision somewhat and see that the 20th century was a very important century not only in terms of the 'colour line' but in relation to immigration, diversity, immigration legislation, race relations, social change and social policy. In practice it was the combination of all of these processes that helped to shape the key social and political questions around the issues of race and ethnicity in the past century as well as the current one.

Let us, by way of example, take the question of migration and its role during the 20th century. Broadly speaking, the 20th century saw three main phases of migration and migration control. In the case of Britain the first phase, up until 1914, reflected the arrival and settlement of Jewish migrants from Eastern Europe who had escaped pogroms from the late 19th century. By 1914 the Jewish population had reached around 300,000 and this had led to legislative measures beginning in 1905 with the Aliens Act, which set limits on the numbers of immigrants who could enter Britain and deportations increased (Solomos 2003). The second period, from 1962 through to 1988, was in response to not only the post-war migration from Commonwealth countries but also the arrival of South Asian refugees from East Africa. Legislation was concerned with curtailing migration from Commonwealth countries and brought to an end virtually all primary migration from the Caribbean and South Asia. The third phase, at the end of the 20th century and the start of the 21st century focused on the control of asylum seekers. Previous legislation had closed nearly all available routes for entering the UK as a new migrant, with family reunion and asylum being the two main ways of entering the UK. Conflict, political oppression, discrimination and abuses of human rights have all resulted in migration and increasing numbers of refugees and asylum seekers arriving in Britain and elsewhere. In response to increasing numbers of asylum seekers, legislative responses have tried to control the numbers of asylum seekers entering Britain as well as to exclude and marginalise them from social and economic life through dispersal, exclusion from 'mainstream' welfare provision and exclusion from the regular labour market.

Why people migrate, who actually moves and migrant destinations are important questions that concern sociologists and policy makers, not least because the characteristics and patterns of international migration and international migrants affect both the sending societies (countries of origin) and the receiving societies (countries of destination). Migration impacts on a range of processes, including economies, development, politics, culture, community, family and household relations. Migration is high on the international policy agenda due to the increasing Scale of international migration as well as the challenges and opportunities that this can present (Global Commission on International Migration 2005). The precise numbers of international migrants is unknown but in 1990 there were 80 million migrants and this had increased to 175 million, or 2.9 per cent of the global population, by 2000. Of these global migrants, just under 10 per cent (9.5 per cent) are refugees (International Organisation for Migration 2005).

Globalisation, global inequality, conflicts, oppression and technological advances in transportation, media and communications will ensure that global migration will continue and that migrants will hold multiple identities as well as obligations to kinship groups in their country of origin and elsewhere. Migration has resulted in the formation of new migrant communities. In the case of the UK, numbers within established migrant groups from the Caribbean, India, Pakistan and Bangladesh have increased, mainly due to internal natural growth rather than new migration. At the time of the 1991 Census, 5.5 per cent described themselves as coming from an ethnic group other than white, increasing to 7.9 per cent of the population by the 2001 Census. Britain has also seen an increase in new migrants and the formation of new migrant groups from countries without prior links to the UK. This has included refugees and asylum seekers from all over the world as well as migrant workers with both regular and irregular immigration statuses. The arrival of new migrants from diverse countries of origin has, Vertovec argues, resulted in the emergence of 'super-diversity' and the need to reconsider both social science research and social policy in light of this diversity, which also extends to residential locality and legal status in Britain (Vertovec 2006: 4).

This book has been concerned mostly with the experiences of migrants in the UK though some chapters also compare the UK with other migrant-receiving countries. Chapters in this book have mostly explored the position of established migrant groups who came to the UK from the 1940s onwards, often as a result of the demands of the UK economy but facilitated through the pre-existing links of imperial – colonial ties and then chain migration as a consequence of family and social networks. Attention has also been given to new communities, especially refugees and asylum seekers who come from all over the world and in some cases arrive without any pre-established links or relations in the UK. While multicultural policies have attempted to promote tolerance, equality and respect for Commonwealth migrants, more recently the agenda has shifted to an exploration of forms of segregation and what some commentators see as a crisis in community cohesion (McGhee 2009). It is to these issues that we now turn.

New directions and issues

Responses to migrants have changed in some ways but have remained worryingly consistent in other ways. Anti-immigration discourse, racism and discrimination and the underlying presence of far-right racist political activity have been a feature throughout the 20th century with governments responding in different ways. Anti-racism, race relations legislation, multiculturalism and integration have all been responses to a diverse society and the inequality within it. However, recent global and national events seem to have changed the agenda at the start of the 21st century. Of particular impact has been 9/11 and 7/7 as well as the disorders in English towns in 2001, all of which affected views and fears of Muslim terror activities as well as perceptions and responses to Muslim minorities, especially those perceived to be or actually living in ethnic enclaves.

In the UK the London bombings on 7 July 2005 by young British Muslim men, on top of the 2001 disorders in towns such as Oldham and Bradford with large Asian and Muslim populations, have created not only a whole new Islamophobic discourse but also a new agenda on community cohesion. Alexander notes that popular/media responses to the disturbances emphasised either structural inequalities or cultural differences, observing that 'the riots are constructed as being about recalcitrant foreign cultures and failed integration as much about social exclusion and discrimination' (Alexander 2004: 530). Alexander observes that multiculturalism has become part of the problem rather than, as it was in the 1980s, considered to be part of the solution. The responses to the disorders have combined two strands of policy: community cohesion and citizenship and criminalisation and containment. Certainly the impact of the latter – criminalisation and containment – is explored by McLaughlin (Chapter 5), who examines the ways in which global, national and local events have influenced the way in which policing is carried out and the operation of the criminal justice system. The focus is very much on youth and gender with young men pathologised as criminals.

The disorders in 2001 resulted in as number of reports including the Ouseley Report on Bradford (Ouseley 2001) and the Cantle Report on Oldham, Burnley and Bradford (Cantle 2001), with both alluding to cultural differences and self-segregation as key factors triggering the riots due to the social marginalisation resulting from these conditions (Alexander 2004). Cantle's independent report noted, 'communities leading parallel lives delineated by high levels of segregation in housing and schools, reinforced by differences in language, culture and religion' (Cantle 2001: 4). A report by Denham observed, first, that while self-segregation is understandable and has been a pattern that successive migrant groups have maintained, the contemporary concern of this segregation emerges from a lack of opportunity for different groups to meet and work together; secondly, that it might reflect fear of racist attacks or racism; and thirdly, that it might result in little choice over education, housing and jobs (Denham 2001: 11–2).

While recent legislation has been concerned mostly with asylum seekers and curtailing their welfare and other entitlements, the most recent proposed legislation, the Immigration and Citizenship Bill, seeks to simplify immigration law by replacing existing legislation and statutory instruments and consolidating them into one Act. Moreover, the proposed legislation includes the new pathway to citizenship where, 'newcomers **earn the right to stay** by learning English, paying taxes and obeying the law' (Home Office 2008: 3). 'Citizenship will also be slowed down for those who don't make an effort to integrate' (Home Office 2008: 3). Thus, English, Welsh or Gaelic language skills, good character, employment and knowledge about Britain will all be considered as an element of citizenship entitlement (Home Office 2008). The Bill also includes provisions relating to entry into the UK, the expulsion and exclusion of migrants, detention, the prevention of irregular work, regulation of who has permission to stay and naturalisation. The emphasis is placed on migrants earning their right to be in the UK and demonstrating that they are socially and economically integrating and contributing.

While the direction of policy is on citizenship, integration, and social and community cohesion, people are differentiated by citizenship, immigration status and immigration controls as well as geographical, social and economic marginalisation. Citizenship and the hierarchy of rights associated with different statuses is an area that concerns sociologists not only because of its impact on everyday social, political, civil and economic life but also because of the impact of 'stratified rights' on marginalised groups, especially asylum seekers and undocumented migrants. Morris notes that if you deny rights to some groups, you risk 'driving the most marginal into an underground existence' (Morris 2002: 52). While the government has an integrationist agenda, in reality the most marginalised are excluded from this policy and for asylum seekers who might be granted refugee status this can have a negative long-term impact on settlement.

Policies towards asylum seekers and refugees have developed incrementally though the concern for integration has emerged most in the last decade. As with the Immigration and Citizenship Bill, the emphasis on integration is on the individual's capacity and social networks. According to the Home Office, integration takes place when refugees achieve their full potential as members of British society, contribute to the community and access the services to which they are entitled. In terms of achieving full potential, the Home Office identifies two factors as being crucial: 'the ability to communicate effectively in English and gaining employment appropriate to their skills and ability' (Home Office 2005: 20). The government is also concerned that there is social cohesion and integration among new communities in their areas of residence. There is a contention, however, between the immigration regulations faced by newer migrants which impede integration and the government agenda which favours integration. For example, refugees are no longer entitled to stay permanently in the UK but have their cases reviewed, which will affect longer-term integration strategies and motivations among refugees while at the same time the government expects people to integrate and demonstrate this in order to be granted citizenship.

While it appears that different agendas are present for differing cohorts of migrants, in reality the government wants to manage migration through visas and refugee resettlement programmes and for those entitled to stay in the UK, including British citizens from minority ethnic backgrounds, there is a concern around what is seen as a lack of cohesion among some groups. While the focus has been largely on urban enclaves, the migration of Eastern European workers to rural areas to work in agriculture, has extended the discussion to different localities (Flint and Robinson 2008).

At the start of the 21st century, we have seen a continued discussion and analysis of structural inequalities coupled with the citizenship and community cohesion agenda, which, as noted earlier, has been conflated with creating pathology around Muslim culture. The chapters in this book refer to and highlight the socio-economic structural approach by providing an analysis and evidence of the inequalities experienced by ethnic minority and migrant groups in the UK. However, they also note the tensions between this analysis and the more culturally orientated approaches that focus on cohesion and citizenship as facilitators of nation and belonging.

Key themes and concerns

The preceding chapters in this edited collection are for the most part concerned with documenting and explaining the discrimination and inequality that exists in different aspects of social, economic and civil society. They also highlight the complex cleavages between and within groups which derive in part from institutional assumptions and stereotyping. The diversity between and within groups makes it difficult to generalise and theorise about race and ethnicity at the start of the 21st century. Many of the chapters also address the changing policy framework and the growing concern over what is seen as a lack of integration among some groups, and the resulting promotion of the community cohesion agenda. What the chapters clearly demonstrate is the evidence of both variable integration outcomes among minority ethnic groups and migrants in the UK and the ways in which different socio-economic factors intersect. For example, the chapters in this collection by Harrison and Phillips and Gillborn and Rollock demonstrate the relationship between housing, education and exclusion. While the education system is seen as a crucial element in the promotion of community cohesion, other structural factors make such an outcome more difficult to achieve.

A number of themes emerged in the chapters though most evident is the relative disadvantage experienced by minority groups and migrants. Racism and discrimination continues in spite of successive race relations legislation (1965; 1968; 1976; 2000) as well as the Macpherson Report (1999) on the murder of Stephen Lawrence, which identified 'institutional racism' at the heart of policing (see Chapter 5).

The preceding chapters showed variations in the experiences of ethnic minorities as well as some attempts to make structural changes through policy interventions. However, the reality is one where institutional racism by a variety of actors still permeates the opportunities afforded to some groups compared to others demonstrated so clearly through the inequality of outcomes for people from minority ethnic groups in key public services areas, including education, policing and health. There are other factors that directly correlate with experiences and measurable outcomes for ethnic minority groups and migrants, which include gender, migration patterns, social and cultural norms, community formation, skills and qualifications, generational variation, proficiency in the language of the country of residence and citizenship/immigration status. One example is the experience of more recent migrants who have obtained their qualifications overseas finding that their pre-migration qualifications and skills are not transferable to an equivalent level and so need to retrain or work in less skilled employment. Research with refugees has repeatedly shown high levels of unemployment and under-employment among those working and that this results in social and economic exclusion (Bloch 2002; Phillimore and Goodson 2006).

The impact of under-employment among those working is a disparity in terms of earnings. Refugees are paid an average hourly rate of £7.29 compared with the £9.26 earned by ethnic minorities and the UK average of £11.74. Therefore, on average refugees were earning only 78 per cent of what other ethnic minority people were earning per hour and 62 per cent of UK average hourly rate. Levels of pay were affected by qualifications and the place where qualifications were obtained. Having a degree or postgraduate level qualification from a British university increased the level of earnings substantially. The average gross hourly rate of refugees with a degree or higher from a British university was £12.10 compared to an average rate of £8.23 for those who had obtained a degree from elsewhere. Ethnic minority people from longer-established communities, with a degree, earned £13.71 an hour on average so the disparity between new and longer-term migrants is evident even when the degree has been obtained from a UK university (Bloch 2004).

There are other costs too among ethnic minorities and other migrants who experience either unemployment or under-employment in terms of the negative effect on self-esteem and confidence. Among those who are working, the comparatively low levels of income have adverse consequences not only for national income and economic growth but also for the social and economic inclusion of the individual (Cabinet Office 2003). For new migrants there are additional factors such as whether they see their migration as permanent or temporary with aspirations for the migration affecting settlement outcomes. Research with refugees has found that if people maintain the 'myth of return' – that is, aspirations for return migration – they are less likely to take steps to facilitate settlement, such as investing in employment and training opportunities, because it implies a degree of permanency (Zetter 1999). Equally, prolonged uncertainty due to government policy that restricts permanency through visas and limiting the length of stay even for those granted refugee status for an initial five-year period will limit settlement opportunities. Likewise, the policy of dispersal that limits access to social and community networks and potentially more vibrant labour markets (see Hynes and Sales, Chapter 3) will negatively impact on the longer-term settlement of refugees. Certainly the state of the labour market and variations in local labour markets at the time of migration affects the longer-term employment outcomes of migrants and so dispersal will and does impact in the longer term (Ho and Henderson 1999; Valtonen 1999).

The complexity of individual experiences and aspirations, both pre- and post-migration, structural and individual racism and discrimination all mean that theoretical generalisations, as well as policy interventions that have historically failed to address the more micro needs of individuals and groups in favour of a more generalised need to facilitate social and economic integration, can be problematic. With this in mind, the government has emphasised the importance of employment alongside social and civil integration, as well as acknowledging diversity of experience and different barriers and critical issues between groups (Cabinet Office 2003). Policy interventions in the area of employment are to combat inequality in employment, earnings, workplace attainment and progress and levels of self-employment. Although the causes of disadvantage are multiple and complex, and include class, geography and migration patterns, the report argues that the most important factors are education and skills, the ability to access opportunities and discrimination. The emphasis is therefore on tackling individual capacity through, for example, skills attainment alongside social policy measures, including equal opportunities. Virdee (Chapter 4) criticises this capacity-building/human capital approach, arguing that it diverts attention from racism and the restructuring of the British economy as a result of neo-liberal economic approaches by instead focusing on what is perceived as the problematic norms of minorities. To really tackle inequality, a much more profound shift in societal attitudes, the media and policy needs to take place. The focus on individual capacity and equal opportunities does not in reality change the opinion of the public, media outputs, racism, discrimination and stereotyping.

The chapters in this book on the media and public opinion also demonstrate the interactive role of these areas in maintaining social and economic divisions. The chapter by Georgiou on media representation highlights ways in which the media feeds negative stereotypes and assumptions and how media concerns have shifted with changing migration patterns while the chapter by Heath, Rothon and Ali on identity and public opinion shows the racialised responses to questions on settlement and migration of different groups as well as the perceptions about threats to employment; for example, about which public opinion is often formed through media representation.

From the late 1980s the media focus was on refugees and asylum seekers but since the turn of the 21st century attention has shifted to undocumented or irregular migrants. Again such coverage not only feeds into public opinion but also affects governments and their quest to win elections. As a consequence, since 1993, there have been eight immigration acts, and further legislation is proposed, as discussed earlier, under the Immigration and Citizenship Bill, 2008.

All the chapters in this book demonstrate the complexity and interaction of these key areas of social, economic, civil and political life in shaping the lives and experiences of ethnic minorities and migrant populations. One underlying strand, though, is the problematic nature of the data that is available and, as we shall explore later, limited or non-existent for some groups. Though there are debates about whether such data should be collected, the absence of it makes any real understanding of difference difficult. Though Heath, Rothon and Ali explore Berry's typology of acculturation outcomes (Berry 1992), in reality, for some groups it is difficult to know their position due to the lack of or paucity of available data.

Intersections of inequality and disadvantage

In spite of the paucity of data, all the chapters clearly show the intersection of discrimination, inequality and relative disadvantage in key areas of economic and social life among Britain's minority ethnic groups. In some areas of social and economic life this has also resulted in clustering; for example, spatially in terms of housing or in particular sectors of employment. Harrison and Phillips clearly identify the disadvantage experienced by minority ethnic groups in the UK and elsewhere in Europe in terms of housing. They show the much greater likelihood of people from minority ethnic groups of being located in poor quality housing in disadvantaged neighbourhoods. In the UK, for example, they note that 67 per cent of people from black minority ethnic communities live in the 88 most deprived districts in England compared to 37 per cent of the white population. However, the correlation is not linear and depends at least to some extent on whether this clustering is a function of 'benign' or 'dysfunctional' segregation.

Castles and Miller (2009) also reflect on the causes of residential segregation, noting that in countries where racism and social exclusion is strong, spatial clustering persists or even increases as migrants are often kept out of certain areas by racism (Castles and Miller 2009). Where racism is less strong migrants move out into better suburbs as their economic position improves. However, the relationship between racism, economic resources and housing is complicated by the notion of choice or 'benign' segregation. Benign segregation or clustering is where concentrations of minority groups live in close proximity by choice to provide support, networks and economic opportunities in the form of ethnic businesses catering for specific needs of minority groups such as grocery stores and restaurants.

Whether residential clustering is about choices or about inequality, the agenda in the 21st century is to tackle the effect identified by the community cohesion literature, which is separate communities living parallel lives. While Harrison and Phillips focus mainly on longer-established minority communities, Hynes and Sales focus on new communities, especially the dispersal of asylum seekers. While traditionally, and as a consequence of chain migration, new migrants seek out members of their own communities on arrival in a new country, the compulsory dispersal of asylum seekers to locations around the UK has separated people from the family and social and community networks which can be crucial in the early stages of settlement and has changed the geography of refugee settlement (Bloch 2002). The separation of asylum seekers from community-based and other refugee networks has been compounded by the propensity of dispersal to be housing-led. The consequence has been that asylum seekers have often been sent to places that are hostile and economically deprived, leaving them vulnerable to racism and racist attacks. Dispersal (and employment regulations that exclude asylum seekers from the labour market) has left asylum seekers and many refugees without employment. The perceptions of these groups are one of a 'burden' on society and this is reflected in media and public opinion, where hostility towards asylum seekers is displayed (Lewis 2005).

The idea of statutory discrimination emerges not only when thinking about housing and access to housing, where discrimination has been noted in allocations, but also in the areas of employment, policing and health. The chapter by Virdee on employment focuses on established minority groups rather than new communities and shows the pattern of downward occupational mobility that Virdee describes as the 'profound process of protetarianisation'. He notes the diversity of employment outcomes by gender, unemployment levels and pay and the relative disadvantage experienced by Pakistani and Bangladeshi men and women. Virdee criticises the focus on human capital in government-funded research studies as they deflect attention, he argues, from racism and the restructuring of the British economy as a result of neo-liberal economic approaches. Moreover, the focus on human capital and capacity building needs contributes towards perceptions of minorities having problematic norms.

The tendency for ethnic minority employment to be hyper-cyclical means that the position of minorities in the labour market is likely to deteriorate as a consequence of the global economic crisis, not least because of the sectors of employment that these groups often find themselves working in, which are areas of contraction during an economic decline. This is particularly the case among Bangladeshi and Chinese men, who were, in 2004, concentrated in the distribution, hotel and restaurant industries. Three fifths of Bangladeshi men and just under half of Chinese men who were working were in these industries (Office for National Statistics 2006). The links between employment and residential segregation are compounded by the likelihood of ethnic minorities to be clustered in areas with disproportionally high levels of unemployment due to declining industries.

McLaughlin explores statutory discrimination in the police and criminal justice system, arguing that it operates at all levels from the police officer on the beat to the court system. Equally significant are the complaints of an unequal police response to ethnic and racial minorities as victims of crime and work-based discrimination against ethnic and racial minority personnel in terms of recruitment, retention and career progression. McLaughlin notes three key areas of concern in the 21st century: street crime and gang culture; new forms of criminality associated with recent surges in migration; and the threat posed by Islamist terrorism. The criminality associated with migration concerns both migrant crime and also racism and xenophobia against migrants, especially asylum seekers who have been placed on sink estates such as Sighthill in Glasgow. Racist violence is also evident in the chapter by Hynes and Sales in relation to asylum seekers and has been observed by others. The post-9/11 treat of terror and the link with Islam is also racialised with the threats leading to the government focusing attention on the UK's Muslim communities. What has been seen as the potentially problematic nature of these communities in terms of separation and segregation had already been highlighted by the Cantle Report in the aftermath of the urban disturbances in 2001.

The clustering of communities also impacts on education and health. Education and the importance of schools were identified in both the Cantle (2001) and Ouseley (2001) reports after the urban disorders in 2001. Schools are seen as an important instrument through which to promote community cohesion and a greater understanding between communities. Mono-ethnic schools therefore, which link to residential and spatial segregation, enhance the distances between communities. The chapter by Gillborn and Rollock in this book focuses on the ways in which race and racism permeate education policy and practice. Differential outcomes in attainment, exclusions and in-school processes all affect the experiences of pupils and their achievements. Moreover, they note that stereotyping by teachers impacts on the attainment levels of minority ethnic pupils.

Stereotyping also emerges in the chapter by Nazroo on health, particularly the impact of racism and discrimination not only on health but on stereotypes about health which result in the propensity of some ethnic groups to receive certain diagnosis over others. Nazroo argues that health cannot be understood outside its social and economic context and diversity between and within groups needs to be explored in the same ways as in other key areas of economic and social life. Moreover, Nazroo argues that access to health care, though meant to be universal, is in fact subject, like other public services, to institutional racism and so there is inequality in terms of access and outcomes.

While the focus has so far been on inequality, racism, discrimination and differential outcomes, all the chapters note that these are generalisations. There is much diversity between and within groups because outcomes are mediated by a number of things including gender and social class as well as aspects of human capital and generational differences. Even though outcomes are mediated by a range of structural and personal factors, Gillborn and Rollock show that in the education system ethnic minority children achieve less well than their white peers of the same social class.

Choices made and strategies adopted by the majority white population in a number of areas such as education, employment, housing, policing, public opinion and media outputs also interact with outcomes for minority ethnic groups. Racism, discrimination and stereotyping all come into play and intersect with outcomes. For example, the chapter by Gillborn and Rollock on education notes the ways in which black, Bangladeshi and Pakistani pupils are falling further behind due in part to teacher stereotyping but, in contrast, the position of Indian pupils is different. Profiles of minority groups in the labour market also show similar patterns of difference and diversity. Race relations legislation has not, in reality, created a society void of discrimination.

The chapter by Georgiou on the media highlights the power of the media in terms of setting the agenda and influencing public opinion. Though there has been a shift to an anti-racist discourse for long-established groups, this has been accompanied by the growing stereotyping of Muslims and asylum-seeking and refugee groups. Certainly the media are interested in stories about migration, asylum and diversity though the coverage is often negative and scaremongering. Thus, the focus of news can be and is often hostile to more recent migrant groups although, as noted earlier, negative representations of Muslims in relation to terror and separation from the rest of society have also become a feature of the news media.

The power of the media in influencing public opinion is apparent when considering the data presented in the chapter on public opinion by Heath, Rothon and Ali. Striking in the public opinion data is the lack of differentiation made by the British public about different types of migrant or migrant categories such as refugee, labour migrant and asylum seeker. Crawley notes that these different immigration status terms, though different in meaning, are 'often used interchangeably' (Crawley 2005: 10). The result of this lack of differentiation is confusion that is replicated in public opinion. For many living in largely white homogeneous areas, there is also a lack of contact with minority groups and so the media stories are not challenged by personal experience. Moreover, interviews with asylum seekers and refugees found a feeling that 'the media taps into the normal everyday pressures experienced by the average British person and uses these as a vehicle to launch attacks on refugees and asylum seekers, blaming them for everything from NHS waiting lists to stealing boy/girlfriends' (Buchanan and Grillo 2004: 42).

The idea of competition or threat from migrants is something that has long been evident in the immigration discourse and is something that Heath, Rothon and Ali note. Certainly the link between the economy and the immigration controls and attitudes towards migrants has been well documented (see, for example, Panayi 1994), adding to the concerns and potential impact of the current economic crisis. As Trevor Phillips, Chair of the Equality and Human Rights Commission, notes in his speech in January 2009 reflecting on 10 years since the Macpherson Report on the murder of Stephen Lawrence, 'We all know that in the wake of the lean times can come resentment and division, all too often along the lines of race and faith. If this recession lasts more than months we know that there is a greater danger' (Phillips 2009).

The public opinion and attitudes surveys show prejudice among the majority white population with the greatest prejudice targeted at less skilled and more culturally different minorities. However, in spite of the community cohesion agenda and the fears of segregation, in reality, minorities do have a high level of attachment to both Britain and their minority group with most groups following an integrationist strategy. The problem, however, is the barriers that prevent real equality of opportunity for all members of society, which has been well documented in the other chapters in this book.

Looking forward: key issues in the 21st century

Given the fluid nature of race and ethnicity in contemporary societies it may be inevitable that they give rise to a number of issues and questions that remain somewhat unexplored in studies of race and ethnicity. Indeed, a major challenge for scholars working in this field lies in the inherently shifting ways in which racial and ethnic boundaries are made and re-made within contemporary societies (Back and Solomos 2009; Murji and Solomos 2005). As a way of concluding this book we want to touch on some of the questions that are likely to come to the fore as we move more into the 21st century and make some suggestions about how we may be able to move forward to address them through both empirical research and theoretical exploration.

The first area is the paucity of accurate and detailed data relating to race, ethnicity and country of birth. The lack of statistically robust and reliable data for newer migrants, with the exception of asylum seekers, is particularly apparent. While acknowledging that the debates about collecting data on ethnicity are complicated and politically sensitive it is clear that understanding the position of certain groups and developing evidence-based policy and theoretically generalisable sociology is limited by the lack of data. Many of the chapters in this book rely heavily on either census data or other longitudinal data from government surveys. The limitations in the data used are noted by many of the authors in this book. Even where a more longitudinal analysis is potentially possible for long-established minorities groups from Commonwealth countries the longitudinal analysis element is affected and replication made impossible by the changing categorisations used over the decades.

The notion of ethnic group was first introduced as a category in the 1991 Census, while in the 2001 Census a question was asked for the first time on religion. The validity of the data collected through these questions has been questioned on a number of grounds. First, because of the changing categorisation between censuses – the standard output for ethnic group was 10 categories in 1991, increasing to 16 in 2001 (Simpson and Akinwale 2007). Second, as a result of the under-enumeration or low response rate of minority ethnic groups (Platt et al. 2005). Third, because of the complex, changing and often-contextual nature of identity, which is not reflected in the available census categorisations. Ethnicity is a multifaceted and changing phenomenon and because of this its categorisation and measurement has changed over time and has included country of birth, nationality, parents' country of birth and national/geographical origin (HMSO 2003: 12). It is these differences along with a lack of data about new migrants that make a reliable analysis of economic and social trends difficult.

A second key area of concern results form the differential experiences of minority communities, particularly the continued exclusion and/or disadvantaged social class, education and economic outcomes among certain groups. This disadvantage has continued among second and subsequent generations where increasingly young black and Asian men are portrayed as alienated from society and engaged in criminal and often violent activities. The position of young people, usually young men, from minority ethnic groups will continue to occupy policy makers though, as the chapters demonstrate, there is a great deal of diversity in terms of experiences and outcomes between and within groups. While in the US, South Africa and elsewhere affirmative action policies have been adopted to try and alleviate some of the structural barriers to equality and to achieve greater parity between groups, in the UK such a strategy has not been adopted. Successive governments have relied on race relations policies and multiculturalism as the key policy tools to tackle forms of racial and ethnic inequality. In reality, though, policies in the UK and elsewhere aimed at achieving parity on the grounds of ethnicity (or gender, disability and so on) have not been successful for all groups. In this environment it is not surprising that there are recurrent calls for a radical rethinking of policy agendas. Cantle, for example, argues that what is needed is a complete rethink and is critical of the outcomes of multicultural polices, stating that what is needed is a means for changing existing values and attitudes rather than behaviour. With this in mind he advocates the use of community cohesion approaches because they 'represent an attempt to both understand the basis of prejudice and the resulting discriminatory behaviour and to confront their causes' (Cantle 2005: 22). The emphasis of this approach is on engendering community through social and other contacts with the aim of changing values and perceptions.

Linked to the community cohesion thesis is the idea that identification with Britain as a political and cultural entity is crucial for integration. This is a theme that has become particularly important in public discourses in the aftermath of the 2001 disorders and the terrorist attacks of 9/11 and 7/7. For some commentators, these events, along with others, created a climate of opinion in which there was a noticeable shift towards a policy agenda that emphasised the need for minorities to be integrated into British society above all else. It is worth noting, however, that according to Castles and Miller (2009: 245) the concept of integration poses two important questions. First, how should migrants and their descendants become part of the receiving society and, secondly, how can both the state and the civil society assist in this process? Castles and Miller observe that in spite of the different policies adopted by states over the past few decades to incorporate migrants, such as assimilation or multiculturalism, the outcome at the start of the 21st century is what they call a 'crisis of integration' (Castles and Miller 2009: 250). Crucial to the process of 'incorporation' – their preferred term as it is more neutral than integration – argue Castles and Miller (2009), is citizenship because it confers social, political and civil rights on individuals.

Certainly the introduction of citizenship tests in the UK has been part of the process of trying to facilitate a sense of belonging and shared values among migrants naturalising as citizens. The term used, as discussed earlier, is 'integration' but in reality such a process is a paper exercise once again putting the emphasis on the migrant rather than alleviating any disadvantage or discrimination that they might experience. Moreover, the relative inequalities and disadvantages documented in the chapters of this book are not a function of citizenship because they are experienced by British citizens from minority ethnic backgrounds.

For new migrants, insecurity about immigration status and aspirations for return are of course issues that affect incorporation. Successive governments have sought to manage migration through visa schemes and programmes as well as the development of ongoing refugee resettlement programmes in an attempt to curtail the spontaneous arrival of asylum seekers. As legal routes for entering the UK have been reduced, so it is increasingly difficult to settle in the long term and become a naturalised citizen. For some who want to stay in the UK or are afraid to return to their country of origin, becoming an undocumented migrant is one strategy and certainly what is seen as the increasing number of undocumented migrants concerns the government, who want to demonstrate control of immigration and enforcement procedures for those in breach of immigration regulations.

The issue of undocumented migrants as well as undocumented/clandestine entry is a global concern not just because of smuggling and trafficking, which are highly lucrative global businesses, but also because of states' endeavours to control their borders. Well documented with respect to this are the porous land borders between Mexico and the US, and Zimbabwe and South Africa, where fences are constantly breached and then reinforced and patrolled. On the UK agenda is the idea of an amnesty for undocumented migrants with some countries in Europe adopting such a policy, notably Spain in 2005. It has not yet happened in the UK but it is likely to remain on the agenda, not least because the government is concerned about their lack of knowledge about who is in the UK but also because of the effect on communities of marginal and often-exploited migrants living separate lives.

Global inequality also contributes to another area that will remain important into the 21st century and that is transnational links in the form of remittances. Developments in transport and communications technology, such as cheaper airline travel and the Internet, have made it easier and cheaper for migrants to maintain multiple relations across borders and one of the basic obligations of some migrants is remittances. Migration can, and does, in fact form part of a household's survival strategy (Al-Ali et al. 2001a,b; Levitt 2001; Portes 1999). Economic remittances have become an important part of the debate around migration and development and are seen as a crucial component in the alleviation of poverty. However, the marginalisation of some migrants in terms of immigration status and employment and their greater propensity for low pay have the added affect of negatively impacting on economic capabilities and therefore remittances (Bloch 2008). The global economy and the impact on development of the policies of the wealthier, more developed countries is something that will continue to occupy and concern policy makers. Sociologists will continue to investigate transnational linkages and what they mean at the micro and macro levels.

The coming decades are clearly going to be a crucial time for race and ethnic relations globally. The start of the 21st century has been characterised by growing diversity within nation-states and large-scale migration, and the signs are that this will continue in the coming period. The chapters in this book show that Britain, alongside other developed countries of the North and West, is a country where race and ethnicity determine life chances. In the past decade or so there has been a preoccupation in public discourse at least with questions of controls on immigration or refuge. Yet, it seems evident from the tenor of the arguments to be found in the substantive chapters of this book that the key issues to be addressed are not immigration controls or attempts to create a sense of belonging through citizenship tests, but how best to ensure a fair society where choices, stereotyping, discrimination, exploitation and the hierarchy of rights associated with immigration status do not impede opportunities. Broadly speaking, many of the challenges that lie ahead for Britain, as well as other societies, converge around the question of how societies can shape the changing boundaries of inclusion and exclusion in our increasingly racially and ethnically diverse social fabrics.

Whatever the diversity of meanings that have been attached to the notion of multicultural Britain over the years, there are a number of features of contemporary Britain that underpin this notion:

- Britain is a radically more diverse society than it was in the 1960s, with about 8 per cent of the population nationwide and nearly 30 per cent in cities like London coming from an ethnic minority background.
- In arenas such as employment, education and housing questions of racial and ethnic diversity are at the heart of both policy and public debate.
- In political culture the question of the representation of the interests of minority communities have come to the fore in both local and national institutions.

In this context it is not surprising that the notion of Britain as a society being shaped by diversity has become something of a taken-for-granted notion.

Politicians such as David Miliband talk of 'building community in a diverse society' and of the advantages of diverse identities. Reflecting current thinking, Miliband defines multiculturalism in contemporary Britain thus:

> Multiculturalism in this reading is based on a very simple notion that most people have multiple loyalties, affinities and attachments, to their ethnic and religious community, to their geographical community, to their communities of interest, and to their national home. And the choice to emphasise different parts of their identities varies among different people, and at different times and places in our lives. On Saturdays at three o'clock, I am an Arsenal fan first, a Londoner second, British third, and, at that time, I wear my origins, political affiliations, constituency interests lightly.
>
> (Miliband 2006)

In the aftermath of the 7/7 bombings in London it became clear that not all politicians shared Miliband's positive take on the state of multiculturalism in British society. Indeed, some commentators argued that there was a need to question the very idea of multiculturalism and to emphasise the need for greater social cohesion alongside diversity. It was in this context that the Commission on Integration and Cohesion was set up, which produced a report on *Our Shared Future* in 2007 (Commission on Integration and Cohesion 2007). The report argues strongly that it is only through initiatives to tackle deep-seated inequalities as well as measures to promote social cohesion that both majority and minority communities can develop a sense of having a 'shared future' together. Yet it remains unclear how such strategies can be put into practice.

On the basis of both historical as well as contemporary experience there seem to be three main models of response to the challenges posed by immigration and the development of both established and new migrant communities:

- Policies that aim to provide for a limited inclusion of minorities and social and economic rights as long as minority communities do not interfere with the culture of the majority.
- Policies of assimilation and integration which include action to deal with processes of discrimination and exclusion as they impact on minorities.
- Policies that affirm various versions of multiculturalism that allow for some degree of cultural pluralism in the implementation of public policy.

Although these models are considered paradigmatic of, respectively, the German, French and British policy approaches, within the context of contemporary Europe, North America and Australasia there are various models of policy change which in practice may involve a combination of all of the above policy agendas. This is not in itself surprising, since individual nation-states have their own histories of immigration, race relations and patterns of minority incorporation. It does highlight, however, the problematic nature of attempts to construct comparisons between the experiences of individual nation-states. There is a danger of imposing models of interpretation that are based on rather narrow analytical frameworks derived from readings of specific historical periods and national political ideologies.

In spite of the dangers of simplistic comparisons it can be argued that we need to look beyond our own nation-state boundaries if we are to derive a more rounded understanding of the factors that have shaped our contemporary understandings of multiculturalism and citizenship. At the very least we need to engage in a dialogue that allows us to draw on the rich bodies of research that have developed within specific societies about these questions.

A case in point in this regard is the renewed interest in the ways in which migrant and racialised communities across the globe construct forms of community through the performance of collective struggles for recognition of their religious and cultural practices. In the current social and political climate in Britain, and other societies in the West, religion can be seen as providing both a performative articulation and an organising principle through which community interests can be represented and staged. Both locally and globally, religious identities can become enmeshed in the articulation of forms of identity politics and other forms of political mobilisation. Religious identification in this context is strengthened by the manner in which collective identity consequently relates to both reflexive debates on the nature of community interest and mobilised networks of influence and decision making.

Within both popular and academic discourse there is growing evidence of concern about how questions of citizenship and rights need to be reconceptualised in the context of multicultural societies. Indeed in contemporary European societies this can be seen as one of the key questions that governments of various kinds are trying to come to terms with. Some important elements of this debate are the issue of the political rights of minorities, including the issue of representation in both local and national politics, and the position of minority religious and cultural rights in societies that are becoming more diverse. The discrimination suffered by migrants and members of minorities in employment, housing and education and in their treatment by state representatives such as the police and immigration officials remains a perennial problem in many European societies. The question as to what, if anything, can be done to protect the rights of minorities and develop extensive notions of citizenship and democracy that positively include those minorities that are excluded on racial, religious and ethnic criteria is one that is becoming increasingly urgent and demands a coherent response.

Finally, nation states also need to consider the position of those migrants who do not want to settle, integrate or become citizens or are excluded from such opportunities. How do stratified rights (Morris 2002) affect the social and economic lives of these migrants while in the UK or other societies and how can the vulnerability and exploitation experienced by some migrants unable to exercise rights be alleviated? The increasing number of undocumented migrants means that there is a group who are in effect 'rightless'. While the focus in the UK has been on the removal of this group this has not been an effective strategy, not least because of the costs of removal but also because of the lack of knowledge and data about these migrants. It is likely that both national governments and supranational bodies will need to consider questions like amnesties and employment rights not linked to immigration status to better reflect the nature of a globalised market and economic and developmental inequalities.

These are some of the questions that are likely to preoccupy both policy makers and the academy in the coming period. There will no doubt be other issues that will emerge as new forms of migration and mobility help to shape and re-shape the social and political fabric of societies such as Britain. We hope this book makes a contribution to encouraging a more informed discussion of these questions in British society as well as in other societies.

References

Al-Ali, N., Black, B. and Koser, K. (2001a) 'The Limits of "Transnationalism": Bosnian and Eritrean Refugees as Emerging Transnational Communities'. *Ethnic and Racial Studies* 24 (4): 578–600.

Al-Ali, N., Black, R. and Koser, K. (2001b) 'Refugees and Transnationalism: The Experiences of Bosnians and Eritreans in Europe'. *Journal of Ethnic and Migration Studies* 27 (4): 615–34.

Alexander, C. E. (2004) 'Imagining the Asian Gang: Ethnicity, Masculinity and Youth After "The Riots" '. *Critical Social Policy* 24 (4): 526–49.

Back, L. and Solomos, J. (eds) (2009) *Theories of Race and Racism: A Reader*, 2nd Edition. London: Routledge.

Bloch, A. (2002) *The Migration and Settlement of Refugees in Britain*. Basingstoke: Palgrave Macmillan.

Bloch, A. (2004) *Making it Work: Refugee Employment in the UK*. London: Institute for Public Policy Research.

Bloch, A. (2008) 'Zimbabweans in Britain: Transnational Activities and Capabilities'. *Journal of Ethnic and Migration Studies* 34 (2): 287–305.

Buchanan, S. and Grillo, R. (2004) 'What's the Story? Reporting on Asylum in the British Media'. *Forced Migration Review* 19: 41–3.

Cabinet Office (2003) *Ethnic Minorities and the Labour Market: Final Report*. London: Cabinet Office.

Cantle, T. (2001) *Community Cohesion: A Report of the Independent Review*. London: Home Office.

Cantle, T. (2005) *Community Cohesion: A New Framework for Race and Diversity*. Basingstoke: Palgrave Macmillan.

Castles, S. and Miller, M. J. (2009) *The Age of Migration: International Population Movements in the Modern World*, 4th Edition. Basingstoke: Palgrave Macmillan.

Commission on Integration and Cohesion (2007) *Our Shared Future*. London: Commission on Integration and Cohesion.

Crawley, H. (2005) *Evidence on Attitudes to Asylum and Immigration: What We Know, Don't Know and Need to Know*. Oxford: Centre on Migration, Policy & Society.

Denham, J. (2001) *Building Cohesive Communities: A Report of the Ministerial Group on Public Order and Community Cohesion*. London: Home Office.

Flint, J. and Robinson, D. (2008) 'Introduction' in Flint, J. and Robinson, D. (eds) *Community Cohesion in Crisis: New dimensions of diversity and difference*. Bristol: Policy Press.

Global Commission on International Migration (2005) *Migration in an Interconnected World: New Directions for Action*. Geneva: Global Commission on International Migration.

HMSO (2003) *Ethnic Group Statistics: A Guide for the Collection and Classification of Ethnicity Data*. London: HMSO.

Ho, S. Y. and Henderson, J. (1999) 'Locality and the Variability of Ethnic Employment in Britain'. *Journal of Ethnic and Migration Studies* 25 (2): 323–33.

Home Office (2005) *Integration Matters: A National Strategy for Refugee Integration*. London: Home Office.

Home Office (2008) *Making Change Stick: An Introduction to the Immigration and Citizenship Bill*. London: UK Border Agency.

International Organisation for Migration (2005) *World Migration 2005: Costs and Benefits of International Migration*. Geneva: International Organisation for Migration.

Levitt, P. (2001) *The Transnational Villagers*. Berkeley: University of California Press.

Lewis, M. (2005) *Asylum: Understanding Public Attitudes*. London: Institute for Public Policy Research.

McGhee, D. (2009) 'The Paths to Citizenship: A Critical Examination of Immigration Policy in Britain Since 2001'. *Patterns of Prejudice* 43 (1): 41–64.

Miliband, D. (2006) *Building Community in a Diverse Society: Scarman Memorial Lecture*. London: Scarman Trust.

Morris, L. (2002) *Managing Migration: Civic Stratification and Migrants Rights*. London: Routledge.

Murji, K. and Solomos, J. (eds) (2005) *Racialization: Studies in Theory and Practice*. Oxford: Oxford University Press.

Office for National Statistics (2006) *Focus on Ethnicity: Employment Patterns*.

Ouseley, H. (2001) *Community Pride, Not Prejudice: Making Diversity Work in Bradford*. Bradford: Bradford Vision.

Panayi, P. (1994) *Immigration, Ethnicity and Racism in Britain: 1815–1945*. Manchester: Manchester University Press.

Phillimore, J. and Goodson, L. (2006) 'Problem or Opportunity? Asylum Seekers, Refugees, Employment and Social Exclusion in Deprived Urban Areas'. *Urban Studies* 43 (10): 1715–36.

Phillips, T. (2009) Macpherson Speech: Institutions Must Catch Up with Public on Race Issue to Mark the Tenth Anniversary of the Stephen Lawrence Inquiry, 19 January 2009, Macpherson Breakfast Debate'http://www.equalityhumanrights.com/en/newsandcomment/speeches/Pages/Macphersonspeech190109.aspx

Platt, L., Simpson, L. and Akinwale, B. (2005) 'Stability and Change in Ethnic Groups in England and Wales'. *Population Trends* 121: 35–46.

Portes, A. (1999) 'Conclusion: Towards a New World: The Origins and Effects of Transnational Activities'. *Ethnic and Racial Studies* 22 (2): 463–76.

Simpson, L. and Akinwale, B. (2007) 'Quantifying Stability and Change in Ethnic Group'. *Journal of Official Statistics* 23 (2): 185–208.

Solomos, J. (2003) *Race and Racism in Britain*, 3rd Edition. Basingstoke: Palgrave Macmillan.

Valtonen, K. (1999) 'The Societal Participation of Vietnamese Refugees: Case Studies in Finland and Canada'. *Journal of Ethnic and Migration Studies* 25 (3): 469–91.

Vertovec, S. (2006) *The Emergence of Super-Diversity in Britain*. Oxford: Centre on Migration, Policy and Society, Working Paper No. 25.

Zetter, R. (1999) 'Reconceptualising the Myth of Return: Continuity and Transition Amongst the Greek-Cypriot Refugees of 1974'. *Journal of Refugee Studies* 12 (1): 1–22.

Index

Note: Page numbers in **bold** indicate figures, page numbers in *italic* indicate tables.